Conspiracy Reader Presents

EVIL EMPIRE OF THE ETS AND THE ULTRA- TERRESTRIALS

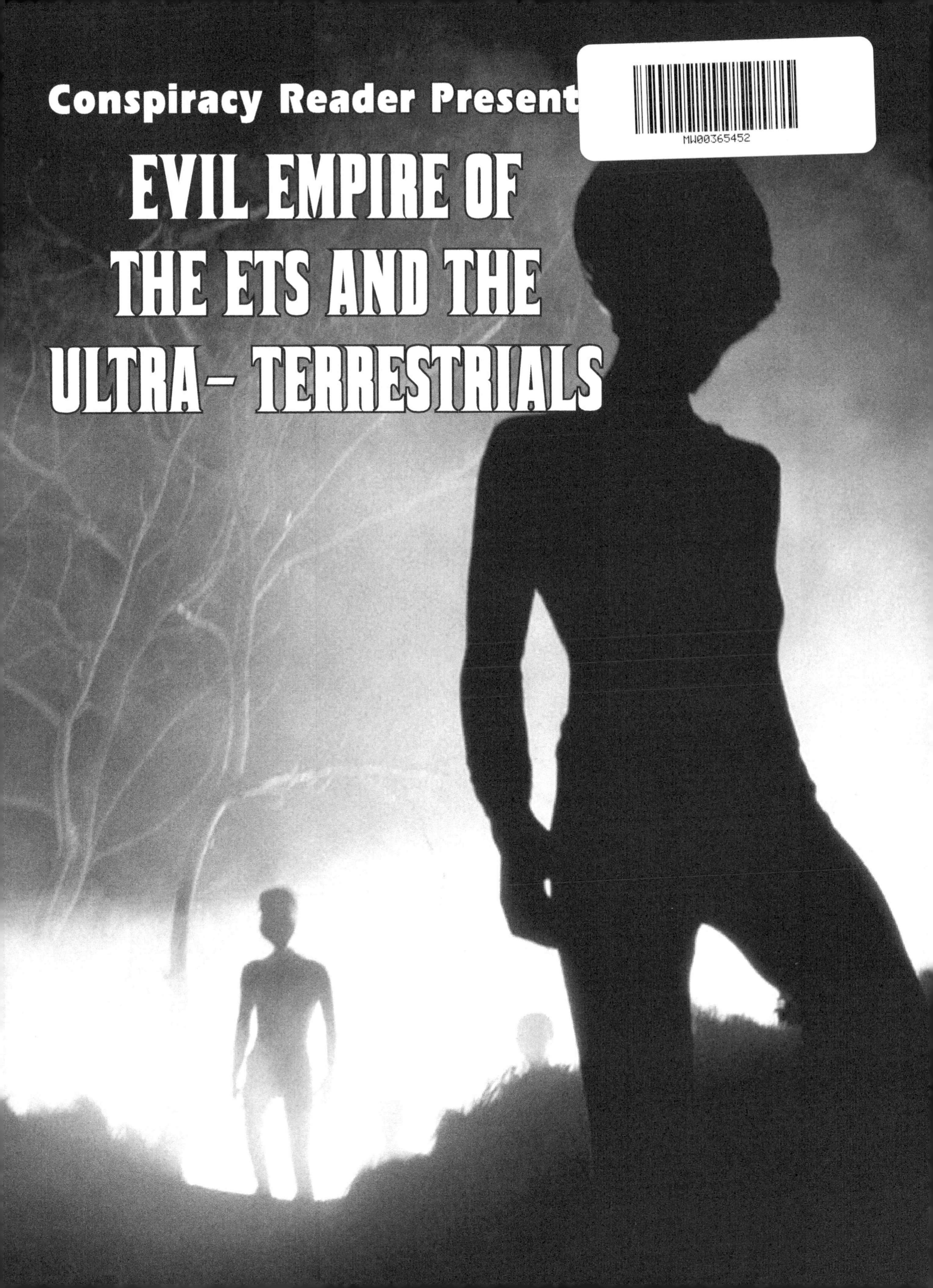

Conspiracy Reader Presents

EVIL EMPIRE OF THE ETS AND THE ULTRA- TERRESTRIALS

by
Timothy Green Beckley
Sean Casteel
Karla Turner
Tim Swartz
Brad and Sherry Steiger

Timothy Green Beckley, Publisher
Inner Light Publications

EVIL EMPIRE OF THE ETS AND THE ULTRA-TERRESTRIALS

Printed in the United States of America
Timothy Green Beckley: Editorial Director
Carol Ann Rodriguez: Publishers Assistant
Sean Casteel: Associate Editor
William Kern, Adman: Design and Layout

For Free Subscription To The Conspiracy Journal Write:
Tim Beckley/Global Communications
Box 753, New Brunswick, NJ 08903
Sign Up On Line: MRUFO8@hotmail.com
www.ConspiracyJournal.Com
www.TeslasSecretLab.Com

CONTENTS

Inner Light
Publications

STRANGE BREW

THE VISITORS ARE A COMPLEX STEW

OF EVIL AND WICKEDNESS

By Timothy Green Beckley

It's not a universe of sweetness and light out there.

There are definitely a few "death stars" aimed in our direction.

Those investigators and wannabe authors that fancy UFOs and their occupants as being totally and unequivocally benevolent are fooling themselves and leading the public around with blinders on.

Sure, some of the witnesses that have been approached by our "alien friends" are dumbfounded and goo-goo eyed upon being confronted by a six foot tall being with long hair and penetrating eyes who speaks candidly of universal peace and love. At first it seems like something right out of an Aryan charm school, but this concept has little basis in reality as the mutilations, abductions, painful medical exams, anal probes and extreme mind control patterns continue forward full speed ahead.

Our penetrating research and that of others of an unbiased mind cannot discount the shocking testimonials of those who have had to deal with the unknown on a face-to-face – mono e mono – basis. Take the less than glowing reactions of a pair of UFO experiencers who had a close encounter and came away totally shaken for the rest of their lives: "The creatures were hostile, and went into attack modes several times, putting up dense fogs. One time when they stopped, it was like a backwards tornado coming from the mouth of the leader of the ships. It was like a ray that he was sending down with the funnel. He did it five times, then we left!"

THE EXTREMITIES OF THE UFO EXPERIENCE

Some readers might think this volume is a bit too "wild," over-the-top or just too damn extreme. For the sake of getting the truth out, I see no reason to sugarcoat what seems apparent by taking the time to digest what several top UFO thinkers have managed to glean about the true nature of UFOs and their sometimes all-too-psycho occupants – be they physical or a supernatural/psychic aberration. We need not coddle the reader. If you want New Age pap we have plenty of books along that line to satisfy your exotic cosmic desires (i.e. the works of the late channel Tuella, who claims to have represented the loving Ashtar Command immediately comes to mind).

But as we shall see, the legends and lore associated with UFOs are many and extremely varied. This is one of the reasons this subject holds a tight grip on those who have become fascinated by stories which science could never possibly explain in rational terms. For, while the public may be familiar with the multitude of sightings of unidentified craft that have continued to be seen in our sky over the past six+ decades, most people are not all that much up on the bizarre aspects of this enigma.

They are probably not familiar with such occurrences as the sighting of "Spinwheel Jack," a "man" dressed in a black cape who, more than a hundred years ago, knocked on the doors of solid British citizens, waking them in the middle of the night, jumping over hedges, landing on rooftops and leaving "hoof prints" in the snow. Nor do they realize that the huge flying creatures nicknamed "Wild Bird," "Moth Man," or the like, have been seen over a wide area from Coney Island to the mountain towns of West Virginia, as well as the smallest rural communities in South America.

Nor is it likely they know too much about the cases where motorists have driven into an eerie fog bank and emerged in an instant only to find themselves transported – or "teleported" – hundreds of miles away. Add to this brief list the sightings of phantom cats, huge black monster dogs, Bigfoot creatures, little men with ray guns, animal mutilations, and you have yourself a mystery that even the great Sherlock Holmes would probably have to give up on. All of the above – and a lot more – "oddities" have time and again been blamed on, or at least associated with, the appearance of UFOs. Is it any wonder that the scientific community, the government and the military all "play ball" together to keep this topic under lock and key? After all, how could they go about explaining such incidents?

Once in a blue moon a truly bizarre UFO story DOES get some attention (as minor as it might be). Such was the case when the "HERALD" out of Sauk Centre, Minnesota, printed a story by staff reporters Roberta Olson and Craig Bihrie concerning an episode that is hard to rationalize even in light of all the oddball things that have happened to date involving UFOs.

The story from the "HERALD" follows exactly as it appeared in the original newspaper report:

"They were completely unnerved, the thin man nicknamed 'Killer' and his wife, sitting in the coffee shop sipping coffee and continually smoking cigarettes.

"'I'm scared to leave,' Robert (Bob) Blair said, and the look in his eyes left no doubt in your mind that was indeed frightened. He was not only frightened, he was terrified, continuously looking and motioning out the window.

"He was terrified, his wife, Jackie, was terrified. They had been experiencing unexplainable phenomena for three days, 900 miles across three states, and when they stopped in Sauk Centre, Minnesota, and begged for help, hardly anyone believed them.

"Bob and Jackie started out from Seattle, Washington, three days before on a routine trip hauling liquid cooking oil to Madison, Wisconsin, in a run they make regularly, weekly.

"Things went smoothly. They were enjoying the trip, and the shiny three-week old paint job on their semi-trailer boosted their morale. Then they got into Montana.

"A couple of miles ahead they spotted lights. 'We thought it was a plane,' Bob said. The story of their bizarre experiences poured out of them, hands shaking as they drew sketches of the creatures, and interrupting each other to agree or expand on a point.

"It was just turning daybreak when they came into Montana, they said. 'It was out there with the stars. They made people think they were stars.' Another man at a rest stop in Montana also saw the lights – nine little ships and one big ship, Bob reported, moving up and down, back and forth in a lurching motion.

"The Blairs continued on their trip, but the ships, or creatures, followed them in their semi. The individual things were described as shaped like about eight-inch people with V-shaped heads, wings on their backs. When the things got hostile with the truck and the drivers, they shot fine needle-like shavings like silver metal through the glass of the windshield. 'They were shaped like a prehistoric bird,' he said.

"'It just ruined the truck,' Jackie said, pointing out paint chips and nicks in the new paint job. 'Every time I touched them I got blisters on my fingers and it turned into a V.' He showed one on his wrist. In the dark, their fingertips glowed from the unknown substance they had touched.

"'We might be dying right now!' Bob said. 'We don't know what it is. We have to get to a doctor.'

"The creatures were hostile and went into attack modes several times, putting up dense fogs. One time when they stopped, 'It was like a backwards tornado' coming from the mouth of the leader of the ships. 'It was like a ray that he was sending down with the funnel. He did it five times, then we left. We didn't think it would harm us any.'

"Not at that point, anyway. They drove on for seven miles, stopping two, three, four times, getting out of the truck and holding on to the top to look at the lights in the sky. Then they experienced 'little black things, thousands of them, coming out of the sky, squiggly things, all around us,' Jackie described. They both experienced it.

"Then, back in the truck and moving, the lights kept up with them, even at 65 or 70 miles an hour. Things that looked like 'vitamin E capsules' began forming on the passenger side windshield as they moved. 'They formed all around the window, the whole inside of the frame was covered with them. At first, they were real little.'

"They got bigger. There were big black ones the size of baseballs. Whatever their size or color they all had a crystal-like thing inside them. Then three appeared as different color things: yellow, lavender and green. They got bigger in size.

"'It would seem like we were hitting them, but when we hit, nothing was there. Like bubbles,' Jackie said, having difficulty describing something that was unimaginable to her. 'When they hit the ground, there was a spot the same color on the ground or on the tree,' she said.

"'There was one about this big,' Bob said, spreading his arms. He was driving around 70 miles an hour at this point, and then there was another and a third of what they terms 'spaceships.' The third one they hit, a cloud burst off, and something shaped like a big peanut fell alongside the highway, about 15 inches thick and hourglass shaped.

"'It hit the ground and it was dirty yellow,' she added.

"At one point, the things shot a piece of metal 'clean through the window and the sleeper and my jacket,' she said, shaking her head and looking out the window.

"Jackie and Bob were trying desperately to get someone to see what they had seen. When they stopped, the 'birds' or spaceships stopped, flocked and waited for them to start traveling again.

"'We don't know why they are following us. Maybe one of them got on the tank or in the trunk somehow,' they said. 'Maybe they were trying to get it back.'

"They had called the UFO Center in Seattle from Montana and had had an appointment to meet an agent in Madison, Wisconsin, after delivery of their cargo. They were afraid to go further than Sauk Centre because when they stopped at Getty Truck Stop to fuel up, the ships had tried another attack and had landed in the trees across the highway.

"'We're not leaving town until somebody helps us,' Jackie said pleadingly. 'We called our boss and he said get a motel and keep the truck running.'

"They spent the night at Travel Host Motel. The motel manager reported they had not seemed distraught or reported anything unusual to him.

"Jackie called this reporter at home Monday night and said unusual things were happening in the motel room, with formation of metal filings on the bedspreads and formation of the same vitamin E-like things in the shower, which would blister her leg when they dropped. Now the blisters formed not only a V, but a T, C and L, she said.

"She was very frightened. 'When we moved the truck over here, hundreds of "birds" followed us. We knew they would come.' Because no one else could see or reported seeing the things, she analyzed, 'I am damn sure they turn invisible.'

"The police and Highway Patrol were in contact with the couple. None of the officials could see the objects the Blairs claimed to be in the trees or on the light posts waiting for them.

"'They were very scared people,' Police Chief Trierweller agreed. 'But I did not see what they saw.'

"Trierweller said he talked to the couple's boss in Yakima, Washington. They had worked for him for 18 years and were the best drivers he had. The truck they were driving is owned by S.D.T. Inc. at Yakima. S.D.T. sent a relief driver to Sauk Centre to meet the Blairs Tuesday morning. They left town about 1 pm, with Jackie driving a rental car and Bob riding with the new driver.

"One or two people believed their stories, but nobody could explain them. At least one witness saw the semi and rental car leave town Tuesday, but saw nothing unusual like fogs, formations or shapes following them.

"Skeptics had their own theories. Many people agreed that they believe things can happen that cannot be explained in terms that people understand. Many people believe there could be creatures, spaceships and unexplained happenings as described by the Blairs.

"Whatever people believe, the true story, the logical explanation, will probably never be found. It will become another folder in the federal UFO investigation files, unsolved."

* * * *

Probably none of us will know what really happened on the open road to these obviously shaken individuals. But if it was all a "daydream," how does one go about explaining the strange markings reporters and police could clearly make out on the cab of the Blairs' vehicle?

A HELL OF A BUMPY RIDE

UFOlogists were never promised a rose garden when they decided to chomp on the bit and enter this field. If they wanted cotton candy they should have gone to the nearest mom and pop confectionary and not to the carnival side show which is plainly laid out for us in the pages of this edition of the *Conspiracy Reader* by such top notch intergalactic chess players as Sean Casteel, Tim R. Swartz and the late Karla Turner, the latter of whom died – some have asserted too early in life – perhaps because of what she found out about the true nature of the alien invasion which consists of many unsavory elements.

By no means is this the first time I have laid down the gauntlet to those who think all we are dealing with is a group of lovey/dovey extraterrestrials who want nothing more than to have us enter an imaginary Intergalactic League of Nations.

EVIL EMPIRE OF THE ETS AND THE ULTRA - TERRESTRIALS

THE SHAPE OF THINGS TO COME

I have always been a fairly good natured guy going through life trying to see the bright side of things.

Recently, however, I came out of the closet UFO-wise upon publishing what has become a rather controversial tome in the field. Before *ROUND TRIP TO HELL IN A FLYING SAUCER* decided to expose the dark side of the ultra- dimensionals (a better word than aliens or ETs) few had dared to tackle the moral complexities involved. In ROUND TRIP we told some really shocking tales that showed that not only are UFOs a menace in the sky but there are shape-shifting, mutilating bastards in our midst.

Some of the stories utilized in this previous presentation are so off the wall we almost thought twice about publishing them but decided honesty was the policy, to utilize a rather worn out expression.

A prime example is the experience of two young ladies. What happened to them defies explanation, but it is a prime example of the total brazen nature of the phenomenon and the despicable nature of the energies that prevail.

Indeed are we not within reason to want to know just how a seemingly metallic structure can change shape? And I'm not talking about just contracting a pair of wings. I'm talking about a disc turning into a triangle, or a square transforming into a cigar. This is the one phenomenon in which what you see is NOT what you get.

As an example, I made an extensive study of the Carl Higdon abduction in which a Wyoming hunter saw a landed craft and was taken onboard and zipped off to a – we assume – far away destination. One of the remarkable aspects of this case – there are several that make this an exceptional incident as detailed in my book "*Strange Saga*" – is the fact that the craft appeared relatively small while on the ground but inside it appeared much larger, holding not only an entire crew but a number of elk that had been grazing near the landing spot.

In Manhattan's Chelsea area on October 13, 2010, crowds watched a cluster of UFOs morph high in the heavens. Some thought they were balloons but a close examination of the videos shows something that appears to be a single object that mushrooms out into several distinct objects before pulling itself back together.

Mickie Eckert's experience goes back a few years, and at the time it was totally unique in the annals of flying saucer-dom. Her story did not seem to fit in with any existing pattern and yet the sincerity showed on her pretty face as she related a bizarre tale that defied explanation.

As she looked at me with bewildered eyes, it was obvious that Mickie, a young woman in her mid-twenties, was seeking answers. She was confused about what had happened and was anxious to find out the reasons she was selected to have a close encounter that goes beyond anything previously recorded.

It was July 22, 1978. Mickie, along with her best friend, Kathy Echard, were driving along Interstate 80 East. They were headed towards Nebraska, a point near the Wyoming border, when they saw what they thought was an accident on the side of the road.

"We turned to get a better look and saw these white lights bobbing up and down. In order to get a better look, we pulled over to the shoulder of the road and aimed our car headlights in the direction of the crash."

It was apparent that Mickie wanted to talk about what transpired that night. We were seated around a large table, in a private conference room at the Royal Quality Inn in San Diego, California. Mickie had come to the privately-sponsored UFO conference (promoted by veteran newsman Hal Starr) mainly because she wanted desperately to talk with some of the top names in the field who are supposed to be trained in the handling of such matters. In attendance on the podium that day were such leading UFO luminaries as Jim and Coral Lorenzen from APRO (since deceased), Walter Andrus, director of the Mutual UFO Network, and Dr. James A. Harder, Associate Professor of Engineering at the University of California (Berkeley). Maybe it was because of their tight speaking schedule, but none of those present seemed to be able to find the necessary time to speak with Mickie Eckert. It was only after she was introduced to me by John DeHerrera (a practicing hypnotist who has been involved in the investigation of several contactee cases, most notably that of Brian Scott) that Mickie found someone who would listen intelligently to what she had to offer.

Going back to the evening in question, Mickie maintains that the sun had just set as they drove on a desolate and very isolated stretch of road eight miles north of Whelock, Nebraska.

"Our spotlights were trained on what we thought to be a mishap, but all we could see was three round circles hovering a few feet above the ground."

At the time, neither of the two young women realized that they were headed for a journey to a Twilight Zone more real than any TV program about the supernatural could ever hope to be.

"In front of our eyes these lights turned into two sports cars that were coming toward us."

One moment they had been confronted by the mysterious presence of airborne lights and the next thing they were aware of were two automobiles speeding in their direction. To say the least, they didn't know what to make of this transformation.

"We wanted no part of what was happening so we took off in the opposite direction. As we turned the car around to leave, in back of us we saw this whole bunch of lights. We backed up on the Interstate and now there were two trucks that had appeared out of thin air. On the trucks were teeny little lights. The trucks were following us, of this I'm sure."

The two tractor-trailers kept a steady pace on the highway in back of the girls. It was as if unseen eyes were watching their every movement, perhaps seeking an ideal spot to overtake them for some fiendish purpose.

"For some reason, Kathy asked me to stop and she got out of the auto and stood in front of the car. It was then that we saw all these other cars parked along the side of the road. They were just stopped there. When Kathy got back into our vehicle she wanted to drive and so I let her take the steering wheel. To her it felt as if something – some force – was trying to take control of our car. She got scared and eventually turned the driving back over to me and I too felt this strange pulling."

Putting as many miles behind them as possible, the two girls sped on through the night, anxious to get back to their home in California. "As we were passing through Salt Lake City, we stopped off at a Safeway store to get some gum and cigarettes." Mickie makes no bones about the fact that they were still shaken but says they were trying to pull themselves back together again, not having seen anything unusual on the road for quite some time now.

"As we were about to leave the Safeway supermarket, I noticed a reflection on one of the large windows coming from either inside or outside. Initially, I just assumed the reflection was caused by either the store lights themselves or from some street light nearby.

"Out in the parking area I discovered this was not at all the case, for directly across the lot was this little light about the size of a basketball just sitting near the ground."

There seemed to be so much that Micki had to say that the words wouldn't come out fast enough. Several times I had to slow her down so as not to miss any part of her narrative.

Totally freaked out by what was transpiring all around them, Micki's friend was anxious to push on as quickly as possible.

"As we entered Wyoming, we stopped again to get some bottled water. We were in a pretty good-sized town called Evansville, and it was still pretty early, but there wasn't a light on in the entire city. Everything was closed. None of the houses had lights on either. I looked out of the window on the driver's side of the car and there were these two ships hanging there. One was orange, the other yellowish-white. We continued on toward Green River, and the objects passed through the trees on the side of the road. At this juncture in time, we lost control of the car once more. No matter how fast we put our foot down on the gas pedal the car refused to accelerate past a certain speed."

In the middle of nowhere the car died completely. With this, a light came into the auto, passing right through an open window. The light touched Kathy Echard and, for no explainable reason, Mickie began talking to that light. "Come on, little light, why don't you touch me, too?" she remarked, despite the fact that everything up until this point had frightened her.

Not long after it had appeared the light inside the car vanished.

"All of a sudden we didn't see the ship anymore, but we started seeing trucks. Northwestern, American – and other big-named rigs. They were traveling in both directions, up and down the northbound and southbound lanes. The only way I can describe it is as a caravan of big lights going back and forth. This one particular truck stopped directly in front of us and we knew something was wrong. It was freaky – the trucks were now ships; dome-shaped, 3 sided ships about the same size as a compact automobile, and they were no longer on the road, but traveling about six feet off the ground."

Micki admits that she was too bewildered to be an excellent observer. She finds it hard to estimate the number of trucks or dome-shaped ships but she does know that the car they were in got pushed forward about 20 feet as if it had been lifted by a terrific force from underneath.

Despite their accelerated heartbeats, the girls decided to get out of their car to have a look, to see if anything might have gotten caught underneath their wheels which might account for the sudden tug forward. There was nothing there that would offer a solution to the puzzle, and so they climbed back into the relative safety of their vehicle.

"Soon there was this other car that pulled up directly in back of us and Kathy said she wanted to get out and see who was driving it." It was quite apparent from Mickie's comments that the girls were anxious to seek help from any other companion of the road they might find driving so late at night.

"When Kathy got back into the car I was anxious to know what she had said to the individuals in the car behind us. She just looked me straight in the eye and said, 'Turn around and tell me what you would have said to them.' There was this black dog, tail curved up and two red eyes blazing, just outside our car door."

The girls were understandably terrified by this new development.

Cowering in fear, Mickie happened to glance into the rear view mirror. What she saw only added fuel to a fire of panic that was so near to bursting out of control within them. "I saw what appeared to be a kid with his arms bunched together on the back seat."

The girls got out of the car in an attempt to escape this potential menace. Luckily the dog-like creature they had seen was nowhere in sight. However, directly behind them were two bright lights which were joined by several other duller-looking lights. After several minutes, they all blended into one light. "As the light went past us, it was no longer just a light – but a ship. We heard this rumbling sound and our hair stood on end. Our skin was covered with goose bumps."

At this point it seemed as if Mickie and Kathy had been transported to another dimension, another sphere of reality, for all at once things started looking peculiar, totally out of whack.

"Then the sun started to come up, but it was only an orange ball and it was coming toward us. And then it was not orange anymore, but its color turned suddenly to gray, and it was about 100 feet across, just enormous. And people started to appear out of nowhere, walking across the freeway carrying tubes or pipes. We didn't actually see them come out of any ship because the sun – or whatever it was – had landed in a valley out of our immediate viewing range."

The beings – or whatever they were – were standing in the middle island that separates the north and southbound traffic.

"There were this bunch of blue lights and we knew something was going to happen. We were terrified. We felt like we were going to be taken to another planet and would never be heard from again."

Without warning, the car started up. "I got mad at Kathy because I thought she had slammed on the brakes and I hit my head on the dashboard. We saw this ship coming down the Interstate and we also saw an 18-wheeler truck towing one of the sports cars we had seen earlier in the evening. Something pushed us from behind but we couldn't get the car to run of its own accord."

From out of nowhere a man appeared and asked the girls where they were headed. "He said he was heading toward Chicago and we said that's where we were going, too. I'd have gone to Timbuktu just to get out of the spot we were in."

From what I was able to gather, the man did not know anything was happening. He seemed totally unaware of the frightful state of the girls' minds caused by a terror that was real enough to them even if nobody else was able to perceive what was transpiring around them.

"I was so scared that I crawled all over the driver. He stopped at a truck stop to get coffee and we got out and walked to a nearby motel. We didn't have very much money. But we had about $35 and so we got a room. We unlocked the door and turned on the light and the TV went on by itself. Also this little teeny light flittered around the room and we knew we hadn't escaped."

Realizing that they were being observed, the girls tried to intimidate the light that was buzzing around their room.

"'Kathy, did you mail that letter telling about the flight pattern of the UFOs to my lawyer?' I asked with a purposeful slowness. She said she had, playing along with the game.

"We called the police and finally, at 5 o'clock the next afternoon, they came and took us back to the spot where we had abandoned the vehicle. As it turned out, the car wasn't where we had left it. And when we went back to the valley where the ship had been, the area wasn't the same. There was no little road on the side of the road. The freeway railing wasn't even the same. There was a sign MOUNTAIN ROAD 189. There is no Mountain Road 189 in all of Wyoming. We had a full tank of gas and we were about 250 miles into the state and there wasn't a gas station anywhere."

It was like they were driving without consuming fuel.

"The one item of interest was the corpse of a cow and a sheep off in a nearby field. The cow was all bones and the sheep had all of its skin peeled off, which made it look like a blanket lying there."

Mickie says that the police made them fill out a complete report. "After they had finished hearing our entire story they shrugged and told us we'd seen swamp gas!"

Moving the tape recorder closer to Mickie, she reported that both her life as well as her friend's have been drastically altered because of the events of that night.

"Kathy is only 31 years old, but she's been in the hospital at least 20 times since this happened. It's hard to explain, but somehow I feel we are the same people, but then again we aren't. Kathy had always been a slob and I have always been neat and clean. Now my house looks like the wreck of the Hesperus, and Kathy's is really neat, tidy, and very well cared for. Before I had always been the type to make my kids breakfast, lunch and dinner, while Kathy believed her children should prepare their own meals. It's just the other way around now. It's almost as though we've somehow exchanged personality traits. In other words, I'm still me, but it's as though I'm having my personality altered – taken over. I have always been a reader, for instance, and now I'm reading much more. I'm reading as much as I can on UFOs. That's the one subject that fascinates me the most."

Under hypnosis, Mickie was made to draw what she had seen. When it came to sketching the trucks that had appeared on the highway, she rendered a skeleton-type being instead of a moving vehicle.

"Is it possible that they altered your whole thinking process that night?" I asked the witness. Mickie acknowledged that this is what might have happened and that what really transpired could be entirely different from what she perceived. For some unexplainable reason, Mickie and her friend, Kathy, have grown farther apart in their friendship. "Before the experience, we had been the best of friends for 17 years. Now we speak to each other only once a week, tops."

Mickie is anxious to undergo further hypnosis. She wishes to find out what really took place on July 22, 1978. She is not satisfied just forgetting about the incident. The whole episode is a true puzzle. Taken as an isolated encounter, most UFOlogists would probably do their utmost to doubt the word of those individuals who were personally involved. The rule of thumb seems to be, "If you can't explain it, or it doesn't support existing evidence, brush the whole affair under the carpet." If we were to do this, we wouldn't be any better than the government agencies who have tried so hard to hide the very existence of UFOs from the public.

This case is a prime example of just how mysterious the entire UFO phenomenon can be. Just when you thought you might have pinned down the answer, it darts right away from you again!

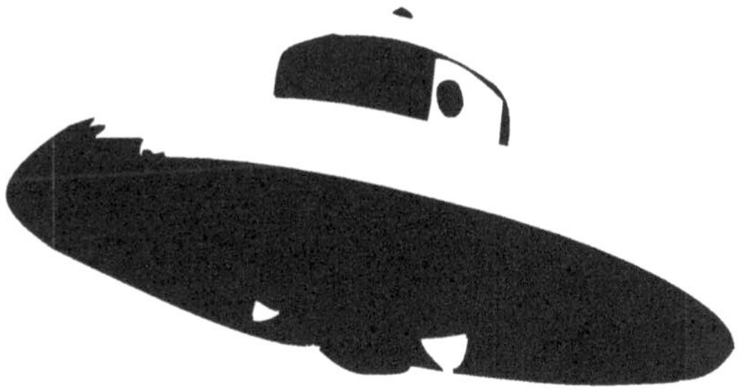

Has "Mr. ET" Taken Control Of Leading Figures In Politics, Religion And Economics In Order To Manipulate Earth's Destiny?

The Shadowy Universe Of Alien Thought Control

By Sean Casteel

In the New Millennium, as in decades past, the appearance of UFOs and their shadowy crew members may in fact be a political tool being used to reshape the patterns of our collective thought processes to the aliens' advantage, all of which forces us to ask questions like:

· Are the extraterrestrials here implementing plans to take control of the planet?

· Are the aliens offering solutions to mankind's problems as a kind of Trojan horse in order to get their foot in the door so they can lead us to a totalitarian form of world government?

· Do the ultra-terrestrials utilize religion – and fundamentalism in particular – to influence and even control the current program of terrorism?

· Will mankind one day be ruled over by hybrid human/aliens whose superior mental powers will completely subjugate us?

· Have we secretly achieved a new military technology that may one day provide us with effective weapons to use against an alien invasion?

· And finally, have the extraterrestrials found an ally in high-profile UFO researcher and advocate Dr. Steven Greer and his very popular Disclosure Project organization?

According to journalist and author Michael Brownlee, the answer to all of those questions is a resounding yes!

In 2003, Brownlee published a two-part essay on what he sees as the potential peril certain researchers such as Steven Greer may be placing our civilization in – either knowingly or unknowingly – by helping to popularize the unproven notion that the extraterrestrials are here to be helpful, benevolent friends of mankind. (Dr. Greer declined to be interviewed for this article, citing his busy schedule, but we extend a standing invitation to him to rebut any of the points made here by Brownlee.)

Brownlee initially viewed Greer as a hero.

"In 1997," Brownlee said, "which was a pivotal year in this field, I went to a conference in Phoenix, Arizona. It was a Prophets Conference, and one of the speakers there was Steven Greer. I'd heard of Steven. I had been reading some of his material and was very interested because he was the only one who, at least in the title of his organization [which is the Center For The Study Of Extraterrestrial Intelligence], was talking about studying the extraterrestrials themselves. I thought his efforts toward disclosing the presence of extraterrestrials were very courageous and heroic.

"And I know he was suffering a lot of persecution at that time," Brownlee continued. "The person who was closest to him in that work died of cancer. Dr. Greer also suffered from cancer, and they felt very strongly that the cancers were implanted by someone who wanted to stop them. I was just very touched. I thought he was a very compassionate, brilliant man, passionate and doing something worthwhile."

But since then, Brownlee says his opinion has changed.

"Whether for him it's knowingly or unknowingly," Brownlee said, "it would appear that Dr. Greer has been essentially 'co-opted' by the extra-terrestrials who are visiting the Earth at this time."

In other words, the aliens have taken control of Greer, at least in terms of what he says publicly.

Meanwhile, Brownlee credits a reclusive spiritual leader named Marshall Summers with helping him to gain what he now feels is a more accurate viewpoint on both Greer and what the aliens really want.

"At a UFO Expo in California," Brownlee said, "I ran into people who had an underground version of a book that I had not heard of. It was called 'The Allies of Humanity,' written by this man named Marshall Summers. The book's had a galvanizing effect on my life, certainly, and it has on a lot of other people as well, because the perspective that it presents is just totally unprecedented in this field. It's not research. It's not about the phenomenon per se. It is a look at what's happening."

The "Allies" of the book's title are a group of friendly extraterrestrials who are sending a warning to mankind about the coming colonization of the Earth by less benevolent aliens intent on manipulating mankind into an ultimate submission.

"This book contains information," Brownlee said, "that just unravels the whole mystery of the extraterrestrial activities and presence on this planet. And I say that not based on something I just want to believe, because there's a lot of material in it that's damned uncomfortable."

Our prior attempts to understand the situation, Brownlee says, have been woefully inadequate.

"The biggest problem we've had in the UFO/ET research community," he said, "is that this whole business of UFOs and extraterrestrials has been thoroughly enigmatic. It has just been a mystery. We haven't been able to penetrate it no matter how much research we do. After more than 50 years of hammering away at it, we haven't gotten much closer than we were in 1947. We have a lot of different ideas and theories and experiences, and they're all conflicting."

But Summers' book, while it is helpful to Brownlee in terms of getting a handle on the phenomenon, hasn't been welcomed with open arms by the UFO community.

"One of the things that I have noticed," Brownlee said, "is that the material presented in this little book is highly unpopular in the UFO community because it presents a viewpoint that a lot of people would just not like to be true. The aliens are, just like [well-known UFO researcher] David Jacobs says, implementing plans to take control of this planet.

"Not to destroy humanity," he continued, "but to take control. And Steven Greer has become their most effective ally and ambassador with the human race. He's gone from responding to a deep passion within him to being used by the extraterrestrials. And as I say, I don't know whether he's aware of it or not. But, unfortunately, that's the position he seems to be in. So in my eyes he's gone from being a hero for being so courageous to being a very, very dangerous force in the world today."

Brownlee vigorously contests certain opinions expressed be Greer, including Greer's claim that the majority of UFOs sighted are really manmade devices.

"Of course," Brownlee said, "the literature is filled with stories of how we have captured craft or downed spacecraft and we have been working very hard to reverse-engineer them at Area 51 and other places. We've been hearing all that for years. And Greer was talking about that, of course, in his early years. But recently, in the last two or three years, he's started saying that, 'Well, what's really going on is that most of the UFOs in the sky are manmade.'

"Now, there is absolutely no evidence for that. It is an assertion on his part that is not backed up by evidence. He said, 'And we can prove it,' again and again. But he doesn't offer any proof. He doesn't offer any documentation whatsoever. I have no doubt that the government has been doing its best to reverse-engineer alien craft technology, but it's a long way from that to saying that the majority of UFOs are manmade."

Brownlee also disputes Greer's claim that the abduction phenomenon is again a human effort.

"This is called 'Escalation of Rhetoric,'" Brownlee explained. "Years ago, and I have heard Greer talk about this, he was saying that, based upon the work of Helmut Lammer, who wrote about MILAB abductions, he said it looks like we're in the business of doing abductions. It's absolutely true that Helmut Lammer wrote about military-based abductions, human-based abductions. He says he doesn't know why it's happening. He just said it appears to be happening but he also makes crystal clear that, based upon his research, this amounts to a very small fraction of abductions that are taking place.

"So Greer started using Helmut's research on MILAB abductions," Brownlee went on, "and he escalated the rhetoric in the last couple of years to start saying that all abductions are perpetrated by humans. All of them. Now, again, there is absolutely no evidence to that effect. There is no way he could even know that. If you look at the evidence, if you look at the studies that have been done, if you look at all of the abduction research, on balance you'd have to say that it is a completely ludicrous claim. Why is he making it? It's very odd. It's even odder that no one calls him on it."

But what if Dr. Greer is right, at least partially? How would a "hoaxed abduction," the kind put forth by Greer, typically play itself out?

"My understanding is," Brownlee replied, "that it follows much the same course. The one difference sometimes is that the abductees are taken to an underground facility. An underground, apparently MILITARY facility where they see lots of armed soldiers and things like that.

"Now, if you ask David Jacobs about this, he will say, well, it's pretty obvious now. We know from research on hundreds and hundreds if not thousands of abductees that human-appearing beings often show up in abduction scenarios. And what he proposes is that those are not humans at all but are in fact hybrids. The hybrids are increasingly responsible for the abduction program. So to assert that they are human is a wild assertion, devoid of evidence."

However, in spite of what Brownlee considers to be Greer's false claims, Greer still provides an accurate barometer of what the aliens really want, says Brownlee.

"What I have learned about Steven Greer," Brownlee said, "is if you want to know what the extraterrestrials are concerned about, what they're worried about, what they're up to, pay attention to what Dr. Greer is saying and doing. He can give us the best insight into their strategy of almost anybody on the planet. But you have to look at it from the perspective that what's going on here is essentially a clandestine takeover of the planet. And again, this is not about destroying humanity or destroying the planet. That's ludicrous. They want control. It's just that simple."

One method the aliens are using to manipulate our thinking is the time-honored ploy of making humanity feel guilty.

"The really stark thing that comes through everything else," Brownlee said, "is the statement that humans are the real problem in the universe. That's an outrageous statement. It is based upon a species-wide guilt, if you will. It's like, 'Oh, man, we're really bad. We're really screwed up.' And that's exactly where we're most vulnerable. So the extraterrestrials come and abduct our people and they tell them, the point they make is 'You guys are screwing up your planet.'

"Well, they don't say it this way, but the feeling is, 'You're bad. You're screwed up. You need us to come and straighten things out.' From a psychological perspective, that is the basis of a codependent relationship. That's exactly what they're trying to create. They want us dependent on them. They want us controlled. We're useful to them, because their numbers aren't very large. They've got a lot of work to do here and they need our labor."

One primary motivation for the alien takeover may be simple, old-fashioned greed.

"The world holds incredible resources that are pretty rare in the universe," Brownlee theorizes. "Those resources include biological resources, they include mineral resources, and perhaps some other things. They don't want us, for instance, destroying our ecological system because it's bad business for them. It screws up their plans."

EVIL EMPIRE OF THE ETS AND THE ULTRA - TERRESTRIALS

The aliens offer solutions to mankind's problems as a kind of Trojan horse in order to get their foot in our door so they lead us to a totalitarian form of government.

"The message of fascism," Brownlee cautioned, "is always 'This will solve all problems.' What we're looking at are signs of a fascist takeover that, if it is not exposed and resisted, will wind up being not just a fascist state, but a fascist world.

"It's not like the aliens are going to come down as aliens and run things. No, they don't function that way. The Allies [the informants in Marshall Summers' aforementioned book] present a very interesting idea. And that is that the aliens are breeding hybrids to be the new rulers, the new leaders, of this world. They will look like humans, only they will be very, very powerful, particularly in what the Allies refer to as the 'mental environment.'

"The particular aliens that are here now, while they're technologically advanced, they don't have great legions, they don't have great military forces. That's not how they work. You can only take physical technology to a certain point in the evolution of life in the universe. What's beyond physical technology is the technology of the mental realm. And that's where they excel."

Brownlee made reference to the late Harvard psychiatrist and abduction researcher Dr. John Mack to drive his point home.

"Even John Mack," Brownlee said, "who took a fairly positive view towards the alien presence here, he said the most common form of contact between humans and extraterrestrials is in the dream state. In other words, they can enter our dreams. They can plant images, ideas, emotions, thoughts, impulses. They're very good at that. And we're just so wide open that we don't even know it's going on, for the most part.

"In the mental realm," he continued, "they are very, very effective and we are unfortunately very naïve. So one of the ways that this plays out is in one of the key areas of alien activity – the manipulation of our religious and spiritual beliefs. They are very aware of our naivety and they are able to easily manipulate people who are particularly prone to fanatical beliefs, fundamentalism in all of its varieties around the world. They can be very influential."

This has frightening implications on a global scale, according to Brownlee.

"One of the astonishing things that we ultimately learn out of this," he said, "is the extent to which the extraterrestrials are operating behind the scenes in world affairs today, influencing key people. And one of the great problems that we have in the world today, that's pushed us to the brink of global warfare, is this explosion of Islamic fundamentalism."

Brownlee again cited "Allies Of Humanity" as his source for this belief.

"The suggestion is that the extraterrestrials are meeting some resistance in the Western World," he said. "Meaning that we just aren't falling over for their program here. So they have decided to stir up some reprisals and extract a little pain. Those are the roots, if you will, of the September 11 attack and the whole terrorist effort that has been building and escalating and has pushed us into war. Now, I think that's a pretty extraordinary hypothesis, and if there's any basis to it at all, it's something that we should be looking at. I mean, talk about a conspiracy theory! That's about as big as it gets."

On top of that, the aliens have begun a form of warfare of their own.

"Craft have flown over military bases with nuclear missile," Brownlee said, "and shut them down. They just shut the missiles down. People couldn't even restart them. There is no way that that could not be interpreted as a blatantly hostile act. If we did anything like that to, to any other country, what would happen? It would be an instant cause for war, right?

"It's a pretty universal principle. You enter my territory and you brandish weapons – or not even weapons, but just give a show of force, a show of power – that's throwing down the gauntlet. I mean, you've violated my territory, damn it! And what's interesting is our response to that. Our military forces, when events like that have happened, have found ourselves to be completely powerless. There was nothing that they could do.

"Do you want the world to know that you were humiliated by someone like that? Absolutely not. You don't even have to talk about over-flights. As Jacobs and others have done, you could simply talk about the abductions that are going on. They are a flagrant and fundamental violation of human rights and freedoms. You can't interpret it any other way. That's hostile.

"So the rhetorical claim that Steven Greer makes, that the aliens have no hostile intentions whatsoever, is preposterous. Again, it is an illogical, undocumented, unproven claim. Why is he making this claim? On whose behalf is he making such a claim?"

The aliens are also concerned that humanity may one day be able to defend itself militarily against an alien invasion.

"I know of people," Brownlee said, "who are involved in space defense projects and who are very consciously aware that what they're doing is developing systems to defend against the extraterrestrials. It's happening. It's not just pie-in-the-sky or a rumor; it's actually happening. They're working on it.

"There are pretty good indications," he continued, "that the whole Star Wars missile defense effort has very little to do with terrorism and rogue states on this planet. I think it's much more likely that those systems are early attempts to design systems to build a shield against extraterrestrial incursion. I know that's not a politically popular viewpoint, but I think it's worth considering. And if that were true, it would kind of explain the way that some of those programs have been handled, the secrecy around them, the kind of skittishness that our government has had about them."

In spite of those possibly heroic machinations behind the scenes, there is still the REAL conspiracy to be dealt with, as Brownlee sees it.

"We talk about this dark conspiracy," he said, "of the wealthy and so on. It's not difficult to imagine that those people in positions of power are again either knowingly or unknowingly co-opted by the extraterrestrials. Yeah, there's a conspiracy, all right, but it's much larger than our conspiracy theorists have been talking about. We've been talking about human conspiracies here. Well, all human conspiracies are being manipulated by the extraterrestrials, essentially.

"We need to start understanding what they're up to. We need to start seeing the patterns of manipulation. We need to start seeing their strategies and their programs. We need to know what this hybridization program is about. We need to understand why they're manipulating religious and political and economic leaders throughout the world. We need to understand why they're acclimating us to their presence in every possible way they can, through the media, through entertainment, a variety of ways. They getting us comfortable with the idea that aliens are among us."

All of which paints a dark picture indeed. But there is more.

"We are on the brink of losing our freedom," Brownlee warned, "of losing our sovereignty, and we're not aware of it. And we need to become aware. We need to help other people become aware. And that's a very big challenge."

[If you enjoyed this article by Sean Casteel, visit his "UFO Journalist" website at www.seancasteel.com to read more of his articles or to purchase his books.]

Michael Brownlee is an author, publisher and journalist reporting on "the transformation of consciousness now unfolding on this planet." He co-founded Visibility Unlimited, LLC, a publishing venture committed to "communication that creates," and edited and published "Awakening World," an online magazine.

Brownlee was the chief editor and coauthor of "Just In Case: Dispatches From the Front Lines of the Y2K Crisis," a critically acclaimed anthology of essays published by Origin Press in 1999. Brownlee was a frequent public speaker, media interviewee and workshop presenter on this controversial topic. He is also the author of "The Creator's Workshop: A Complete Course In Creation."

Brownlee has conducted workshops on "Understanding the Extraterrestrial Presence in the World Today," an introduction to the mystery of "contact" and the growing challenge to human freedom; "The Extraterrestrial Crisis: The Challenge of Our Lifetime," a wake-up call for those who suspect their destiny is somehow connected to humanity's emergence into the Greater Community; "Awakening the Creator Within," a profound experiential journey into the underlying design of human evolution, from the personal to the universal; and "The Cultural Creatives: An Awakening Culture," an introduction to the new paradigm of consciousness that is rapidly reshaping our world.

Steven Greer, M.D., is an emergency room physician and the founder of the Center for the Study of Extraterrestrial Intelligence, an international nonprofit scientific research and educational organization "dedicated to the furtherance of our understanding of extraterrestrial intelligence." CSETI was founded in 1990 by Dr. Greer, who also served as the organization's international director. Greer later founded the Disclosure Project, a nonprofit research project "working to fully disclose the facts about UFOs, extraterrestrial intelligence, and classified energy and propulsion systems."

According to the Disclosure Project website, "We have over 400 government, military and intelligence witnesses testifying to their direct, personal, firsthand experience with UFOs, extraterrestrials and extraterrestrial technology and the cover-up that keeps this information secret."

"DR. TURNER HAS PROVIDED THE READER with an extraordinary glimpse into the lives of her family and friends. With curiosity and courage, she has explored their UFO encounters; with compassion and commitment, she has helped them to deal with their anxieties, doubts, and fears. Dr. Turner has shown intellectual integrity in describing her detailed records of events, and writing skill in expressing her concerns about the implications of these encounters . . . "

—R. Leo Sprinkle, Ph.D., Counseling Psychologist, Founder of the Rocky Mountain Conference on UFO Investigation

". . . the stunning correlations among these accounts will give the cautious researcher a reason to pause and reconsider the boundaries of his own beliefs."

—John S. Carpenter, MSW/LCSW, Psychiatric Hypno-therapist, Mutual UFO Network Director for Abduction Research

INTO THE FRINGE

A TRUE STORY OF ALIEN ABDUCTION

Karla Turner, Ph.D.

ACKNOWLEDGMENTS

Without the help and support of several people, the experiences described in this book might have been overwhelming. I want to thank my dearest friend, Bonnie, for her faith in my sanity and honesty, for always being there when I needed to talk, and for offering an objective perspective. Sandy and Fred, two others who had experiences of their own, were great confidants, and I thank them for their friendship. I also thank James for his courage and perseverance, and especially for his generosity in allowing me to include his story with ours.

Barbara Bartholic proved to be the greatest ally that Casey and I could have had in our quest to understand what we were going through, and there are no words adequate to express our appreciation to her. Without her tireless work on our behalf, this story would be greatly diminished.

Finally, every woman should be blessed with a husband as strong, supportive, and loving as Casey. Thank God I am.

A NOTE TO THE READER

All of the people in this account are real. Because of the nature of the events they experienced, however, several people involved have chosen to be identified by pseudonym or by first name only. Whenever a pseudonym is used, it will be noted at that name's first appearance in the story.

DR. KARLA TURNER PRESENTS A CHECKLIST OF EVENTS AND EXPERIENCES TYPICALLY SUFFERED BY ABDUCTEES. THIS PARTIAL CHECKLIST ESTABLISHES VARIOUS FACTS:

* Aliens can alter our perception of our surroundings.

* Aliens can control what we think we see. They can appear to us in any number of guises and shapes.

* Aliens can take us – our consciousness – out of our physical bodies, disable our control of our bodies, install one of their own entities, and use our bodies as vehicles for their own activities before returning our consciousness to our bodies.

* Aliens can be present with us in an invisible state and can make themselves only partially visible.

* A surprising number of abductees suffer from serious illnesses they didn't have before their encounters. These have led to surgery, debilitation, and even death from causes the doctors can't identify.

* Some abductees experience a degeneration of their mental, social and spiritual well-being. Excessive behavior frequently erupts, such as drug abuse, alcoholism, overeating and promiscuity. Strange obsessions develop and cause the disruption of normal life and the destruction of personal relationships.

* Some abductees report being taken to underground facilities where they see grotesque hybrid creatures, nurseries of hybrid humanoid fetuses, and vats of colored liquid filled with parts of human bodies.

* Abductees report seeing other humans in these facilities being drained of blood, being mutilated, flayed, and dismembered, and being stacked, lifeless, like cords of wood. Some abductees have been threatened that they, too, will end up in this condition if they don't cooperate with their alien captors.

* Aliens have forced their human abductees to have sexual intercourse with aliens and even with other abductees while groups of aliens observe these performances. In such encounters, the aliens have sometimes disguised themselves in order to gain the cooperation of the abductee, appearing in such forms as Jesus, the Pope, certain celebrities, and even the dead spouse of the abductee.

"It becomes clear," Turner writes, *"from these details that the beings who are doing such things can't be seen as spiritually enlightened, with the best interests of the human race in mind. Something else is going on, something far more painful and frightening, in many, many abduction encounters."*

Dr. Turner's Checklist

INTRODUCTION

In December 1987, Casey (a pseudonym) Turner was a successful computer consultant in a large southwestern city. He had a happy second marriage, good health, professional respect, intelligence, and a kind, good-humored nature. At the same time, David Trayne (pseudonym), a bright science student at the local university, was living on five acres of a 35-acre area on the edge of the city. He had a roommate, James (pseudonym), a girlfriend, Megan (pseudonym), also a science student, and three dogs.

Today, almost three years later, it would seem that things are still much the same for Casey and David, but I know better. Casey is my husband, David my son, and Megan is now our daughter-in-law. Together, we have all struggled to understand an astonishing phenomenon that revealed itself in our lives. It has altered our whole reference of reality in ways we could never have imagined.

We discovered that we were victims of abductions by some alien force. We learned that this force, this alien presence, had in fact been a part of our lives for many years. And through sharing our experiences, and seeking answers and help from others who had also encountered these beings, we learned to survive with our sanity intact and our perspective on life immeasurably expanded.

Stories of humans abducted, examined, and crossbred by alien beings of unknown origin are nothing new, not since Budd Hopkins's, Whitley Strieber's, and most recently, the media's interest in the subject. But that interest itself, a serious interest, is new. There hasn't been so much discussion on the air and in print about UFOs and ETs since the 1950s. And although UFO activity never ceased in the past forty-five years, it certainly has changed, most noticeably since 1981.

Undreamed-of numbers of people have discovered that they, too, have encountered this alien presence. Abduction activity affects all types and ages of people, and for the victims there is no shelter and no one to offer any real help. They are victims of affronts which no official power— political, spiritual, or social—admits to be real.

When we discovered this phenomenon in our lives, I began keeping a journal of events. At first it was only of Casey's experiences, but it soon expanded to cover mine and those of David, as well as of Megan and James. Awareness and involvement in the phenomenon, it seems, was spreading.

What follows is an integrated account of our experiences, taken from the journal entries from May 1988 to the summer of 1989. Many of these events were consciously experienced and remembered. But other occurrences were blocked from memory and known only from the evidence of marks on our bodies, episodes of "missing time," or strange phenomena in our homes. In several instances, hypnotic regression was used to uncover more about the blocked episodes, although many of our experiences have yet to be explored in this way.

This account also includes information from television reports, from books and other research documents, and from the stories of new people who came into our lives because of this phenomenon. I have not limited our story, as has been done in other abduction accounts, to only that information I judge to be believable, or palatable, or conforming to some theoretical explanation of my own choosing. Instead, this is the whole story of our first year after the discovery of alien intrusion, with all our fears, doubts, trials, and successes.

The information in this book is very personal, yet I believe its focus is of great, immense importance. We are in the midst of a reality-challenging mystery, and although I once said that this story couldn't be written until it was over, we no longer have the luxury of waiting. Like some species-wide recurrent nightmare, it may never be over. Or the mystery might all be made clear tomorrow, with revelations that mark the end of the world as we know it.

EVIL EMPIRE OF THE ETS AND THE ULTRA - TERRESTRIALS

The people in this book are victims. They are also my family and friends, both old and new, and it matters very much to me what happens to us. It should matter to everyone else, too, because our story is proof that no family, no child or friend or mate, is safe from intrusion and abduction. The experiences of our small group, in fact, are being repeated in thousands of homes right now.

Finally, the things we've experienced prove that our global reality is not what we once thought. This phenomenon continues to spread, and, no matter what the actual nature of its cause, the world will change irrevocably. For us, it already has changed, and we can't help but fear to discover the direction it portends.

—K. T.

INTO THE FRINGE
by
Dr. Karla Turner

CHAPTER 1

In the spring of 1988, our world ended. Life went on, but everything we had always known about reality—our trusted perceptions of ourselves, of the present and the past, of the nature of time and space—were destroyed. The end of one's reality is truly the end of a world. Another world follows, of course, but exile from the first one is permanent. We were thrust into new territory, a place of missing-time episodes, of UFOs and unhuman beings and all sorts of bizarre phenomena that wouldn't go away. Yet we hardly noticed its beginning, and later, when it became clear that something strange was occurring, we had no idea that the very fabric of reality was about to change for my husband, Casey, and myself, as well as for our family and friends.

This is the story of how we came to this new reality. It is an account of the experiences that erupted in our lives, of our entrance into that other world of altered realities we "sane" people merrily deride or ignore. In the beginning, we kept these things to ourselves, out of fear and confusion, but now we realize the story should be told, for two very good reasons.

First, what happened to us is not unique. It is occurring all over the world, yet until now such an account, involving a cluster of people, has never been presented in its entirety. What follows here is the complete truth, with nothing omitted or added to make the story more believable or more fantastic. Second, the implications of our experiences are global, in fact cosmic, and they point to a very disturbing future. If our world has truly changed, so has yours, for we occupy the same world.

Please don't assume that my friends and I were unbalanced or fanatics of some sort, given to extreme beliefs, when this all began. Instead, we were generally open-minded about most things, which I'm sure would have included the existence of aliens if the subject had ever come up. But it didn't, at least for me, until quite inexplicably while teaching a freshman course in argument and logic I did something I'd never done before in my eight years as a university instructor: I brought up the subject of UFOs in class, as part of an assignment.

UFOs were one of three topics, actually, including the Loch Ness monster and Bigfoot, and my students were asked to make an objective evaluation of the evidence pertaining to one of these phenomena. I chose these three because I assumed the evidence would be weak and inconclusive when examined from a clear-thinking, insightful, educated point of view. In truth, however, I had never really looked at the evidence with more than a passing curiosity.

But in reading these research papers, I became familiar with titles of available books on these subjects. Perhaps that's why I suddenly decided to buy a paperback I'd seen for months at the mall bookstore, one which had never interested me before: Communion, by Whitley Strieber, a bizarre account purporting to be factual, about his experiences with some sort of alien entities, from some undetermined source. I read the book skeptically, yet was intrigued by his emotive story of intrusion, terror, and the groping for understanding.

In late April I was on my way to the West Coast for a few days, leaving Casey alone at home. Before I left, my son, David, borrowed Strieber's book and took it to his house. At the airport I looked for something to read on the flight and, remembering that Strieber had mentioned Budd Hopkins as a researcher into UFO phenomena, I bought Missing Time, Hopkins's account of several abduction experiences.

In California I read the book late at night, with very strong reactions. For one thing, I wondered how on earth Hopkins and Strieber could get away with claims that their books were factual, since the material—strange alien beings, small and gray and clone-like in their actions—was so obviously impossible. Hapless humans abducted, medically examined, then released with little or no memory of such events? Who were they trying to kid? I also remember thinking how glad I was that these stories were not true. How, I wondered, could you ever live in a world where such things could happen?

It was hard enough, I thought, to cope with the real world, even for the sanest of us. Casey and I, for instance, were financially solid and very happy in our marriage. Yet for several months, we had been attending separate counseling sessions in an effort to find out why we'd developed physical symptoms of stress.

For me, it was the onset of TMJ,' with all its painful clenching of the teeth and jaws, and for Casey it was a variety of things. He was usually a calm, centered person, but since Christmas he had grown increasingly tense and short-tempered. His eyesight worsened, he had frequent headaches and stomachaches, and he suffered from tingling, numbness and pain that ran from his hip all the way down his left leg. Counseling helped us deal with the apparent problems in our lives, but the stress didn't disappear as promised. In my therapy, hypnosis had been used, so I became familiar with a relaxation technique involved in achieving a trance state. Since I'd been unsuccessful in finding the source of my stress with the first therapist, I began seeing a second counselor, Dr. Riley (pseudonym), who helped me work on consciously relieving the symptoms through mental relaxation.

I was also keeping notes on my dreams during this time, again as part of my therapy. I'd studied Jungian theory and found that these ideas deepened my insight into the psyche. At the time, I believed that explanations for all human behavior, including the experience of visions, lay in the archetypal structure of the human mind. Examining my dreams gave me entrance into the nature of my own psyche, and looking back now, I can see in those dreams the presence of a looming shadow.

A brief chronology of events shows how rapidly this new subject surfaced in my life, which until then had been completely free of extraterrestrial interests. In mid-April I assigned UFOs as a possible research topic in class. On April 21, I dreamed of seeing my husband and a group of his friends sitting happily together in a round environment, either in a round room or at a round booth, or both. His friends were all males in black attire, and I somehow knew they were vampires. On the twenty-second, I dreamed that a worldwide disaster or catastrophe had occurred, and my son was missing along with some of his friends. On the twenty-fourth, I began reading Communion. I asked my husband if he'd ever seen a UFO, and he said he hadn't. I replied that I hadn't, either, yet I remembered seeing a puzzling light zig-zagging high in the Oklahoma sky in 1959 or 1960.

On April 25, I had two significant dreams. In the first, I went from dime store to dime store with my husband, and in each one I saw a doll in a cage. The dolls became more and more lifelike, until in the last store the doll was a miniature living little girl. She cried and reproached me as her mother, for leaving her there so long. I also dreamed of seeing a UFO land. I went toward it in great excitement, but the UFO suddenly exploded, and I knew that the government was responsible. The explosion somehow set off a land rush for Canada. Awake, I did not recall ever having dreamed about UFOs before. On the twenty-seventh, I bought Missing Time and read it in California.

It may seem a long way from UFOs and aliens to the vampires, catastrophes, and caged living dolls that appeared in my dreams, but I've learned that each of these images is directly relevant. Not so obviously, perhaps, but very significantly, and that's what makes me believe the dreams were in some way foreshadowing the events yet to unfold.

And I'm aware that UFO scoffers reading this account will say that the books were the sources of everything that followed. But that is not, from the distance and experience of the past three years, how I interpret it now. Instead of these books causing all the turmoil that was to follow, I believe I was drawn to them because of the discoveries I would soon have to confront. The alien phenomenon forced itself into my consciousness and directed me to the subject, to the books, as a means of preparation. I was being made ready, I feel certain, to deal with what was looming ahead.

May 1988

When I returned from my trip to California, Casey was suffering from back pains, the numbness in his left leg and foot which had recurred for several months, a headache and an upset stomach. So on May 2, after dinner, I offered to show him the relaxation hypnosis technique I'd learned in therapy, hoping he could relieve these symptoms. He lay down on the couch and I began to lead him into a trance state. It was the first time I'd ever helped hypnotize anyone but myself, but he was a good subject. Before long I'd taken him through some of the tests my therapist had used to prove to me I was really hypnotized: one arm floating like a feather, for instance, while the other hand weighs heavily into the chair.

When I saw that Casey was clearly in a trance, I decided to imitate my own therapist, in hopes of helping Casey uncover the problems that must be contributing to his stress. First I asked him to look back over his life and see if any particular event or person seemed especially important. And Casey responded easily, scanning back to recall mostly fond memories. He talked about his parents, his childhood, and the wonderful times he spent with his grandparents. But no particular problem came to his mind.

So I tried another of the therapist's tactics. "Why don't you ask your unconscious to communicate with you?" I suggested. "Ask if it will reveal to you anything that might be disturbing or significant."

Casey was silent a moment, and then he nodded. "Yes," he answered, "it says it will talk to me." Sitting back, then, I expected to hear any number of things—friction at work, mixed feelings about his children, or, more likely, I thought, unresolved emotions left over from his first marriage.

My expectations were blown away, however, as Casey spoke. First, he saw himself in his father's 1940 model Ford, with the windshield and dashboard bathed in such a blinding light that his eyes hurt. He was less than two years old, standing in the front seat as his father drove, and he recalled a dark afternoon storm before the light flooded in. He saw his father at the wheel, unmoving, as if frozen in place, before the memory jumped to the drive home through the hills around Grass Valley, California, near the Nevada border. Although the scene was clear enough, he didn't know why it had presented itself to him.

Then Casey again asked for subconscious help to uncover anything significant or disturbing that was being suppressed and causing his painful symptoms. But the next image he received was of a wall, a long, curving gray wall marked with strange symbols, and he couldn't see beyond it. I used a technique to help clarify his vision, directing him to imagine a thick curtain and to open it very slightly at first and peek through. He envisioned the curtain and mentally pulled it apart, and then he suddenly jumped in fright, literally levitating horizontally off the couch with a great start.

"What is it?" I asked anxiously, wondering if I'd strayed into something neither of us could deal with.

"A face!" he told me, still obviously terrified, as he described a strange countenance, grayish-white and deeply wrinkled, with an O-shaped open mouth and two huge, circular, black, staring eyes.

Just then the phone rang, and I quickly tried to relax Casey long enough to let me answer it. I picked up the receiver, said "Hello," and then heard the most unusual sounds I'd ever heard over the phone. Someone or something was talking to me in a rather thin, erratic, rapid voice, but I could understand nothing. The talking didn't sound as if it came from a machine, but it was nothing like a human voice, either. Surprised, I listened for perhaps twenty seconds and then repeated my "Hello." Abruptly the talking stopped, and all I heard was a faint static back- ground. This lasted for another few seconds, and then the line went completely dead.

Puzzled, but too concerned about my husband to think about the call, I hung up and rushed back to Casey and asked him to continue his description.

"His face looks sort of like putty," he said, "and it's so wrinkled and old-looking." He felt that someone was holding him, lifting him to see this face up close. "I don't want to go to him," he continued. "I still see the wall, it's transparent, and there are some symbols on it."

He talked about seeing a black sky, with pinpoint stars, and then he gasped, shaken again, and described what could only be considered a space craft. "It's so big!" he kept saying, and it was giving off an orange glow.

After having read Communion and Missing Time, I didn't want to hear about alien faces and flying saucers, especially from my own very sane husband. I was upset by Casey's descriptions, and all I could think to do was bring him out of the trance immediately. But he was still agitated, trying to describe what he'd seen in better detail, and finally he drew pictures of the face and the orange craft. When I looked at the face he'd drawn, I too was terrified and repelled, so much so that I simply couldn't stand to be in the same room with it. And I didn't understand why it upset me so much, for it was not identical to the gray-faced aliens discussed in the books I'd read—books, by the way, that Casey hadn't seen.

At first I thought that Casey had somehow, perhaps telepathically, picked up on the material I'd read. Not that I'm a big believer in telepathy, but I was reaching for some understandable explanation. When I thought back through the hypnosis, however, I saw that Casey had described events and scenes different from those in Hopkins's and Strieber's books. If he were really reading my thoughts, I reasoned, his descriptions should have matched more of the details. Casey had told me of a blinding light, a paneled, curving wall with symbols, the enormous orange spacecraft, and the wrinkled, dark-eyed alien face. Yet these things weren't familiar from my reading.

Furthermore, it didn't seem likely that Casey had simply invented these images, because his emotional responses had been genuine and intense, surprising him as much as me. Yet it seemed just too coincidental that I would have suddenly read those books, with no previous interest in UFOs, and then would hear my own husband talking about such things, with such conviction. The only thing I felt sure of was that I hadn't intentionally influenced him, during hypnosis, to describe the UFO or the alien face. All I had done was ask him to consult his subconscious mind and see if it would show him the cause of his stressful symptoms.

Casey and I were both quite shaken by his descriptions. I slept poorly that night, and in the morning I was still so frightened that it was hard to leave my bedroom. That picture, I knew, was still in the living room, and I dreaded going in there. So, although I'd only seen Dr. Riley twice, early that morning I phoned him, asking if he would talk to my husband and try to sort out the reality behind the things he'd seen. I didn't believe Casey had actually ever seen such a face or spaceship. Yet both our reactions were so strong that I wanted reassurance of another more logical and acceptable explanation.

The therapist refused to talk to Casey. Instead, he said he wanted to see me and deal with my strange fears, but I insisted that it was my husband who needed looking after! We needed to know that his memories stemmed from a movie he'd once seen, perhaps, or from a forgotten nightmare, and we wanted someone in authority to tell us that. "Won't you talk to him for a minute?" I asked repeatedly.

The therapist lost patience with my insistence. After warning me again that I was the one in need of help, he ended the conversation on a sarcastic note. "I can tell you this," he concluded vehemently. "Whatever it was that your husband recalled, it certainly wasn't flying saucers and little green men!"

I desperately wanted to believe him. Images from the books I'd just read kept running through my mind, though, and I began to think that perhaps such tales weren't impossible. We needed a hypnotist, but the only one I knew refused to help. So two days later, our intense curiosity won out. We turned on the tape recorder to keep a record of what might follow and put Casey into a trance again. This time we were looking for something specific: the origin of the images he'd first recalled.

The story that unfolded was not a repeat of what I'd read by Strieber or Hopkins, so I felt confident that Casey wasn't subconsciously picking up his material from me. But that's all I felt confident about. Here was my husband of almost ten years, a man of caution and intelligence and great analytical ability, telling me about two different childhood encounters with nonhuman beings.

We began by focusing on the creature he'd drawn on May 2. He brought up the image and told me, "I saw a strange eye. It's close. It goes from left to right and it's big and close and dark and open, just looking like a big deer's eye, not a human eye, just big." Throughout much of this session, I noticed that Casey spoke in a more childlike manner than usual, as if he were recalling these events from the child's perspective.

I asked, "What color is the eye?"

"The outside is like dirty white," he told me. "The outside, the skin around the eye, like thick paper. The eye, it's black or brown. Close to my face, about two inches away."

"Can you see who the eye belongs to?" I questioned.

"I know," Casey nodded.

"Can you tell me?"

"It belongs to, uh," he hesitated, "I don't know if it's real or not. It's the man I drew." And then he saw another head, bald and more human-colored. "This one," he said, "it's very bulbous, like a dolphin."

I tried to elicit more details, but Casey was unable to see much more of the scene. So I instructed him to become more tranquil and to focus his mental vision.

"It's hard to see," he admitted. "It's hard to look at, to bring into focus."

"Is that because you don't want to look?" I asked, "or because you can't?"

"'Cause I'm not supposed to," he replied. And then he said he couldn't tell where he was, that he felt like he was moving between two incidents: the scene on the large craft, and a different memory he'd told me recently, of being in a strange school.

"I feel almost like I'm going back and forth between the other time," he said, "and looking through the wall, and the school is very, very real. I walk through the halls. The janitor just left."

"Are you able to see the janitor?" I asked.

"No, but I know he left. He was nice. I remember him saying it was time to go. And so time to go. Yes, I remember that. He said it was time to go. And so I'm looking for my aunt and mother."

"Where's home?" I questioned.

"Dallas."

"All right," I said. "So, now do you know how old you are?"

"I'm five," he answered. "Before I was in school."

I asked Casey to move ahead with his recollection, and he told me that everyone was gone, the school was empty, and he wondered where his mother was.

"I go back to the room," he said.

"Do you know what you're doing in this room?" I asked.

"I think I've been, I don't know if I was studying," he replied. "I can't remember. It's real comfortable. So nice I don't want to leave. But I stayed too long. And outside the sky is green and orange. That sounds weird. It's green and orange and white. Like the sun's going down through thick clouds. But there's no clouds. It doesn't feel right, like normal clouds. It's not clouds."

After a few minutes of trying without much success to learn more about this scene, we moved on to his memory of being in the 1940 Ford and seeing the bright light flood into the car. Once again, he saw himself and his father driving down the rural road, with storm clouds whirling in the sky.

"The light comes straight down," he said, recalling the event as if it were happening again. "Oh! No! It came at us! The light hit the dash. Boy, it's extremely bright, it was almost so bright it went through the car."

"What does your father do?" I wanted to know. "Can you tell that?"

"Oh, my God, yes!" he replied.

"Is the car still moving?"

"It seems like it's not. No, it's not moving at all."

"Is your father moving?"

"He doesn't seem to be," Casey said. "The car is stopped."

"Can you see anything out around you?" I wondered.

"I don't believe that I see this," he murmured. "Yeah. There's somebody coming to get us. But they're okay, I'm not scared, they're not moving fast."

"What do they look like?" I asked. "How many are there?"

"Four," he told me. "Uh-oh. I see this, and I don't know if I'm really seeing it or not. They're just coming. It's like they beckon."

Casey said they took him from the car, carried him away, and then he experienced a strange backward sort of movement. But I interrupted the flow of events and asked him for a better description of the beings who took him away. And this time, the description somewhat matched that of the typical gray alien.

Their faces were "cartoon-like," he said, "and they're wearing cover-like things." But it was their eyes that most fascinated him. "They're just big, real pretty circles. Very smooth and don't blink. The light's so bright it hurts their eyes, so they cover their eyes from the light." He described their skin as some sort of dirty white covering, which he felt as he was carried by one of the beings to a small "saucer-shaped" craft resting on the roadside.

And he told of going to the huge orange ship and encountering the Old One, the being whose face he'd seen two evenings earlier. Casey describe deep fissures in the Old One's "putty-like skin," vertical wrinkles, and black eyes. "He has the darkest eyes," he said, "like he knows all, and sees so much, knows so much, and he doesn't care."

"Does that Old One look like the other four beings?" I puzzled. "Or is it one of the four?"

"No, this is the Old One," he insisted. "Those were young ones, They're not the same. This one does not have a covering on its face. It's the Old One I saw last time."

Casey remembered some kind of physical examination, and as he relived the experience, he became very agitated. He'd just begun to feel hungry on the ship, "a feeling of emptiness in the pit of my stomach," he explained, and then he was suddenly talking very rapidly.

"There's a, there's a light! And there's a, uh! Uh! A thing that looks like a rearview mirror, but it's not, it's thick, and it's got a plate glass, shiny glass or cover, and it's, it's coming at me. And then there's that other thing, that looks like . . . metal . . . teardrop-shaped. And over that teardrop there's two dots, two silver dots. They don't have heads, like screws, they're just dots. It touches here," he gestured, pointing to his stomach.

Finally, he remembered a strange sense of backward movement as he was returned to the car, where his father was still waiting, frozen, clutching the steering wheel. Before ending the session, I asked one last question.

"Can you ask your unconscious if you're familiar with the Old One? Is this the only time, can your unconscious tell you if this is the only time?"

"It says no," Casey replied, "no, it's not the only time. It says I know him."

Intrigued by his answer, yet reluctant to delve any further into the experiences without some expert guidance, I helped Casey return to a normal state of consciousness.

For the next week, it was all we could think about, and I continued to feel afraid when I was alone at times. After Casey's revelations under hypnosis, I certainly didn't want to put him in a trance again myself, yet we both wanted to know how much reality his memories had. I was concerned about Casey, sometimes wondering if I should doubt his mental grip, yet knowing deep down that he wasn't the sort to fantasize such things, much less to fabricate them deliberately.

Casey had always been an earnest, honest, intelligent, practical person. He'd excelled in high school in everything from science to music, and when he enlisted in the military, the Army put him to work as a linguist in a branch of military intelligence. The assignment took him overseas where he traveled extensively. After the service, Casey and his first wife eventually divorced. She remarried and moved with her new husband and Casey's two children to another state. Casey finished college with a computer science degree and within five years established himself as a successful consultant. His work demanded expertise, reliability, and confidentiality, and he was recognized as one of the best. Professionally or personally, no one could accuse Casey of being a liar, a joker, or unstable.

Yet the memory of the face and the ship wouldn't go away. And during that week, other things, other memories began popping into his mind, especially an incident in California. In 1971, when Casey's son was about two years old, there were poltergeist activities in their house and an earthquake that apparently only Casey experienced. It was at this time that his son began talking about a "black man" who appeared through the wall in his bedroom. When Casey tried to find out more about this being, his son replied that the black man talked to him, but he refused to say what they discussed.

We both felt that we needed to find some sort of "expert" on UFOs and alien beings, if there were such a thing, but we had no idea where to look. Finally, I noticed a listing of a UFO research organization in Hopkins's book, and I called the international director, hoping he could direct us to some local person for help. Through him, we contacted a metropolitan chapter of a loosely related organization, Metroplex Mutual UFO Network (MUFON), and arranged to meet with a few of the members later in May.

The date seemed impossibly far away, considering our states of mind. One night I dreamed of seeing a house with its roof shaking, bouncing like a lid on a boiling pot, and I understood this was a sign that UFOs were coming. And then, a few nights later, I had my own bizarre experience, this time fully awake. On and off all night I woke up hearing strange sounds in the house, but I was too apprehensive to get up and see about them. There were bumps and clicks unlike the usual creaking house sounds we were familiar with. At one point I felt almost sure that someone was in the house, but I was too frightened to open my eyes.

Then I heard several people, in the corner of our bedroom near the door, speaking to me. It sounded like one voice, but it seemed to come from the whole group. I realized that the voice had been talking for a while, although I couldn't remember it, and then I clearly heard it say, "This is 'eliomi' (or 'elianni'?), the longing for that you've asked for." I was terrified, clutching tightly to Casey's arm, and then the voice was gone.

Casey, meanwhile, was rediscovering more old memories that had always seemed odd. He remembered once when he was thirteen, waking up to see a strange woman, dark-eyed with white wispy hair, approach him in unfamiliar surroundings. She got on top of him and engaged in sex, yet it was not at all erotic for Casey. He never told anyone of the experience and finally dismissed it as a dream. He also recalled being frightened one night while out parking with his fiancee, hearing pounding footsteps approaching the car. He had told me of this incident years ago, in fact, how they immediately started the car and tore out of the deserted area to go home, but when they arrived it was almost two hours later than it should have been.

And one other thing, a memory much more recent, came to mind. Casey reminded me of something he'd seen the past December right in our own town. Driving home, he glanced toward downtown and saw a strange, spherical metallic object stationary above the courthouse. He said when he arrived home, he parked and walked up the hill less than a block away to get a better look at the object, which he could tell was not a balloon. He walked around and stared at it for five or ten minutes, but when he turned to go back down the hill, he was shocked to see that the sky had grown very dark, as if time had passed that he wasn't aware of.

I remembered the incident then, that he'd told me about seeing the sphere, and that I had helped him look through the Sunday papers to find any news item that could explain what it was. Our town was sometimes used as a filming location for movies, and we thought the sphere might have been a movie prop. But there wasn't a mention of such a thing, so we both forgot all about it. And not once did either of us think of it as a UFO. Casey did, however, sense some relationship between the thing he saw and a deep, straight scar on the back of his leg that he found a few days later. He recalled accidentally touching it and being instantly angry about it, wondering how he could have gotten such a cut without knowing it.

When the evening finally came for our meeting with the UFO research group members, we were both anxious and apprehensive. We drove into the city, about forty miles away, and met several gracious and interesting people. I didn't understand all of the questions they had, but they seemed to know quite a bit about UFOs and even about alien abductions, so we opened up to them. And, although it was only Casey who seemed to be involved in this strangeness, I told them about a few odd things in my own life, even though I didn't think they were relevant.

But they insisted that I talk about any unusual events or recurrent dreams I'd had, and I related an early-childhood nightmare that happened several times. All I could remember was a tall, insectlike being standing next to me, holding my hand, and telling me it was my mother. But more interesting was an experience I'd had in 1980, something that I'd always treasured as a genuine vision, since I had no other explanation for it.

Returning from a neighbor's and walking into my backyard, I was suddenly hit by a strange feeling, a sort of electric, shimmery feeling, and I began to see colors and movement around everything in the yard. I walked on and then saw four people standing side by side beneath a large tree. I thought of them as people because they were about my size—five feet tall—and had the usual appendages, but their appearance was actually like a shadow. They seemed gray and featureless, yet somehow I knew there were two males and two females. They greeted me warmly and told me they were my ancestors, that I carried all of their memories and wisdom in my body. I laughed at that, but they assured me that there were ways I could tap into that knowledge and use it.

I was coming home to prepare dinner, and since I was a notoriously insecure cook, I asked them why I was such a disaster in the kitchen. After all, I said, surely one of my ancestors was a good cook, so why couldn't I use that knowledge myself? At that point they began to direct me in the preparation of the meal, at least the two males did. While I was cooking, the two females stood close behind me, talking quite rapidly to some part of my mind other than my consciousness, but I couldn't understand what they were telling me. When I asked, the males said that I shouldn't worry about it, they were only giving me certain "instructions."

The entire incident lasted about forty minutes, and then I was aware that the ancestors were no longer with me. When Casey and David came home that evening, I excitedly told them both about the vision I'd had, and Casey noticed that I seemed to recall very little detail about the forty minutes.

We told the UFO group about the various memories as well as what Casey had related during hypnosis, and then we asked to be put in touch with a knowledgeable hypnotist. To our surprise, however, no one in the group came up with a name. So our one hope for help came to nothing that night, and we drove back home feeling as lost as ever. And, although Casey didn't tell me about it until the second time it happened, he noticed that we were followed for over twenty miles by a white Chevy. It pulled out of the neighborhood when we left, about 12:30 A.M., and stayed with us until we reached the outskirts of our own suburbs several towns and almost forty miles away.

Our contact with the MUFON group paid off a week later, with the news that their June speaker was a hypnotist and UFO researcher whom we could meet. At this point our spirits lifted a bit, and when Casey's parents came to visit, we decided to question them about the time Casey remembered being taken from the car. To our surprise, his father did recall a trip when Casey was a year old, through the foothills of the Sierras.

At the time, Casey's grandfather ran a restaurant where his mother and father helped out. It was a holiday weekend, and the great number of customers had depleted the steak supply, so his father took Casey and went to a couple of other towns to buy more meat.

"Was there anything unusual about the trip?" Casey asked.

"Not really," his father replied.

"Well, you were gone an awfully long time," Casey's mother interjected.

"Why?" Casey asked. "Did you have to stop anywhere other than the meat markets?"

"Yes," his father answered, "but only for a few minutes. There was a tree down across the road, I think."

"What happened there? Did you have to move it, or detour, or what?" Casey probed.

"No, I didn't move it," his father said. "Some men came out of the woods and took it away."

Casey's father was a gregarious, helpful person who would have volunteered to help anyone in trouble, so it seemed odd that he wasn't involved in removing the blocking tree.

"What did you do, then?"

"I just sat in the car, and they moved the tree," he replied. "It only took a few minutes."

"But we were pretty late getting back to the restaurant?" Casey asked, hoping to prompt some further memory.

"You sure were," his mother answered. "I was really getting worried about you by the time you got back."

It was the first time Casey had heard this story yet the details—the location, Casey's age, his mother's absence, the missing time—all fit with his recollections while under hypnosis. His father's confirmation that such a trip had really happened somehow made things even harder for Casey and me. All along we were still hoping that the strange memories had no basis in reality, for we just couldn't accept the existence of space ships and little green (or, in this case, gray) men. Yet we were more anxious than ever to meet the investigator, a woman named Barbara Bartholic, from Oklahoma.

CHAPTER 2

June 1988

At the MUFON meeting, we introduced ourselves briefly to Barbara and sat back to listen to the talk, intrigued by her information yet still skeptical. She began with accounts of multiple UFO sightings throughout northern Oklahoma, witnessed by hundreds of people including local law enforcement officers and increasing dramatically since 1987. In that same period, she said, many people had come to her telling of their abduction experiences. She mentioned the crossbreeding experiments and sometimes painful physical exams, none of which I wanted to hear. After the session, though, we went with Barbara back to her hotel to discuss the possibility of working with her.

And the more we talked, the more we liked her. A wife and mother in her late forties, she was completely unpretentious and very warm, humorous, and knowledgeable. Her UFO research began almost a decade earlier when she assisted one of the most respected scientific "names" in the field, Dr. Jacques Vallee, in cattle mutilation research. Dr. Vallee had done important computer work for NASA's space program, and his investigations into the UFO phenomenon resulted in such books as Passport to Magonia, Dimensions, and, most recently, Confrontations. He was the model, in fact, for the French scientist in the movie Close Encounters of the Third Kind.

Barbara's work with abductees started first with the help of a qualified hypno-therapist, but when the number of cases exploded, the therapist taught her his technique and she continued on her own. Her serious dedication to the research was very clear, and she took no payment for the hours she devoted to each case. We talked late into the night, and finally when it was arranged that we'd visit her in a few weeks, we took our leave, at 2:15 A.M.

About halfway home, while discussing the meeting with Barbara, Casey suddenly changed the subject. "Do you see that white car behind us?" he asked, peering into the rearview mirror.

"Yeah," I said, glancing back. A white American model was in the near distance, but I couldn't believe it was really following us, as Casey insisted. "How can you be so sure?" I countered.

"I saw it in the parking lot of the hotel," he replied. "It pulled out when we did, and it's been on our tail ever since. I've tried changing lanes and changing speeds, but it stays right there."

"That's crazy," I told him. "Why would anybody want to follow us?"

"I don't know," Casey answered, "but this is the second time it's happened. Once might have been a coincidence, but not twice."

Then he told me about the first white car, the night we met with the UFO group, and we both began to worry about what we had gotten ourselves into. Two months before, our lives were normal and the world was a familiar and comfortable place. Yet here we were, being followed in the middle of the night, having spent the evening actually considering the existence of alien beings, and the absurd possibility that these beings had somehow touched our lives.

Our pasts, we now feared, held some mysterious and frightening secrets. Was it better, we wondered, to leave those secrets buried? Our lives had been good, and these new, unsettling developments were very unwelcome. We didn't realize, at that time, just how deeply and irrevocably they would change our world, yet we couldn't help but fear what was coming. Our instincts told us to be conservative and protective, to keep this new knowledge to ourselves, and so we did. That meant, however, that inevitably we began to withdraw from our close friends. They loved us, we knew, but how could we expect them to accept such outrageous, fantastic stories? At this point, we still weren't sure we believed them ourselves. So the prudent, sensible thing to do was to keep silent, at least until we knew much more about what had happened.

But pulling on our emotions in the other direction was a strong need for answers. We felt angry, as if our lives had been broken into and robbed of some very precious innocence. We wanted an explanation, maybe even an apology, for our forced encounters with these beings, so we decided to find out everything we could about our dimly remembered experiences. For Casey, especially, this was important, since he had always known that strange events had happened to him, without remembering enough detail to know what any of these events really comprised. He was like a man with partial amnesia, who cannot feel complete with such perplexing gaps in his memory. So, in spite of our fears, we decided to explore this phenomenon, in our own lives and in whatever research material we could find. In our concern for the past, however, it never occurred to us that the same strange events might start up again in the future.

Once our research began, we found a great deal of ambiguity in the UFO-ET phenomenon, stemming mainly from the nature of the evidence. Eyewitness accounts, which make up the bulk of UFO material, are ultimately unverifiable, to most people's thinking, no matter how many witnesses confirm each other's story. Sure, they may all have seen something at the same time, but given the brevity of the usual sighting and the distances involved, accurate descriptions must be very rare. Photos can be faked, and so, for that matter, can video. Physical traces are admittedly evidence of something, but the "something" itself isn't there to identify reliably. And there's always the chance of deliberate deception. So what is one to make of the tons of material in the book stores claiming to deliver factual accounts of UFO and alien activity?

It would have been much easier to dismiss the whole bizarre notion if I didn't have someone I loved and trusted telling me similar things about his own life. But I still couldn't seriously accept Casey's memories as factual, and I'm not certain that he could, at that time, either. We were involved in something so strange that we tended to treat it like a fiction, as if we'd just discovered we were actors in a movie we didn't realize was being made. We knew, of course, that something was going on, but we held to the idea that his memories were symbolic, not actual. And as we left to visit Barbara late in June, we both hoped that regression would uncover the hidden truth about Casey's experiences, a truth that had nothing to do with UFOs.

Soon after our arrival, Barbara and Casey began their first session. She kept him in a trance state for several hours, patiently encouraging him to dig deeper into his stored memories. Before they started, Casey told Barbara about a few of the odd things he'd been recalling, as well as the events he'd discovered in the earlier regression with me. So she directed his thoughts to these memory cues, and I listened in rather shocked attention to the incredible story he unfolded.

The first strange memory they explored was of a "waking dream" Casey had as a preschool child. In the "dream," he was taken to a sort of school, and he recalled at one point feeling very abandoned and afraid. Under hypnosis, he now recalled being in a school environment with the Old One and another unidentified being, and of feeling that he was being tested in some way.

"It feels like I'm there to learn something, I know I learned something. I feel something in my heart, and yet at the same time I feel like I'm—and that's silly," he interrupted himself, "because I'm so young—but I feel like I'm teaching. I don't know how I could. Something is being learned from me," he said, "and at the same time I'm being given feelings that are much bigger than I am, that go well beyond, go far beyond me."

Barbara asked Casey if he'd ever seen the Old One before, so Casey once again went through the abduction experience when he was a year old which he'd first related to me. He described the small craft again. "It's quite solid," he said, "and it's just a dull, not very spectacular piece of work. It's sitting there and I can see it, and it's standing on about three legs, or four."

"Please be more specific," Barbara requested. "Is it on three legs or four legs?"

"I can't, I'm sorry," Casey replied. "I just remember that as a kid. My mind's just so interested in what I'm seeing. It's the people that are coming to get me. They're little, and yes, they do have . . . I don't know if you've ever seen them, they are quite diminutive. The people aren't very big. I mean,

I'm just a little kid, and they're picking me up, and they feel small. Like maybe an eight-year-old child. And they pick me up, and I feel through the fabric they're thin. I feel like I'm being held by somebody that doesn't really know how to hold people."

I noticed that this time, telling Barbara about it, he showed much less emotion than before, as if he'd come to terms with the incident in some way. He was able to view the whole thing with clearer vision, also, so Barbara elicited much more information than I had. And then she asked him, once again, if he'd ever seen the Old One or any of the shorter "cartoonlike" beings before this abduction experience.

"Yes," he replied, and then in a bewildered voice he began telling of seeing himself as a ball of golden light and of watching a group of beings "make" him. "They got me ready to be born. They're excited. I'm watching what they make. I feel like I'm watching them make me. I feel like they wanted me to be born, like I was their thing there with them before I was, with somebody. They're workers, they're not makers. And I'm watching them work. And after I was born, they watched, and they came, and they took me back there again."

"Can you describe the process that was taking place?" Barbara wanted to know.

"What I see when you ask me that," he explained, "is a series of very intricate red and white patterns. They are interlocked, and they are being fixed. One of the people is pushing these patterns around with their fingers. It's like a box or panel, like a computer terminal with totally different keys. And it feels like they're moving things around, chemicals, I'm having to say, speculation, because what I see is red and white patterns, lines interconnecting. They're adjusting these lines, they're moving them around, pushing them to different levels. And I don't know what that means. It feels like it's very important."

"What happens after that?" Barbara asked.

"It's like instead of watching," he replied, "I'm inside."

"Inside of what? Can you give me a description?"

"I'm inside of Mother," Casey said. "You can see the light in the daytime, it's pink and yellow, it's living." After this surprising revelation, Barbara questioned him about why he was "made" by these beings and then born.

"Are you receiving directions or instructions?" she asked.

"Feels like I'm making the decision myself," Casey responded. "I make the decisions. It's time. My feeling is that it's a difficult decision to make, but that, knowing I really change, knowing I will not be myself, that I elected to do it. I wish to be . . . solid. To feel more than just inside, to feel outside, too, to feel the outside world, to have it affect me. And so I made the decision to be born."

"Were there any instructors," Barbara probed, "any others above you who gave you a choice to be born? Who gauged this movement for you?"

"An agreement," he told her, "just an agreement."

"And who did you make the agreement with?"

"I'm getting into an area that's almost incomprehensible, without sounding strange," he admitted. "But it's like, there is reason, there is purpose, and I have to do it and want to do it, and it's time to do it, and I can, and I go." When pressed about the worker beings he'd watched, Casey said that they were in effect carrying out instructions from a higher authority. "There was another source," he explained, "and we all know that the source is the instrument of this. They are under the control of that Old One. The Old One makes the thought, and they 'do.' The Old One sees, and they see."

Barbara asked, then, if Casey considered the Old One to be synonymous with the ultimate Creator, and he said no. "The Old One is an instrument, a vessel that contains the wisdom and the art and the mind and the knowledge and the experience. And knows its future and knows its past, and it's sad and not sad, and happy and not happy."

By the time they finished with Casey's pre-birth recollections, I was truly disturbed. Casey normally shied away from metaphysical ideas, yet what he'd just described was far beyond the merely metaphysical. It was crazy. My mind was almost numb, but there was still more to hear.

The last incident that Barbara focused on was the sighting of the metallic sphere in December 1987. Once again, Casey told of seeing the object from his car, parking at home and walking up the hill, and then watching the sphere above the courthouse. But this time he recalled much, much more.

"Tell me what is happening now," Barbara directed.

"I don't understand," he said. "I feel like I'm seeing myself being brave and going into a beam of light. I'm watching it. It's just like everything narrows into a very tight beam. And I disappear into that. And that doesn't make sense. I wish I could see."

"What are you experiencing around you," Barbara asked, "what are you aware of?

"Oh!" he said, startled. "There's a big eye. I just saw it again."

"What is the source of the big eye?"

"It's like a lamp, like a big lamp," he replied. "It just goes through everything, you know? It just washes you with something. Washes everything."

"Can you give me a description? How does this lamp wash you?"

"No, well, it's very trying. This whole feeling at this time is real trying."

"What do you mean, 'trying'?" Barbara questioned.

"I don't want to be here," Casey answered. "Wherever this is. Feel like I'm in a small, cramped place. Not like a coffin or anything like that, but just in a small . . . it feels claustrophobic, the room."

"Can you look around and describe it to me?"

"Oh, I'll try, Barbara," he said, becoming agitated. "I'm so upset about being here that I don't want to look. These don't feel, it doesn't feel like the other feelings that I've had. It feels grubbier and dirtier and mechanistic more than spiritual, or loving."

"Tell me your feelings. What are you experiencing?"

"Feel like I'm on my back, with my legs pushed up to my chin. Feels like I'm just balled up in a gray cloud on my back. It feels small and dank. Like a cellar but not a cellar. It's not wet, but it smells yucky. Closed quarters, like an old gym, old locker room. It feels cluttered, it feels real cluttered, busier. It doesn't feel smooth and expansive, like a big ship does. And I don't even know if I'm in a ship. I can't tell, it just feels like I'm in a room and there's all these small scatterings. I mean, it's got walls. Feel like I'm in a room with walls and laying on my back, and I'm being pushed here and shoved there, and . . . I'm really shutting my mind now to what's going on up there."

"Are you alone?" Barbara continued patiently.

"No," he admitted, "there's somebody doing this stuff, but I don't know him."

"Can you tell how many? Is there one or many?"

"There's more than one," Casey said, "but I can't tell you how many. I'm the only 'person' that I feel here, but I could be wrong. It's just, I'm pissed off."

"Are these the same beings that you have known before?" Barbara asked.

"No, doesn't feel like the same."

"Do they have you with your permission?" Barbara pressed him.

"No."

"What could be done to prevent this from happening? Is there any recourse?"

"I refused to go this time," Casey said. "I don't know what more I could do next time."

"You refused, and yet they'd take you, right?"

"Yes, and they cut me," he told her. "They lifted up my, when my leg was lifted up, they cut me. They wanted something. They might have made me do something, and they wanted to see something happen, or they wanted something. They didn't tell me, they won't tell me. I don't know, I don't like that."

"Can you tell me why they're doing this to you?" Barbara asked. "Do you know?"

"Yes, I think so," he answered. "It sounds too unbelievable, but it seems that they must have pieces of us . . . so that we can stay alive. They need pieces of me so that there is a way to continue. They need something so they can repair, so they can make, so that they correct and fix. And I shouldn't be angry, but it makes me angry when they take me away and don't let me know. I'm old enough now. I know I'm old enough and I care enough. And I don't understand why. And that makes me mad."

When Casey was brought back to full consciousness and questioned, he said the memories seemed very real, and I could hear the amazement in his voice as he went back over the experiences. I was anything but calm, understandably, and equally amazed, but I still couldn't let myself believe that these things had actually, factually, occurred.

Not to my husband, not in my reality. I was frantically searching for psychological explanations and coming up empty as we went to bed, and

Casey was very quiet. On the trip to Oklahoma we had discussed the possibility that actual contact with UFOs and aliens—whatever they really were—might have happened to him in the past, telling ourselves we could surely learn to live with that knowledge, now that it was all over. But December 1987 was far too recent for comfort, edging much too close to our present lives.

A second regression took place the following evening, Saturday, after we spent the day visiting with two of Barbara's friends and Jack Lee (pseudonym), a guest of hers who was a counselor from another state. Barbara and her husband lived in one house, but they owned the house immediately to their left, where Jack, the other guest, was staying. Casey and I were staying in a third house they owned, directly across the street from Jack.

Casey went into trance easily this time and proved to be much more clear-sighted and responsive than he'd been the night before. The first incident to which Barbara directed him was a day in Kansas, 1960, when he'd remembered having a bad pain in his nose, for no apparent reason. Barbara asked him to describe the setting and the situation.

"It was when I was about, in the sixth grade," he began, "so I was thirteen. And some boys have just told us, told me and my friend that they saw a UFO land at the top of the field that's across the street from my house. And I think that they're silly, that . . . couldn't happen, but I want to go see it. We used to play there, it's a big field. It was summertime. And I was scared, because I didn't know what it meant. I thought they knew what they were talking about. I can see it.

"It really was there, Barbara," he continued. "I remember that I was terrified to go over there, across the street from my house. The field was like a city block. It was a real long block, must've covered ten acres or more. I remember, I'm trying to see why that hurt my nose. I remember telling my mother that I thought I broke my nose. But I didn't have a fight, but it sure hurts. Hurts inside. It shouldn't hurt. Feels big.

"I remember Bill and I went to explore, then that's all I remember, except that my nose hurts. It felt real, real swollen around the bridge of my nose, at the top. Near the eyes. It feels like I've been hit! Except we didn't have a fight."

"Tell me again what you see when you go to look," Barbara requested, hoping to learn more detail.

"God, there really is something over there, you know it," he said. "Oh, it makes me tingle all over! Ah, yeah, I know there's something there, there really is. I can't, I'm not supposed to see that, Barbara, I'm not supposed to see that. I'm really not supposed to see anything there."

"What are you experiencing?"

"Tugging," Casey said uneasily. "Bill's going, too, and I, it feels like I've got to go, too. I feel like I'm stumbling, I'm falling, and then . . . I'm real tired, and my nose hurts."

When Barbara led him back over these memories and helped him clarify his vision, Casey told of encountering three beings whom at first he thought of as strange children. They took him and his friend Bill into a landed craft where he was placed on a table. Quite clearly reliving the pain, he told of some sort of instrument being pushed up his nostril and feeling a sharp "popping" sensation as the instrument penetrated a membrane into his brain. I listened, utterly shaken, and felt terrified for the first time that Casey was telling the literal truth. The pain in his face was real.

The next memory explored also dealt with Kansas, and once again Bill was involved. While spending the night at Bill's house, Casey recalled looking out a bedroom window for some reason. Then he found himself back aboard the same ship where he'd had the nasal examination. This time, as he lay on the table, after having been made to drink a cinnamon-smelling liquid, he saw a white-haired woman walking over to him. He said she seemed gentle and perhaps caring. She got on top of him, initiating sex, and when it was over she left. Casey saw that the Old One was in the room, watching.

"Did he watch while she was on top of you?" Barbara interrupted.

"Yeah."

"Did he seem to enjoy watching you?"

"No."

"Why was he watching?" Barbara pressed.

"Because the Old One is like my teacher, my master," Casey tried to explain.

"I see that you like your Old One, that you have great depth of feeling for your Old One," Barbara mused. "Is he a part of you?"

"I don't feel like a relation," Casey disagreed. "I feel like a pupil."

"Do you have any idea why they selected you?'"

"No, but they're excited," he said, referring to his experience with the woman, "they like it. They seem to be darn certain that I'm the one they want. Certainly don't leave me alone."

"What do you mean by that?"

"It just seems like they've bothered me, bothered, busied themselves by keeping track of me for such a long time," he told her.

Quite a long time, apparently, for the next exploration was of a memory from 1966. Visiting his fiancee that December, Casey took her parking on a remote, newly widened road outside the city. Their night was quickly interrupted, however, by ominous loud footsteps coming toward their car, so they sped away. But when they arrived home, almost two hours had inexplicably disappeared, and they were in trouble with his fiancee's parents for being so late. With Barbara's help, Casey was able to discover much more that happened that night.

"Well, the lights aren't right," he began, "with the radio on there's a little light on the radio, and all the other lights are off. And then it seems like, I have not been able to see any of this experience since it happened, ever, once. It was terribly frightening."

"Was your fiancee scared, too?" Barbara asked.

"Yeah, she was real scared, too. Because what happened, what I can remember happening, was we're touching each other. Then the car is flooded with a feeling of immobility, and it seems like confusion. And something comes out, watching. . .."

"Are you still embracing her?"

"No, not, not at all," he replied, visibly frightened. "I feel like I've got to run, I want to get out of the car and run. I get out of the car! We both get out of the car. I have to get out. Feels like I was told, compelled to get out of the car and walk to the front of the car. And I do. I can feel the dirt beneath my feet. I can feel the warmth of the engine, and I can see the front of my car. Down the road there is in the darkness, from the darkness there's something coming at us from the front."

"Are you able to move while you're standing there?" Barbara inquired.

"No."

"Is she able to move?"

"No."

"What do you see coming?" Barbara kept questioning him.

"Darkness," he told her, "dark figures. Four."

"Do you recognize them?"

"No," he said, "I don't recognize these. These seem to be taller and dark all over. And they're really scary."

"How tall are they?" she probed.

"They seem to be almost up to my chin," Casey indicated. "Almost five feet tall, but they're so thin and black. Covered in black clothing. I can't see their faces. It's so dark I can't see."

"How does she react?" Barbara asked, referring to the fiancee. "Can you talk to one another?"

"No, but I feel like she just wants to run like a rabbit. We're pulled, held still. We're just held still in front of the car. It's tiring. My heart's just going ninety miles an hour. I feel hot."

"What are they doing? Are you being touched or communicated with?"

"No, it feels like I'm being leered at, doesn't feel like I'm being studied." Casey's face showed deep concern and fear. "It doesn't feel like the same kind of feeling I have when the little ones are around, or the Old One. It seems like a different group. It seems like they're more interested in something else."

"What are they interested in?"

"They're interested in my fiancee," Casey replied. "They're not interested in me. Not these people. And they take her. She goes with them. And I'm just stuck. Just frozen."

"Can you tell where they take her?"

"I don't know," he said, "but I don't like it."

Casey showed strong, frightened emotions as he recalled that night, standing paralyzed by his car. When his fiancee returned, much later, he said, they got back into the car, heard the loud footsteps, and drove away in a panic. Yet neither of them was aware that almost two hours had passed, and they recalled nothing of the thin black beings or the woman's abduction.

The regression was running late into the evening, but Barbara asked

Casey once again to look at the December 1987 abduction. His recall had been so vivid, she hoped that he might offer more information. In the previous session, Casey seemed to think he'd been taken into an unfamiliar room, by a different group of beings. But this time as he looked at the experience, it was more recognizable.

"It's the same one that, when I was a child, but it's now smaller, I'm bigger," he said. "And it's just busier, these people are so busy. They're in a hurry."

"Then they were the same people that were with you when you were young?" Barbara clarified.

"Yeah. It feels, it has the same light, the same feel about it. It's the same area, it feels like I'm in the same place again. But this time, they're just there to say, 'Casey, you, are . . . you've got to remember, you got to know yourself. Remember!'"

He became very agitated, and Barbara brought him out of the trance, calming him. But the emotions were overwhelming, and Casey couldn't help crying in relief. So much had been kept hidden for so long, and now he felt he'd recovered great pieces of his past. He sat up a long time after the session, describing details of the incidents—the cinnamon-scented liquid, for instance, and the pale yellow, slitted "cat eyes" of the thin, black ones in 1966—but he was no longer agitated. There was a real sense of relief and certainty about him that gave away his state of mind: I could see that Casey now believed these things had truly happened to him, just as he'd recalled them.

I was shaking, unable to hold a cup or even a cigarette, the shaking was so intense. I had an irrational desire for Casey to suddenly burst out laughing, to deny that he'd been telling the truth, but it wasn't going to happen that way, and I knew it.

Barbara was exhausted and went home shortly before 2 A.M., but Casey and I were still far too agitated to sleep. That night I experienced real terror for the first time—Casey's memories were utterly terrifying if they were true, and I felt they were now—and I wasn't about to let Jack, the counselor who was visiting Barbara that weekend, go to his guest house and leave us alone. He had been resting in another part of the house during Casey's session with Barbara, and when he finally insisted on going back to his own quarters, I asked if we could accompany him, and he agreed. We went upstairs to his bedroom in the house across the street and-talked, telling Jack about the regression, which he hadn't heard.

Going back over the story, I was still frightened, but at least the shakes had stopped. And Jack was a good listener. He was a large, friendly man ten years our senior, and, like Casey, a former member of military intelligence. Since his retirement, two things had developed for Jack: a career in private counseling and a terminal heart condition, which he faced with calm acceptance and an assurance of a rewarding hereafter. I found his presence comforting, and even though I was much calmer myself, I was still too afraid to leave the room alone, even to go to the bathroom.

And then, about 3 A.M., something happened. A moment before, I would rather have died than been left alone, yet now I was suddenly compelled to go outside.

"I can't stay in here anymore," I told them, getting up from my seat and pacing. "I've got to get out, right now!"

Casey looked at me as if I'd lost my mind. "It's the middle of the night, Karla," he objected. "What on earth would you do out there?"

"I don't know," I admitted, "I just need to be outside, really bad."

"Come on back and relax," Jack said, but I was already hurrying down the stairs. Both of them jumped up and followed after I burst through the front door, out into the darkness.

Jack and Casey caught up with me in the middle of the street, and I just stood there, feeling silly. They both asked me why I had rushed out, but I had no explanation, only that I couldn't resist the urge. We were looking around, up through the trees at the nighttime sky, and within a few minutes, maybe two or three, I noticed they were both staring up toward the east.

Then Jack pointed, in silence. I looked up and saw a bright white light flash once, and my heart sank. "It's got to be a firefly," I whispered to myself, but then it flashed a second brilliant time, larger than a tower beacon, in a different location, and I felt as if my heart stopped beating. This is what it feels like to die, I remember thinking, but I kept watching the light. It flashed on and off in a leisurely zigzagging fashion, moving around to the north, and then it stopped moving.

"I think we've got something here," Jack said fearfully, staring up at the stationary light.

We watched in silence for a few moments, and then the light began to change. Instead of a single bright white light, we now saw changing colors of white, red, and green. The light grew perceptibly larger, until the colored lights appeared to make up, or be attached to, a horizontal row. It finally dawned on me that the light was growing larger because it was coming closer and closer to us, and I panicked. I turned to run back inside, but in my last glimpse I saw a dark pie-pan shape beneath the row of lights. It was a craft of some sort, coming straight down towards us, and all I could think of was to run indoors and hide. Jack was right behind me, but Casey stayed outside a few moments longer and then hurried inside, torn between wanting to comfort me and wanting to stay and watch. He, too, had made out the pie-pan shape beneath the row of lights and the dull reflection they cast on the dark body of the craft.

If I had been shaky before, I was near hysteria now, and we all three huddled closely together in the living room, waiting for whatever might be coming next. Every sudden noise made me jump in fright, and the men were visibly upset and anxious, too. My pulse was racing, as was Jack's, and we hoped the strain wouldn't cause him any harm, given his serious heart condition.

His own thoughts, however, were of a very different nature. For a while he said nothing, and then when he spoke there was a different sound in his voice, a quaver of uncertainty.

"I thought I had it all figured out," he said, slowly shaking his head. "I mean, I thought I knew what life was all about. And all those things I've studied, I even thought I knew what to expect after death. But now," he paused, "now I think that I don't know anything."

It was an utterly humbling realization, and we shared it with Jack. The craft with brilliant colored lights had truly been in the sky over our heads, which in the flash of a moment turned our universe into an entirely different place than it had been before. But as the minutes slowly passed without any further incident, we began to calm down, discussing the craft and wondering what it was.

Comparing notes to make sure we'd all seen the same thing, we realized the craft had certainly not been a conventional airplane. The sighting occurred at a few minutes past 3 A.M., there had been absolutely no sound associated with it, and the lights were all wrong, we knew, having watched planes overhead from our home as they came into the large metropolitan airport nearby. Besides, what sort of plane can zigzag at 45-degree angles as the initial large white light had done?

When we finally went to bed, each of us knew we'd seen a UFO which, coming just after Casey's second, pain-filled regression, seemed a clear confirmation of the reality of his recollections. Neither Jack nor I slept that night, although Casey drifted off eventually, exhausted by the emotions he'd been through, and it was a long time after that before I again enjoyed a peaceful night's sleep.

CHAPTER 3

July 1988

After returning from Oklahoma, Casey and I both felt compelled to spend a lot of time outside at night. We'd walk up the hill near our house, where Casey had been abducted in December, and watch the skies in vague expectancy. It may sound foolish, but we wanted another contact. We were angry enough and determined enough to want answers, and the aliens were the logical place to find them. We referred to them as aliens because they certainly weren't human, but we didn't know if they were interplanetary beings, entities from a different dimension, or something even stranger than we could imagine.

"Is there any way you might be able to contact them?" I once asked Casey as we stood staring up at the stars. "They've apparently been in your life for years. Don't you think they know your thoughts, then?"

"Maybe," Casey conceded, "but I don't think it works like that. They just do what they want to do. I never called out for them to come get me before, anyway, I know that."

"I wonder what I'd do if one of them actually appeared in the house," I said, visualizing such a scene. "I think it would scare me to death. I've been practicing every time I open a door, pretending there's some alien creature standing there staring back at me. And every time I do it, I get weak."

Casey squeezed my hand. "Don't worry about it," he told me. "Whatever happened, it's over. They don't show up by invitation."

Still, it was a time of great fear for me, wondering if the alien beings were going to come back. I continued to call out to them mentally, asking them either to leave us alone or to appear to us consciously and give us some explanation of what they're doing to us. Or, if that wasn't possible, I asked that they give us warning of their return so that we wouldn't be so frightened if anything else happened.

And then, less than two weeks after our sighting of the UFO, another strange experience took place. On July 7, after entertaining a visitor in our home, we went to bed, but our sleep was anything but peaceful. All night I felt uneasy, the way I'd been back in May when I'd heard the voice in our bedroom. This time I heard several unusual sounds in the house, including a distinct knocking, and I also remember hearing another voice, saying a single word that began with a "K" sound but which was unfamiliar, when I woke up once in the middle of the night. But again I was too frightened to open my eyes, much less to get up and look around.

In the morning when I went into the kitchen to start breakfast, I was shocked to see that our television was on, with the sound muted. Casey and I were both certain that the television had been off when we went to bed, yet it was playing now, and we couldn't figure out how it could turn on by itself. I asked several people who understood televisions and electricity if there were any way a power surge might have activated the set, but the answers were negative. And the fact that our remote control operated on infrared made the event even more puzzling, unless there had been some other infrared source in the house.

We phoned Barbara, knowing she had much more experience with this strange phenomenon than we did, and told her what had happened. She urged us to check our bodies, to look for any unusual scars or marks, and we did so. That was when I discovered two things: a pair of small puncture, wounds about a quarter of an inch apart on my inner left wrist, and three solid white circles on my lower left abdomen. The circles formed an almost perfect equilateral triangle, with sides of 15 millimeters. The puncture marks looked as if they could have been made by two hypodermic needles, and they were fresh, still scabbed, but there was no sensation of pain associated with them. The circles forming the triangle didn't appear to be a wound of any sort—no broken skin, no itching or pain—just three white areas where the pigment had disappeared.

I had no idea what could have caused either of these sets of marks, until Barbara explained that many of the people she worked with turned up similar scars on their bodies after abduction experiences. Now I was really frightened. Consciously, neither Casey nor I remembered any event which could account for the marks, only the strange sounds in the house and the television being on, but that, too, she explained, wasn't unusual.

My later research into books about UFO experiences confirmed this fact, as I read about several instances in which people had encountered UFOs and their occupants and then began experiencing events that were commonly associated with poltergeists: lights turning themselves on and off, for example, and electrical appliances behaving in unusual ways. Even more frequent were reports of UFOs passing over automobiles and causing them to completely lose power, as well as stopping watches which the passengers wore. And airplane pilots coming into proximity with UFOs often complained that the electrical equipment on their craft malfunctioned.

We already knew from Casey's experiences that abductions can occur without the person consciously being aware of the experience, and Barbara confirmed this. Our feelings of helplessness were overwhelming. If these strange beings could come into our homes undetected, do whatever they wished to us, and then leave us with no memory of their presence, how could we ever defend ourselves or resist their intrusions? To this question, unfortunately, Barbara had no answer.

But we didn't give up. We started reading books on the subject, searching for more understanding and hoping to find an account where someone had been able to stop these things from happening. All through the summer I raided bookstores and ordered other books from the library, yet nowhere in my reading did I discover an answer. Still, we were learning a lot. We found out that this phenomenon had been going on for years, at least since the late 1940s, and that in itself was some sort of relief, knowing that we weren't the only ones who'd been through such things. And we kept in touch with the MUFON group in the city, just in case they could help us in some way.

August 1988

In August we received a flyer announcing an upcoming MUFON meeting with a guest speaker we'd never heard of, a man named John Lear, and we decided to go. By this time we had told our son, David, about our experiences, and he simply didn't believe such events could be real. Still, he decided to go with us to the Lear lecture.

The only other person I had confided in was Bonnie, my best friend. I couldn't just blurt out that Casey had been contacted by aliens, so I started by describing Casey's first hypnosis for relaxation. "When he was under," I said, "he began exploring his subconscious, looking for causes of stress. And he had some pretty strange memories come to the surface."

"What sort of memories?" Bonnie asked.

"Really strange," I hesitated. Bonnie was my closest, oldest friend, yet I was afraid of her reaction to Casey's story. Who could blame her if she thought we were crazy? But I had to take the chance because I needed her support. Gripping the paper with Casey's drawings, I went on. "What he remembered was so strange that we don't know what to make of it."

Bonnie glanced at the paper in my hand and then back up at me. "Why? Is it something horrible?" she asked.

I shrugged. "We have no idea," I said. "But he drew some pictures of what he remembered. Do you want to see them?"

She nodded, and I handed her the paper. Her response was immediate. When I showed her the face, she literally jumped in her chair and tears came into her eyes.

"What's wrong?" I asked. "Why did you respond so emotionally?"

"I don't know, I don't know," she insisted, shaking her head.

But I knew there had to be a reason, so I pressed her. "Why did that drawing make you cry?"

Finally she replied, "I didn't think anyone else knew," but then immediately denied again that there was any reason for her tears.

It occurred to me that Bonnie might have had experiences of her own, for why else would that drawing have brought tears to her eyes? But she assured me that nothing unusual had ever happened involving UFOs or alien beings. Still, she was very supportive. She'd known me for twenty years and had every faith in my honesty and sanity, and she too wanted to go with us to the meeting. At the last minute, David announced that his best friend, James, in whom he had confided, was also interested in going, so the five of us drove into the city in two cars, ours and James's.

Fortunately, we arrived early and managed to get seats near the front, for by the time Mr. Lear began to speak, a crowd of over three hundred had packed the room, spilling out into the hallway. The room was hot, yet we didn't notice once the lecture began, because the information we were hearing was riveting. Lear told about his research, his countless interviews with people who'd had similar experiences, but the most shocking and unbelievable part concerned an alleged government involvement with these alien beings.

Lear, an expert pilot, had flown missions for the CIA and thus had contacts in the intelligence community, and he insisted his information was true. There were bases, he told us, hidden throughout the country where the aliens carried on a variety of bizarre activities, including crossbreeding experiments with humans. And he said that the "invasion" of these beings was already a fact, that the government had made a secret deal with them, giving permission for the abductions to take place in exchange for promises of advanced technology.

But the government had been duped, he said, and in fact had received very little in the way of useful technology, while the aliens had carried on their abductions and experiments far beyond what was allowed by the agreement with our government. And now, he concluded, the government was in a real quandary. For years they had officially denied the existence of UFOs and aliens, but now with the escalation of ET activities, they didn't know how to go about warning the population, much less how to prevent these things from continuing.

Our little group sat listening in apprehension and disbelief. One part of my mind realized how wild and frightening and unsubstantiated Lear's words were. These things could not be true, I insisted, not in the world that we know. "That's just the point, though," another part of my mind interrupted. "The world you knew didn't accommodate UFOs and aliens, but you have them now anyway, don't you?" This split in my feelings confused me as I watched Lear very calmly, very seriously, deliver his message of doom.

"I'm not here to warn you about an alien invasion," he concluded. "The invasion is over, it's already happened."

I glanced around occasionally, wondering if everyone else in the room was as astounded as I, and I noticed that James seemed rather strange. He appeared almost to be in a trance, staring down at the floor, unblinking, and when the lecture ended he hurried out of the room with only a few words of good-bye. Assuming he must have been in a hurry to get back home, perhaps for a late date, or that he had thought Lear's lecture was a waste of his time, we didn't pay much attention to his odd behavior. So the rest of us rode home together, discussing the things we'd heard.

I had promised to let Barbara know what we learned at the lecture, so I almost decided to go to Oklahoma and deliver a report in person. But at the last minute I changed my mind and stayed home. As it turned out, that was a fortunate change of plans, for things were about to get very strange here at home.

The lecture was on a Wednesday, and two days later something happened which gave a whole new turn to the situation. James called David and asked to meet him for drinks at a local bar. David told us about the events of that meeting the next day. He said that when he got to the bar, James was acting strange, untalkative and generally unresponsive, almost wooden. After a couple of drinks, however, James began to loosen up, suddenly telling David some very disturbing things.

James said that all his life he'd been visited by strange beings in his bedroom. When he was young he also sometimes heard noises in the house, and when he got up to check them out, he'd seen a skinny, unknown man dressed entirely in black, who was picking up various things around the house as if examining them. But whenever James would rush into his parents' bedroom to tell them a prowler was in the house, they would reply that he shouldn't worry about it and to go back to bed. Having known James's parents for years, I couldn't believe they would be so unconcerned, yet James insisted they never once bothered to get up and see if he was telling the truth.

But the visitors to his bedroom were different. At first, as a very young child, he was visited by a small creature he called Mr. Greenjeans, because of the greenish glow the creature emitted. The first time this being appeared, James woke up to see all the toys in his room moving about by themselves, and then Mr. Greenjeans approached his bed and told him not to be afraid. James was always paralyzed when the being appeared, and, petrified with fear, he could never remember what Mr. Greenjeans talked about to him. In later years, another being began showing up, a taller, featureless creature who periodically came into the room and also spoke with him, and during these times, too, James would be unable to move or speak aloud, communicating only telepathically.

But more recently, in the past several months while James and David were living in a farmhouse, yet another type of being had been showing up, and this time the visitor was a woman. He said that she always entered his bedroom from an adjacent interior room rather than through the door that led outside, and he found himself paralyzed until she left through the same door. As soon as the woman disappeared, the paralysis left him, and James had often followed after her, searching through the house and out into the yard, yet he'd never been able to locate her anywhere else.

In her last few visits, he told David, which had been almost weekly, he had been able to remember consciously some of what the woman told him.

"One time she was in my room, but it was just her head and her hands," he said. "She was holding two big, round black orbs, and she told me they wanted to remove my eyes and replace them with those things."

Terrified, James objected, saying he didn't want to be blind, but the woman replied, "You'll still be able to see, but you'll see differently." She had also spoken of replacing various other parts of James's body, leaving him in great fright. And in her last visit, the day before the Lear lecture, she had urged James to go somewhere with her.

"Why don't you just come with us?" she had asked.

"I can't," he said, "I'm too afraid."

"What are you afraid of?" she wanted to know. "Are you afraid of the dark, or of something you think is out there in the dark?"

"I don't know," he admitted. "I'm just too scared."

And the woman departed, leaving him once again to question his own sanity, as he'd secretly done for years, ever since he was old enough to know that other people simply didn't encounter bizarre visitors in the night as he'd been doing all his life.

The only reason that James had decided to tell David about these experiences was that he had actually seen the same woman who'd been coming to his room—or someone who looked identical to her—at the Lear lecture, and this convinced him that he wasn't crazy after all. She was standing in one of the crowded doorways when James spotted her, and she kept staring over the audience to where our group was sitting. After the lecture, James saw her leave and hurried away to follow her, determined to confront her and demand to know what she had been doing to him. He said he trailed after her into the parking lot, and when she turned at the corner of the building he was only a few steps behind. But, turning the same corner, he was stunned to see that she was nowhere in sight.

That was the story David heard as he sat drinking with James. Its impact was strong, following on the heels of our own revelations to him, and David urged James to come talk to us. But James said he couldn't do that yet, he'd kept this explosive material to himself for so long, and he was afraid we might tell his parents, something he desperately didn't want. He did give David permission to discuss it with us, however, providing we promised to keep his secret, and David came to us the next day with the entire account.

Our son had not been able to believe the things we'd told him, but now, trusting the story of his best friend with whom he'd grown up, his disbelief was shaken. In fact, he remembered, as we also did, that James had long ago told us about Mr. Greenjeans, but of course at the time none of us thought it was anything more than the active imagination of a very intelligent child, which James was. He and David, a year apart at the same private school, had both been valedictorians, and we'd never known either of them to make up such preposterous tales before.

We listened that Saturday, however, with serious concern and asked David to urge James to talk to us in person. A few days later, James did come over, and we went through the material with him in greater detail. He had difficulty in talking about it, though, struggling to get out the words, and at times our hearts ached for him as tears ran down his face. But when he had finished, he said that for the first time in years he felt a sense of relief, that sharing his experiences with us somehow helped him feel more whole, and certainly more sane.

He talked about some information that had just recently emerged in his mind, apparently from the conversations he'd been having with the woman in his bedroom. For one thing, he now remembered being told that the woman and her group were "interdimensional," rather than physical extraterrestrials from some other planet, and were benevolent toward humans. But, she had said, there were other beings here who weren't interdimensional and who cared nothing about our human feelings and rights. These are the ones, she told him, who do great harm to humans, who think of us as we think of insects.

He also said that the crystals which so many New Age devotees carry can help the interdimensional ones monitor us more easily, although he had no idea how that worked. And, finally, he said that he now felt compelled to make a trip to St. Louis, where his parents grew up and where many of his relatives still lived. He wouldn't tell us why he wanted to make the trip, only that it had something to do with his current experiences, and that he would be leaving the following week.

David and his girlfriend Megan came over with James, and they added more, very disturbing, information to what he was telling us. Megan worked 15 miles away in the afternoons, and when she got off work at 10 P.M., she met David and James at the bar the night James had revealed his story. We were surprised to hear Megan's account of that evening, for she told us not only about what James had said, but also about David's responses and actions.

"When James began talking about the woman he'd seen at the Lear lecture," Megan said, "David suddenly interrupted and gave a complete description of the woman, including her clothing. But when they left and went back to their house, David claimed he'd never said any of it."

"I don't remember that," David commented, shaking his head.

"You did it twice!" Megan exclaimed. "James told you that you really had just described the woman, and you repeated the description word for word, how the woman looked and what she was wearing! And then a couple of minutes later you denied ever having seen her, much less described her!"

James confirmed what Megan told us, that at three different times that night, both at the bar and back at the house, David described the woman and then acted as if he'd never said anything. We questioned David about it then, and he still insisted he hadn't seen the woman at all.

And that wasn't the only strange thing he had done, apparently. When they all left the bar, James drove his own car and Megan drove David home in her car, since David had had too many drinks to drive safely. When they reached the house, an old farmhouse, Megan said that David had acted very strangely, frightening her with his bizarre behavior.

"David just suddenly changed," she told us, "his voice and his eyes changed. And he was scaring me."

"What was he doing?" Casey asked. "How was he scaring you?"

"At the farm, when we got out of the car, David grabbed me by the arm and tried to drag me out into the backyard," Megan replied in bewilderment. "He kept saying, 'Something out there wants to see you,' but I was fighting him and refusing to go," she told us. "He was really scaring me, pulling on my arm, trying to get me out into the dark part of the yard. Then when James finally drove up, David changed back to normal," she concluded, "and he didn't remember doing any of that. He didn't even remember when we got to the farm."

David grinned in embarrassment and insisted again that he didn't remember what happened that night, not his description of the woman or his attempts to drag Megan into the yard. And that really worried us. He tried to blame his behavior on the fact that he'd had a lot to drink at the bar, but that wouldn't account for the complete change he exhibited when James drove up the driveway. In my next phone call to Barbara, I told her about that night, and she too seemed worried, even more about David's odd behavior than about James's revelations. But she kept her reasons to herself, saying only that she would like to work with David if the opportunity ever arose, and of course with James.

A few days later, James left for St. Louis, after making us all promise not to tell his parents the real reason for the trip. If he'd been any younger, Casey and I wouldn't have hesitated to talk to his parents, but he was twenty-two years old, and we felt we had to respect his wishes, at least for the present.

And we were still very much preoccupied with our own situation. On August 25, as I was taking my shower, I was thinking hard about these recent events and also about a book I'd just finished reading, Transformation, Strieber's second book about his relationship with alien beings. I felt that I had to do something, find some way to communicate with the beings myself, and I remember thinking, "If you are around me right now, invisible, won't you please just give me some sort of sign?"

And when I stepped out of the shower to dry off, I found a solid red triangle had suddenly appeared on my upper left forearm. At first I thought it must be an insect bite, although I hadn't felt anything bite me, or perhaps it was a hive, but the triangle wasn't itching or swollen. Remembering Barbara's instruction to take photos of any unusual marks, I got out the camera and awkwardly managed to shoot a couple of photos. When I took the roll of film to be developed, the mark was still very visible, and the man at the photo shop looked at it. But by noon, three hours after it first appeared, the triangle was completely gone. Whether it was mere coincidence or a deliberate signal, I don't know, but it has never happened again.

Meanwhile, we all waited anxiously for James to return from St. Louis, hoping he'd finally tell us why he'd felt compelled to make the trip. He came back on the twenty-eighth, but we didn't have a chance to talk to him until the thirty-first, and he had an astounding story to tell.

But on the night of his return, I got a phone call from Nancy (pseudonym), a woman James had dated on and off, and Nancy was upset and worried. She said James had just made a very strange call to her, asking her about what she'd been doing while he was gone. I didn't learn any other details except that Nancy felt worried about James's state of mind.

"His voice sounded really strange," she told me. "He wasn't making very much sense." So we waited impatiently to hear from him, and when we did, the things he told us added greatly to the mystery.

On the way up from Texas, where we all lived, the route took him through Oklahoma, the same route he'd traveled for years with his family and with which he was very familiar. At MacAlester he filled the car with gas and reset the trip odometer to zero, at his father's request since he was using the family car. By the time he reached Highway 44 near Tulsa, however, he was aware that something strange was going on. For one thing, that part of the journey had been incredibly short, taking only about 45 minutes, and for another his odometer registered only 37 miles. In actuality, the trip should have taken much longer, since the distance between the two places was at least 100 miles. And, conversely, on another stretch between two small towns only eight miles apart, James insisted that he drove for an hour.

"Later on that day," he said, "I suddenly felt something in my mind telling me to pull over to the side of the road and look to the left. So I did, and there was a very bright light in the sky, making a circular motion in the sky. I watched it come to a dead stop, and then it just sort of hovered, but there were a lot of colors flashing all around it. When it did that, it shot off really fast, out of view."

He told us that the reason for the trip was a command that had been given him by the woman in his bedroom, that he was supposed to go to a certain hill on Saturday night.

But the closer it came to the time for him to go, the less he wanted to do it. "The weather was sort of misty, real spooky," he said, "and I thought it would be crazy to go out on a hill somewhere like that. So I tried to turn the car around and go back to my grandparents' house, but I couldn't make myself do it. I had a really strong urge to drive to the hill, and I fought it with all my strength. My arms wouldn't do what I wanted them to. I kept saying 'No, no!' over and over, but finally I just gave up."

Once he reached the hill, he parked and opened the trunk of his car to get out a camera and tape recorder, but again, as if not in control of his will, he couldn't take the equipment with him. "I saw them lying in the trunk," James said, "but I must have lost my mind because I just figured, why bother?"

Night came on as he sat on the hilltop, feeling quite alone and rather silly, he said. For a while, nothing unusual happened, and then three bright lights appeared in the sky. He watched as they went through an intricate series of motions, making a circle in unison and then stopping, as the single light he'd seen earlier had done, emitting colored sparks before departing.

After they vanished, he heard a voice in his head saying, "See how easily we made you come to this place? You don't have any control over it. In the future, when you're supposed to go to a certain place, you'll be made to go there. Don't worry about it, there's nothing you can do to stop it."

At that point, thoroughly upset, James left the hilltop and drove to his relatives' home. There he undressed and went to bed, only to suddenly find himself back on the hilltop, completely dressed, in the company of the woman who'd been coming to his bedroom!

Whereas before, at home, the woman had appeared in a variety of ways, sometimes in full form and at other times showing only her head and hands, this time the woman seemed very corporeal.

"She was dressed like a real person," James explained, "in jeans and a T-shirt. And she was nice that time, nicer than she'd ever been before."

In fact, James said he actually felt comfortable with her, talking and listening to the many things she told him. "She wasn't scaring me, talking about replacing parts of my body," he told us.

"What was she saying, then?" I asked.

James shrugged. "I think she was trying to make me feel better about all this stuff. She told me that very long ago I'd made a decision, and that had really decided every other decision since then."

She said he had a specific task—a set of tasks, in fact—to accomplish in the future, within five years. And as she told him all these things, he saw images of David, of us, and other people he knows involved in this future task together. She also told him, without explaining what it meant, that we would be "moved" into other bodies.

And, as proof that her messages should be trusted, she gave him bits of information about the future which, as they occurred, would show him that she could somehow see across time and know the future events that awaited humanity. One of the things she told him was a conversation taking place far from St. Louis, back in our hometown. James's ex-girlfriend Nancy, the woman said, was conversing with her date at that very moment, and she told him details of that conversation. When he got back home, James called Nancy, questioning her about the date, and Nancy's description of what was said matched that of the woman on the hill. Much more was told to him by the woman, but he hasn't been able to remember it all. The next thing James was aware of was sitting on the front porch of his relatives' home, fully dressed, with no idea of how he'd gotten to the hill or been returned.

A feeling of great apprehension, a real sense of fear, pervaded the room as we all sat listening to James's story. We asked him if he had any idea what was actually going on with these beings, hoping that some of his unremembered information might be nudged to the surface. And, at a later time, James did tell us more about the overall situation, what he understood to be a coming time of battle. But at first he only discussed the personal significance he'd felt about the events of his trip. To him, it seemed that the whole exercise was designed to alleviate his doubts about his sanity. "The lights in the sky, the odometer, the speeding up and slowing down of time, the woman on the hill—all these things had been very, very real," he concluded. "I think that was why I was sent to St. Louis. They wanted to prove it to me, so I couldn't deny it was real anymore." Casey and I could only look at each other, bewildered. If his experiences were real, and if he were truly involved in this bizarre reality, then so were we. He had been shown a future time when he would be activated to perform his "task," and he had seen us working with him.

CHAPTER 4

Sometimes I still tried to pretend that it was all in our imaginations. We overreacted, I told myself, we let paranoia into our thinking, so that now we saw evidence of alien influence everywhere. Afraid to sleep at night, compelled to watch the stars, sometimes disturbed by the books I read about UFOs, yet I couldn't keep from reading more. Conventional logic insisted that such things couldn't be true, and so did the honest desire of my heart. This was not what I wanted reality to be.

I traced the sequence of events back to the very beginning, trying to rationalize the situation. How to account for all the people in my life who now claimed to have had experiences? James must have got it from David, who heard it from us. Casey picked it up from me, I picked it up from Hopkins's book, Missing Time, and the book was motivated by the class project I assigned on unusual phenomena. But where, I wondered, did the motivation for the assignment come from? And why would so many people pick up on the topic and proclaim their own experiences falsely, especially these usually skeptical individuals? Did it make more sense to believe in telepathy, to believe that people I trusted would all suddenly fabricate such stories, than to believe they were telling their own truths?

No matter which way I thought about it, the one thing I couldn't get around were the crafts we had variously seen. I remembered Casey talking about the metallic sphere in December, and I believed James had seen the craft twice on his trip to St. Louis. Most compelling, of course, were the lights and the craft witnessed by three of us in Oklahoma. At the time it seemed like a confirmation of the reality Casey had seen under hypnosis, and that's how it worked now. Every time I'd be just about convinced that there was nothing to fear, I'd remember the dull metallic darkness of the flattened hull reflected in the green and white and red lights, coming directly down toward us, and I knew it was all real.

Still, it was one thing to face such a reality privately with my husband, for we were mature people with plenty of experience in the surprises and crises of life. But it was quite another to see the same bizarre phenomenon descend upon my child. At first, I had thought that only Casey had ever been involved, then I'd begun to have my own experiences, and now there was James. How much longer, I wondered, before David would be waking up hearing things in his bedroom, or seeing strange lights in the sky over the farm? Research showed that the phenomenon often occurs among members of the same family, or among a group of friends, so I sometimes asked people I knew, very discreetly, about their own unusual experiences. We'd asked David early on, of course, at a time when he didn't believe such things actually occurred, and he assured us he'd never gone through anything that didn't have a logical explanation.

Research also indicated, however, that many experiences of alien encounters are only remembered as dreams or as occurring when the person is in a dream state of some sort. And now David was beginning to have UFO dreams—and doubts. The first dream early in August involved the landing of two spacecraft and mental communication between David and an alien occupant of the ship. Later in the dream, another type of UFO craft appeared and also landed, and the odd little alien who emerged delivered a message: the time had come for "the human diaspora." When David told me about the dream, I thought it was something brought on by all the things we'd told him about our own experiences. Still, the alien's message was a total surprise. Nowhere in our conversations had such an idea ever arisen, and David didn't even know what "diaspora" meant.

Then, on August 11, he went through a very real experience that couldn't be dismissed so easily. He went to bed late, about 1:30 A.M., expecting to fall asleep quickly. Instead, he began to feel a strange sensation, building up suddenly and rapidly, in his head.

"It was something I felt," he said, "not saw or heard. My immediate thought was that my persona was about to leave my body through my head—up and out."

He was frightened at first, but then he tried to concentrate on the feeling and form some objective description of it. That's when he became aware of a sound, "like a loud electric buzz," yet he knew it wasn't an overtly audible sound. It felt more as if he were hearing it internally, as if, he said, "something was getting on the auditory nerve between my ears and my brain."

The second thing he became aware of then was a great pressure inside his skull, a feeling of inflation that gave him, oddly enough, no sense of pain. "When I thought about it some more," David said, "I could sense that it wasn't just a general pressure, but seemed focused at a certain point behind my forehead, as if there were an incredibly, enormously powerful light there, although," he added, "I could see nothing, as my eyes were closed."

This point source of pressure was hard for him to describe. It seemed like "a cylinder of energy/force/light/ buzz/pressure" coming in through the top of his skull and reaching about halfway down into his head. After concentrating on this feeling for a couple of minutes, David said, he stopped focusing and just relaxed, and that's when it stopped.

For David, the whole experience had been curious but brief, apparently nothing to really worry about. But I had learned enough from Barbara, as well as from Casey's past experiences, to know that such memorable brief events were often all that was consciously recalled from much more significant, complex situations. I was afraid, with good reason, that my son was no longer exempt, if he ever had been, from alien intrusion.

And I wondered about his girlfriend Megan. Taking Barbara's advice to question our acquaintances, I asked Megan if there'd ever been any strange occurrences in her life.

"Oh, no," she answered, "there's never been anything unusual." I was relieved to hear it and was about to change the subject when she unexpectedly continued.

"Except there was that time," she said, "when I saw the monkey in the window."

Megan had lived all her life in a large city, and I couldn't imagine how a monkey might have turned up in the neighborhood, so I asked her to explain.

"I was ten or eleven," she replied, "and I was taking a nap in the den one afternoon. I woke up and sat up on the couch, and that's when I saw it. There was a gray monkey bobbing up and down outside the kitchen window."

"What did you do?" I asked. "Did you get up to have a closer look?"

"No," she said, "I just sat there watching the monkey."

"Well," I pressed, "didn't you say anything? Did you yell for anyone else to come see it?" But she shook her head negatively.

"And that's all," she continued, "unless you count the time I woke up in my sister's bedroom—I was maybe twelve at the time—and there was a slide show or something going on, up on the wall."

"Slides of what?" I asked.

"Oh, a lot of different things," Megan said. "I can't remember everything, but I do remember seeing the moon. At least I thought it was the moon, and there were two spaceships of some sort flying around. Then they crashed into each other and exploded, and the whole moon blew up. A lot of white stuff started falling onto the earth, and I saw all the people running out to pick it up and eat it."

It was a pretty strange thing to see on the bedroom wall in the middle of the night, we agreed, and I asked if she remembered anything else.

"Well, not really," Megan said, "although there was this thing in the sky. I saw it when I was real young. I was playing outside with some other kids, and I remember looking up and seeing a huge gray shape going over the garage. I thought it was a giant fish."

Of course, I didn't want to frighten Megan by telling her how much these things sounded like screen memories, protective disguises of events too frightening to face. I wondered what she might discover if she ever went through regressive hypnosis. And I also wondered how many other people had strange recollections, strange events in their past, that had been dismissed because they couldn't be understood. Casey and I had done the same thing, relegating those odd scenes and memory gaps to the very back of our thoughts, until events forced them to the forefront once again.

"There must be other people like us out there," I remarked to Casey, "with no idea of the things hidden in their pasts. I wonder if they are also beginning to find out. And I wonder why we haven't heard anything about this before. There are several million people in this part of the state! Surely some of them must have been abducted or have seen UFOs, too."

At the end of August, one of those people came into our lives. I received a phone call from a man in the city named Fred, who had gotten our number from the MUFON group. He had been plagued with nightmares and frightening memories of a strange night in New York the previous October, and when he'd discussed it with a friend, she'd suggested he contact the study group to see if they could help. And they passed him on to us, since we were the only ones they knew who were going through current experiences.

When Fred first came out to meet us, it was apparent that he'd been through a real trauma. He was visibly agitated and excited at the same time, and after we began talking, his story poured out. He had a bizarre UFO sighting back in 1973, with two relatives. They watched a flying craft cavort through the sky, and then it transformed into a giant image of a bearded man dressed in a long, belted robe, with his arms outstretched.

But it was his visit to New York in October that concerned him most. He was staying alone in a friend's apartment, collapsing in bed after hours of walking the streets alone, and when he awoke he was covered with bruises and scratches all over his back. But he had no memory of how they got there, only snatches of memories that made no sense. And now he was suffering from nightmares and fears, all associated with UFOs.

We couldn't do anything more than listen to Fred's story and share our own experiences with him. He left, however, feeling less alone in this strangeness, and we promised he could contact us any time he needed to talk. We also said we'd tell Barbara about him and make arrangements for them to meet. Fred had read Communion and knew enough to want to try hypnosis, to explore the things that had happened to him in New York. He also was worried about a few episodes of missing time he'd experienced recently, working alone on the night shift. We talked about all these things and assured him he could phone us whenever he was frightened or went through some new experience. Sympathetic support was all we could offer, though, having no answers ourselves and not even being sure of the questions.

September 1988

In early September we went back to Oklahoma for another round of regressions, and this time I planned to undergo hypnosis myself. On our first visit there, Casey's experiences were all we really knew about, but since then enough odd things had happened to me to warrant my own exploration through regression. While we were with Barbara, a constant stream of people passed through her house, so we learned in a very short time just how pervasive this phenomenon can be. Several people we met there told us of their UFO sightings and experiences, but the most astounding story came from Ellen (pseudonym), a woman who lived on a northern ranch with her husband. A UFO had once caused a stampede of their herd, Barbara told us, but Ellen's visit to Oklahoma had nothing to do with Barbara's research.

Having tried repeatedly and unsuccessfully to have a baby, Ellen was in town visiting a woman who'd agreed to be a surrogate mother for her and her husband. She told us of the many pregnancies she'd been through, only to have them terminate in miscarriage, and her dream of finally having a child now seemed to be within reach.

As we talked, Barbara asked if Ellen had had any unusual dreams lately, a common question to all her visitors. Ellen replied that, yes, she'd had a frightening dream a few nights earlier, in which a woman had threatened to take the baby from the surrogate mother. In the dream, Ellen had to fight very hard to stop the woman from taking the unborn child and had awakened in great fear.

Barbara asked if she'd dreamed of this same woman in the past, and Ellen said no. "But I've seen her when I wasn't sleeping," she added.

Prompted by Barbara to tell us her story, we sat listening as Ellen described her first encounter with the woman. She was in a doctor's examining room, lying on the table alone, when a strange woman suddenly appeared. Ellen didn't tell us all the details of their conversation, which had been several years before, but her impression was that the woman was somehow an ancestor who had previously lost her own children. Ellen thought the woman was resentful of her pregnancies and therefore had been responsible for the miscarriages.

There had been two other such encounters, she said, and that was why she fought so hard in her recent dream to protect the surrogate mother's fetus. Then Barbara asked Ellen to describe the woman, and we listened in astonishment to an almost identical description of the woman who was coming to James's bedroom!

This wasn't the only surprise for us. I had decided to attempt a hypnotic exploration of one of my own unusual memories, but I didn't expect to find anything alien such as turned up in Casey's regressions. Odd things had happened to me during the summer, to be sure, but I still felt that it was Casey, not I, who had been touched by the alien phenomenon earlier in life. I held on to the belief that all the unusual memories from my past would turn out to have mundane explanations if I explored them. Barbara, however, had questioned me about anything strange I remembered, and one puzzling but apparently inconsequential memory caught her attention. So, on the last day of our visit, she put me into a trance and led me through an event which had occurred years before.

I had been driving back alone from my parents' home, a trip of 240 miles, when I saw ahead of me on the interstate a large black cloud descending rapidly. It covered both lanes and the shoulders, so there was no way around it, and it appeared so suddenly that I couldn't apply my brakes in time to avoid it. It was daytime, and the darkness of the cloud stood out in stark contrast, with curling edges and a density that made it almost appear to be solid. I remember driving up to it, and I also remember driving down the interstate past the cloud, seeing it behind me in my rearview mirror, but I never remembered actually driving through it. That, and the cloud's sudden appearance, were all that had made it stand out in my memory.

Barbara began the regression by setting up the scene, having me describe the car, the countryside, and the weather.

"This is such a boring drive, mostly," I told her. "But this is the pretty part, so I can look around and enjoy it, the trees and hills. There must not be much traffic now, I'd just be looking around. And I look back to the road. It's like the sun's not so bright anymore. I'm just wondering if it's gonna rain because the sun's overcast now.

"And then there's this crawling, sort of curling black stuff. It's like smoke, coming from the right and just going across the road. And it's making me feel bad, Barbara," I stopped, beginning to feel afraid.

Barbara expertly reassured me that I was safe and able to look at the experience, so I started up again.

"It's coming, crawling black stuff," I said. "Something dark is coming across the road beside me. At first, I just seem to see these 'finger' tendrils, and then it's all a huge black cloud. It sweeps in front of me, and it's so fast I think it's a storm, but it hasn't been like a storm before now. So I'm wondering what this sudden weather thing is. And I'm going to just drive through it, because I can't slow down in time to stop."

"Are you aware of any other cars passing you or in back of you?" Barbara asked.

"I was looking off to the left before I looked back to the road," I explained, "and when I looked back there weren't any cars between me and that cloud, I don't remember looking behind me. And I think I'm driving into it. Suddenly I can't see anything, it's dark all around the windows. I'm looking up trying to see if I can see the sky through it. I don't see anything."

"Can you still see inside the car?"

"Yeah," I replied, "I can still see inside the car, I just can't see outside. There's nothing on the windshield. I'm holding the steering wheel real tight, and I'm leaning up close to it, looking up to see why it's all over me. It's like being in a black room, only there's light where I am."

When I seemed unable to get beyond this scene, Barbara deepened my level of concentration and then moved me ahead to the next thing I could recall happening.

"Oh, Barbara," I told her, "I don't know if this is it, really." Even in the trance, I wanted to reject the images flooding into my mind. "But I'm lying down, and I see that I don't have any shoes on. I'm covered up with something white, but it's not over my feet, about to the middle of my calves. That's what I see. It's like I'm waking up or trying to wake up. I can move my head just this much. I don't know what I'm lying on."

"Can you move your body at all?" she asked.

"I can't even feel it," I replied. "I can move my head. I'm not thinking anything."

"Look around you," she instructed. "What can you see?"

"It's like real soft lighting, sort of peachy or pink. And I can't see above me."

"What is taking place?" she prompted.

"I feel like I just woke up, I don't feel aware of very much. There's more space over here that I can't see, but the white goes all around as far as I can tell. I can't feel my body. I don't see what I'm lying on, it's not showing down there. I must be perfectly comfortable, I can't feel anything. But I feel my ear hurting."

"Which ear?" Barbara asked.

"The right ear, just at the edge of the inside," I tried to explain. "There was just a burning sort of thing, but I can feel it. It's not bad."

"How long did that pain last?"

"I can still feel it a little," I admitted. "It's not bad. But I feel it again a little harder now, down low. I feel my ear being pulled over this way, and that hurts. My ear, the lobe stretches a little."

"Is it stretching by itself?" Barbara asked, hoping to find out exactly what was being done.

"I don't think I'm looking," I answered evasively.

"Can you experience anything at all?" she persisted.

"I know there's some motion," I said after a moment. "I mean, there's just a sense of movement. And I don't know anything at all about what's going on. I feel like there's movement, if I could look, like some people moving. But I can't see anyone, not yet."

"But you're aware of movement to your left," she repeated.

"Uh-huh," I told her, "because you can see that the light changes as things move around in it. That's why I think there's more than one person moving. I think I feel reassured. I don't feel scared."

Barbara questioned me a while longer, but I was unable or reluctant to remember much more. When she asked if I had ever been in that place before, a pain flared up in my side, and I asked her to bring me out of the trance, which she soon did.

This was my first attempt at hypnotic regression, and I found it hard to relax and give myself up to deep trance. Still, the things I saw seemed very real, even if disjointed, yet I tried to explain the whole thing away as the product of my imagination. I had read enough to know that my recollections pointed to some physical intrusion into my ear, perhaps an implant of some sort, or a probe. But since I'd read so much about abduction experiences, it was easier to tell myself that the recollections had been conjured up from the books, not from my own past. Several months passed before I tried regression again, and looking back now I can see that it was my fear which made me wary and resistant to the experiences I had recalled the first time. My heart still rejected the belief that aliens existed or that they had been interfering in our lives, even though my mind knew differently.

I didn't want it to be true, but I feared, increasingly, that it was. Either that, or there were many otherwise normal people in the world who were all having the same sort of mental aberration. As time went on and we heard the same story over and over again from more people, Casey and I finally had to accept the reality of this phenomenon and find a way to understand and cope with it. But it was too early for that now—we were consumed with discovering exactly what was going on, not why.

One other piece of information turned up during our visit with Barbara which shed light on an experience I'd had earlier, back in May. At that time, I was awakened hearing voices in the bedroom during the night, telling me of the "eliomi" or "elianni." At least, that was the closest I could come to transcribing what I heard, and I knew it wasn't an exact reading. Whatever had been said, the word made no sense to me then. But in a book I picked up in Oklahoma in September, The Goblin Universe, by Ted Holiday and Colin Wilson, I came across references to early Gaelic mythology that echoed that nighttime conversation.

"The Ellyllon were pygmy elves or nature spirits," I read, "a name derived from the Welsh el, a spirit, which in turn came from the Hebrew Elohim-God. Such spirits have always been known to objectify materially on occasion, although this is usually in remote country places." Maybe in Wales, I thought, but there was nothing very remote about my bedroom! Going further, I read, "There are many sorts of fairy or nature spirits ranging from the tiny Ellyllon ... to the wandering Sighes, Elohim, or Trooping Fairies whose illusions and paranormal hoaxes are an intrinsic part of the flying saucer story."

Could that be what the voice in the bedroom was saying? Were the beings who spoke to me calling themselves by the Gaelic term? Later in my research, I did come across other references to alien beings speaking in that ancient language. Most notable was the case of Betty Andreasson, recounted in Raymond Fowler's book, The Andreasson Affair. During one hypnotic regression, Betty Andreasson suddenly began speaking in an unrecognized language, which was duly reported in phonetic terms. One reader of the book later contacted Fowler and said the language matched remarkably well with old Gaelic. When translated, the message read, "Children of the northern peoples, you wander in impenetrable darkness. Your mother mourns." But I could only wonder what message the voice in the bedroom intended for me.

As soon as we returned home, David and James were eager to talk to us. While we were away, James had another episode of missing time, with no memory of what had happened during the two-hour gap.

He and David arrived shortly, and we gathered in the living room, anxious to hear his account. By this point I had begun keeping a journal, first of Casey's experiences and then later adding material about all of us. So, for accuracy, I turned on the tape recorder and got a complete record of James's story.

"It was fifteen till midnight," he told us, "and I decided I'd go to Whataburger and grab a hamburger. So I just got up, got in the car, went and got a Whataburger, and came back."

"Did you eat it in the car?" I asked.

"No," he replied, "I just went to the drive-through and came right back and came into the house and looked at the clock, and it was 2:30."

"Was the hamburger warm?" I wondered.

"No, it was cold," James said. "And I didn't even think about that! There's so many things I don't think about. I reached in there [the sack] and thought, 'Umm, okay, french fries,' and I grabbed a french fry, ate the french fries, and they were cold. And I was mad. I thought, 'Damn,' you know."

That wasn't all that had happened in our absence, James continued. "I was sitting on the couch, and it was late at night. And all of a sudden, the couch started hopping up and down, and then this footstool started hopping, I mean, really hopping. It was shaking me! And then it stopped, just like that, and I got up and looked under the couch, you know, pick up the cushions. I went outside and tried to peek under the house and see if maybe it was something underneath hitting the floor. And I thought, 'Okay, I'm gonna tell David about this,' and then it was two days later before I remembered!"

James paused, still confounded by his forgetfulness of the experience, and David remarked that James had been remembering more of the things the strange woman had told him. We asked James, who nodded in agreement.

"Yeah," he replied, "they said they were nine-dimensional. And for them the tenth dimension was like time to us." The girl had told him this, and he found it odd that more recently she was switching back and forth referring to herself sometimes as "I" and other times as "we."

We wanted to know if he remembered anything about where the woman came from, but he didn't. All he could tell us was that the woman warned him about some other "beings" who have learned how to use the fourth and fifth dimensions, but who weren't spiritually developed.

"She said to be careful of them," James explained. "She said to be very, very careful." And it was his understanding that the woman was warning him about the Grays, the typical being described by so many people who are abducted. The same beings whom Casey had seen during regression, taking him as a young child, later abducting him to perform a nasal implant and to have sex with one of their females, and most recently taking him half a block from our home, cutting his leg and telling him it was time to remember!

It's impossible to describe how we felt then. We had learned a lot about our past experiences through hypnosis, but here we were faced with a current situation in our midst. James was still agitated from the missing time episode and the "hopping" couch incident, and we were frightened for him, as well as for our son and Megan, living in the same house.

A few days later, more strange things occurred, in the onset of what proved to be months of disturbances and encounters. Throughout the fall and winter, we felt literally under siege from forces and entities we couldn't fathom, yet we all tried to keep it secret from the rest of our family and friends. Jobs had to be carried on, houses kept in order, classes taught—the flow of our "normal" lives—but the strain was growing.

One Friday night, I became generally upset, so frightened for David and the others that I begged Casey to take me to the farm to check on them. He drove us over, but since I was so upset he left me in the car and went inside for a few minutes. When he returned, he assured me that they were all three quite all right. The next morning, I simply couldn't wake up. No matter how hard I tried or how much tea I drank, I was in a daze the entire day, yet I had no reason to be so exhausted.

The fear continued, and I became determined to stay up all Saturday night at the farm and watch over the three sleeping young people. My plans were interrupted, however, by the presence of James's younger brother Lucas (pseudonym). Lucas knew nothing about what was going on, nor did James want him to, which meant our conversation was severely limited. By 2:45 A.M. it became clear that he didn't plan to leave before we did. So reluctantly we went home for the night.

The next morning I called to see if anything had happened. At First the only response was that Megan had heard strange noises in the house, waking up three different times. The first sound that disturbed her was James's bedroom door opening and closing, but when she nudged David awake and asked him to check it out, he replied sleepily that she'd only heard the cat.

The second noise she heard was the sound of heavy, crunching footsteps in the front yard, near the picnic table, about twenty feet from her bedroom window, which was open. And the last thing she remembered hearing was a frightfully loud, long train rumbling nearby, which never seemed to pass, followed by the hoot of an owl.

It wasn't until the next day, however, that James told us what had happened to him that same night. He began by saying that two days earlier, when David and Megan were staying at Megan's apartment, James woke up standing in David's bedroom. His arms were outstretched over his head, and he came awake hearing himself say, "I made it! I made it back!" and grinning wildly. But he had no idea where he might have been or why he was in that room instead of his own.

Then on Saturday night, after the others were asleep, James had another visit from the strange woman. She came through the interior door, and this time he was appalled to see that she was angry with him. She scolded him for sitting around and doing nothing. She said he had important things to be doing and that he should get up and start on them.

At that, James exploded. All the anger, frustration, and fear built up inside him came bursting out, and he said he raged at her and at his own inability to understand what was happening to him. He screamed at her, complaining, "Every time I think about all this, I just get more confused, and the more confused I get, the harder it is to think about it! What the hell is going on?" He was demanding answers, but the woman gave him none.

Instead, she suddenly left off her own complaints and began trying to calm him down. She made him lie down on the bed, and then she lay beside him, telling him to rest and find himself again.

As they lay there, three balls of light, about the size of basketballs, suddenly whooshed in through the window and whizzed around the room. A voice came from the lights, saying, "Listen to her, believe it, you're not ready," as if in response to his raging demands. The lights whizzed around a little more before disappearing back out the window, and James eventually fell asleep.

Listening to this bizarre story, we could understand how James had doubted his own sanity for so long. If such a thing had happened to us, we would surely have doubted ourselves, too, and yet James had been visited by many stranger events than this, throughout his life.

On Sunday, the next day, the strangeness continued, this time affecting Megan. In the afternoon she went out into the front yard of the farm, beyond which stretched almost five acres of field bounded by a road and a railroad track.

She was watching the road where a policeman had stopped a car, but then her attention was drawn to a stand of trees by the track.

"I saw this strange, shimmery glow of color formed between the trees," Megan said, "really pretty." And then she heard a sharp, quick noise and felt a blast of cold air, "sort of like the vents of air that surprise you in a funhouse," she explained. The sudden blast sent a shock of adrenalin racing through her system, but just as suddenly as she'd been exhilarated, she was drained of all her energy and almost fell to the ground in a faint.

James and David noticed her erratic movements as she tried to walk back to the house, so they rushed out and helped her inside.

"It was like she was totally dazed out," David said. "Both of us had to hold her up and just drag her to the porch."

Megan collapsed on the couch, unable to speak or even open her eyes for almost half an hour, and then the feeling of exhaustion went away and she recovered. Afterwards, however, she had very little memory of the fainting spell, though she still recalled vividly the glowing color in the trees, the blast of air, and her collapse in the field.

The next night, what little peace of mind I still had was destroyed by an experience I tried to think of as a dream. I was lying down with Casey when I felt the whole bed start to shake, and when I tried to move, I found I was paralyzed. I couldn't even speak, but somehow I finally managed to whisper a prayer, asking the god of truth and love to make this frightening force go away. I repeated the prayer again and again, until the paralysis broke, but the bed shook even more violently as my strength increased.

At last I was able to sit up and pound my fists on the bed, demanding out loud that the force must leave me alone, and then the shaking stopped. I tried to rouse Casey and tell him what had happened, but he rolled over sleepily without responding. At that point, three women came in and approached me. They held me comfortingly and told me, "You did the right thing. You passed the test."

The next thing I recall was actually sitting up in the bed, with Casey asleep beside me. Once again I tried to wake him up, and once again he refused to be roused. I described the dream experience into my tape recorder, feeling the need to remember it in every detail, and then I turned out the light and fell back asleep. But when I woke up the next morning, I was drained and weak. I spent the day completely exhausted, giving in, on and off, to the urge to cry before finally calling my friend Bonnie to come for a visit.

While we were together, I got a phone call from George Andrews, a researcher with whom Barbara was working on a book. He told me about a car wreck his daughter had just been involved in, which had left her seriously injured, a wreck for which there was no logical cause. This news really frightened me, because only three days earlier Barbara's daughter-in-law had been badly hurt in a similar wreck, the cause of which had baffled the investigating police officers. The two young women had received serious injuries to their mouths. I was frightened because Barbara had recently been warned by two different men—one a self-proclaimed psychic to whom she paid little attention, and the other a man whose occasional predictions had proven more reliable—to discontinue her research and not to reveal what she was finding out from the people whose experiences she had explored. That meant, of course, that she shouldn't contribute material to George's book.

They had been warned, and now their children were suffering. What's next, I wondered, scared by the thought that these beings might deliberately be hurting people and afraid of what I might have brought onto my own family by exploring this phenomenon myself. I was filled with the idea that the best thing I could do was to get absolutely out of the entire UFO situation: no more books or journals or notes or tapes or contacts with anyone involved in this thing.

At no time, before or since, have I felt such fear, blinding my logic and leaving me to react instinctively and protectively. We were in a nightmare world, helpless. And then James phoned. He wanted to tell me about a dream he'd had the night before, the same night I'd felt the bed shaking.

In James's dream, he was a little child, perhaps three years old, sitting with a group of other children who were being told a story by an older person. The storyteller looked like James also, but a James twenty-three years old, as he was now, not three. When I heard his dream, I asked him to come over and record it in the journal I was keeping of his experiences. What follows is that account of the dream.

"Once upon a time there was a young prince," James began. "This prince looked around at his world and saw that evil things were happening, and he wanted to stop the evil. So he told his friends, 'There must be someone causing all this evil, so I'm going to go out and search through the world until I find the evil person. Then I'll make him stop.'

"So he roamed all over, meeting and talking to everyone he could, trying to find out who was causing the evil things to happen. But no matter how much he looked, for years and years, he couldn't find an evil person. At last, however, he met a sorcerer, who told him that the cause of the evil was under the ocean. The prince was unable to get down under the ocean, and the sorcerer was unable to help him.

"So the prince returned to his kingdom and stayed there for a year. But he could see that the evil things were still happening and, in fact, increasing throughout the world. Finally, then, he resolved to take up his search again and try to end the evil. Once again, he roamed through the world looking for the evil man, but the man was not found. And once again, the prince met another sorcerer, and this wizard was able to show him how to get under the ocean.

"The prince did as the wizard told him and made his way under the ocean and began to fight against the cause of evil. Meanwhile, back in his kingdom, the friends of the prince waited anxiously for his return, but the prince remained below the sea. After a long, long time passed, the friends became really worried and decided that they would also go down under the ocean themselves and help the prince in the battle. So they managed to get down under the water, and there they found the prince. They rallied around him and fought in unison, and the evil was finally defeated.

"The moral of the story is that you need your friends in the fight against evil: one man cannot defeat it on his own, but by banding together, our strength can be great enough to win."

The message went straight to my heart. An hour before, I was ready to run away, hopeless, and hide, but here was a message of hope. Could we really fight this awful situation, I wondered, did part of the answer lie in uniting with our friends in some way? And how? What is the battle we face? It was no longer merely a question of what is going on, but of how can we make it stop.

CHAPTER 5

James and I weren't the only ones having "dream" experiences that Sunday night, September 12. On the following Tuesday James phoned to tell me what he'd just learned from his younger brother Lucas, who'd been at the farm on the twelfth. Lucas spent quite a lot of time with James and David and other friends at the farm, often staying up late to play video games. On Sunday night, however, he had a very different experience.

He told James that "something like a dream" had happened while he was at his parents' home. "He said he dreamed he was sitting in the living room of the farm," James repeated to me, "when this stream of people began coming in the front door, maybe twenty or thirty. They just, moved through the living room and kitchen into my bedroom, then out my back door and back into the living room.

"Lucas called them 'people' at first," James continued, "but then he thought they weren't real, so he started calling them 'things'."

"What else happened?" I asked.

"Well," James went on, "he watched them for a little while and then he got mad. He said he wanted to stop them from bothering me, so he threatened them. Lucas said when he hit one of them, it just screamed but didn't fight back, even when he knocked it down. They they started running, and he chased after them. He caught one and jerked it around face-to-face. But the thing attacked him, with its mind. Lucas attacked back, pummeling the thing in the face, until the creature began to scream.

"Then Lucas chased after a second being and attacked it in the same way, but when he went back into the farm, he saw a huge creature, much bigger than the other two. He caught it and demanded to know what was going on," James continued. "The creature didn't answer, so Lucas said he was going to beat them all senseless if they didn't leave me alone. That was when they all left."

When James paused, I asked if he'd ever said anything to Lucas about his own experiences.

"Not at all, never," he assured me. "I haven't told him anything. That's why I'm so blown away by the whole thing."

"Did you ever ask Lucas what these beings looked like?" I wondered.

"Yeah," he replied. "Lucas said they acted like they were trying to appear human, but they weren't doing a very good job of it. They were wearing ragged clothes and stuff, like hillbillies in old overalls and hats."

Lucas laughed nervously at the strange description, but I immediately remembered something we'd heard from a member of the study group in the city. This man was at our first meeting with the group, and he'd recounted his own first experience with alien beings. They "astrally" moved him in the middle of the night to a nearby golf course green, where a small craft appeared. Several humanoid beings descended from the craft, the man told us, and he remarked how surprised he was to see that the first one was dressed in a tattered shirt and overalls, with a straw hat and a piece of grass between his teeth as he smiled. "He was dressed just like a hillbilly," the man said.

And now Lucas's dream had shown hillbilly creatures at the farm. What kind of insanity were we caught up in, we wondered, for it seemed that almost daily some new strange experience occurred to one of us. James, however, had more than his share. After so many years of living with his bizarre secrets of alien encounters, James long had suffered the added strain of fearing that his experiences were merely the product of a diseased mind, not a reality. Now at last he had people he could talk to, who understood because they had strange experiences of their own. And after his trip to St. Louis and the outward confirmation of this alien reality, he no longer doubted his sanity.

Instead, James wanted to know more about his situation, and it may have been that desire for knowledge which led him to try astral projection. A few years earlier, James had discussed astral travel with a small group of his friends one day when I happened to be present. He said he'd been able to "get out" of his body in that manner for several years, since he was a young teenager, without going into any detail, but I dismissed the whole subject in disbelief. The only other person I knew who ever talked about astral travel was my brother, years ago, who claimed to be able to do it, and even then I thought he must have been quite imaginative to come up with such stories.

James told us that on September 14 he had tried to astrally project himself earlier that day, just to see if he could still do it. The last time he tried it, James said he had a lot of trouble getting back into his body and so had frightened himself out trying it again.

"This time," James said, "I was just beginning to feel like I was about to get free of my body, but something happened. Something just sort of jerked me out. And the next thing I knew," he continued, "I was in this dark room, sitting at a table. There were some black blocks or cubes and rectangles, and I was supposed to move them around."

"Why?" I asked. "Who was making you manipulate the cubes?"

"I don't know," James said. "There were some others there with me, but I didn't really see them. The room was dark, and the only light was coming down on the table from behind me. All I ever saw was their arms, when they'd reach over my shoulder to adjust a block or something. The arms looked pretty dark, but I couldn't really tell."

"How long did all this go on?" I wanted to know, but James just shook his head.

"I don't know," he admitted, "it was real strange. The phone kept ringing."

"You mean the phone in the house?" I asked.

"Yeah. I'd be trying to concentrate on the blocks, on doing it correctly, and then the phone would ring. It kept distracting me, like I was in both places at once."

After a short while his concentration on the task was completely broken, and he was put back into his body. He told us that the experience was very unsettling and he didn't think he would try astral projection again, since the beings were able to manipulate him in that state.

The next day, Thursday, James once again went through a strange and frightening occurrence. David and Megan had both already left the farm for the night, and James was sitting in the living room, finishing a cigarette before going to his parents' home to sleep. Outside, the two cats suddenly started acting strange, and then the dogs "went wild" barking in their front yard pen. Immediately, James felt the entire farmhouse start to shake, so he raced out the back door and into his car. As he was driving away, he said he could see the house still shaking.

The whole week had been so full of bizarre incidents like this that we were all perhaps a little apprehensive about the coming weekend. Fred was planning to come out on Friday, to watch a television program on UFO abductions and also to meet James. From hearing their stories, Casey and I knew that they had both seen human-looking beings during some of their experiences, and both of them had been told that new bodies were somehow being made or prepared for us. We wondered what else they might discover they had in common.

That Friday afternoon, I was alone at home, reading Our Haunted Planet, a book by John A. Keel, that described Joseph Smith's initial contacts with the angels who led him to the golden plates, the Book of Mormon. It reminded me very much of something James had experienced. In St. Louis, out on the hill with the woman, he'd been told he would have to locate something, a box of some sort, at a future date. Joseph Smith was also told of a box he'd have to find within six years, whereas James had been told that his tasks, including finding the box, would come within five years.

As I was thinking of these similarities, there was a sudden bright flash of light in my living room, a blinding white light, as if lightning had struck indoors. I looked up, startled, waiting for the sound of thunder to follow, but there was none. I ran outside and looked up at the sky, which was clear and bright, so I came back in, bewildered. That was the first silent lightning I experienced, but it occurred several times in the following months, and I never found an explanation for it.

That evening we gathered early for a chance to talk before the TV program. Fred and James arrived around 7 P.M., then David and Megan came over, and finally Bonnie stopped by for a brief visit. After she left, we went to the farm to watch the program, a segment of the now-defunct "Late Show." The entire program was devoted to various UFO subjects, with Whitley Strieber, William Moore, and an ex-astronaut, Brian O'Leary, among the guests. Also, in the audience were over fifty abductees, and the host interviewed several of them.

Each story was different, yet they all shared a basic sameness with the experiences we had had, and it was very eerie to listen to strangers on television and feel so close to their stories. When one of the abductees mentioned finding a triangle mark on his body, Fred laughingly said he wished he'd find one, too, as if it would somehow make the whole thing seem more real. Yet we all felt that it was very real right now, and that it seemed even more ominous now that the media were making these situations known to the general public.

We wondered why, after so much secrecy and the imposition of amnesia on the victims of abductions, everyone was suddenly being told. And many more people seemed to be waking up to the fact of alien abductions going on in their previously normal lives. I had sometimes taken comfort in the knowledge that people had been abducted for years without there being any perceptible impact on society as a whole, but now I could see that a qualitative change was taking place. From Barbara's research, we knew of over two hundred cases in the Tulsa area, where ordinary people were going through extraordinary experiences. Budd Hopkins's books told of many more victims in the New York-New England area. There were over fifty ordinary people in the audience of the television program who claimed to have been abducted, and there were four of us in the living room watching the show! I remembered what Casey had been told back in December, that it was "time to remember." How many other people, I wondered, were also being ordered to remember? And why?

We talked about such things for a while after the program, and then the group broke up. Fred went back to his apartment in the city, David and Megan went to the air-conditioned comfort of her apartment near campus, James left for his parents' house, and Casey and I went home to bed. We slept late the next morning, so we'd only been up for a little while when James phoned, asking if he could come talk to us.

He arrived looking terrible, with dark circles under his bloodshot eyes, and he was exhausted.

"What's wrong?" we asked immediately.

"Something happened last night," he began shakily. "I went to my folks' house and sat up watching TV until 3:00 or 3:30. Then I went to bed in my sister's old room. My parents were asleep already, and so was Lucas.

"So I finally went to bed," he continued, "and the next thing, I'm standing by my bed, thinking I'm so tired, all I want to do is get some sleep."

"Weren't you confused?" I asked. "You didn't wonder what you were doing out of bed?"

"Well, yeah," he replied, "but I was exhausted. I just wanted to lie down again, so I did. And then it happened again."

"What?" I wanted to know, beginning to feel confused myself.

"I was up again," he explained, "standing by my bed. And this time I was really upset. But I was too tired to do anything about it. It kept happening over and over, seems like."

"And that's all that happened?" I asked.

"I don't know," he admitted. "One of the times when I woke up, I was already lying down, but I don't think I was in my real bed. Everything seemed very strange, but then I thought that at least I was horizontal this time, so maybe they'd let me sleep. That's how tired I was."

This phase apparently passed after a while, and then James said he woke up in his bed with a strange female alien being beside him.

"She was trying to get me worked up," he said, shaking his head. "She got on top of me and tried to make me respond, you know, sexually. But I kept refusing, I pushed her away and begged her to leave me alone. I told her there was no way I could do anything like that, I just wanted to get some rest."

"So what happened then?" Casey asked.

"Finally she gave up, I guess," James answered. "She left me and went out in the hall. That's when I saw that there were some other beings out there, too. I could hear them all talking to her, but at first I couldn't understand what they were saying. And then, suddenly it all clicked and I understood them."

"What were they talking about?" I asked.

"They were asking her, the female, what had happened, and she told them I wouldn't cooperate," he replied.

"How long did that go on?" Casey questioned.

"I don't know," James told us. "I was just completely exhausted, and I guess I fell asleep, because that's all I remember."

"What did the female look like?" I asked. "Was she like any of the other beings you've seen?"

"No," he shook his head. "She was different, taller. But the room was dark, and I couldn't really see much detail. She was naked, though, and she felt really cold when she touched me."

"And this type, this group, wasn't familiar to you?" I persisted.

"Not really," he told us. "These were different ones, I've never seen them before. And you know what amazes me? There were a whole lot of them in the hall, right in my parents' house! Like they didn't worry about anyone waking up and seeing them."

We all sat back in bewilderment. Like James, we wondered how such a scene could occur without any of the others in the house being disturbed. Perhaps we could have dismissed it as a nightmare, except that James was so obviously upset and physically exhausted.

"There's one more thing," James said then, standing up. He turned around, showing us the back of his calf. "I found these marks this morning," he pointed, "and I don't know where they came from."

There were three large puncture marks on the skin, arranged in an equilateral triangle. James had never told us of having any marks or scars on his body before, and it was easy to see how deeply the triangle upset him. The arrival of a new group of alien beings and the appearance of the three punctures seemed to be more than coincidental. Until now, I was the only one in the group who'd been marked with a triangle, yet we'd learned that this was an insignia left by at least one of the alien groups.

There was nothing we could do for James but commiserate, and he soon left. Casey and I immediately checked our own bodies, to see if anything might have happened to us. On my right hip I found a single puncture; there was a dried, smeared drop of blood on my ankle; and I had a small scratch, also smeared with blood, just below and to the left of my breastbone. I looked at the bedsheets and found a single thin streak of blood on my side of the bed, corresponding to the scratch on my chest. And Casey had a red scratch, a bit larger than mine, below his right breast. Yet neither of us remembered anything unusual during the night. If we hadn't looked, we wouldn't have known the marks were on us until later when we showered because, like all the unexplained scratches and punctures, they caused absolutely no pain.

Our next thought was of Fred, so we called and asked him if he'd noticed any unusual marks on his own body.

"I don't know," he said. "I haven't looked to see, but I will." He left the phone for a few moments, and when he picked it up to speak again, I could hear excitement and anxiety in his voice.

"They're there, all right," he told me. "There's a puncture, three or four of them, on my arm and leg. Some of them are by themselves, but three of them form a triangle."

Triangles aren't random, and what was happening to us seemed deliberately meant to show a pattern or a connection between us, but we still had no idea what the connection really meant. It seemed like a puzzle to be solved, yet the clues were so ephemeral, only punctures, bruises, scratches that seemed to come from nowhere, caused no discomfort, and healed with remarkable speed. The phenomenon was so that we were like mere children, blindfolded, playing hide-and-seek with invisible prey.

Casey and I were driven to understand the situation, so much so that it became hard for him to concentrate on his business and for me to concentrate on anything. I read more books, kept a scrupulous journal of the events going on in everyone's lives, and I thought about all the things I'd learned in the past few months. There were the classic cases of ufology, available in any number of books, with which we were soon familiar: Mantell, the Hills, Pascagoula, Moody, Coyne, Travis Walton. And there were the standard skeptical explanations that had been put forward for years, which under any scrutiny prove very often to be impossible solutions.

There were the peripheral issues, cattle mutilations and Bigfoot sightings, that were rumored to be closely associated with UFO activity. We knew nothing about these things from our own knowledge, so they were relegated to the "rumors" file. By now this mass of material included stories of secret U.S.-Russian bases on the moon and Mars; blond-haired space brethren from the Pleiades, a star cluster in the constellation Taurus, made famous by the story of Swiss farmer Billy Meier to whom they allegedly imparted cosmic knowledge of their work to assist our spiritual evolution; channeled pronouncements by various extraterrestrials of the Galactic Federation about the shifting of the global axis; and secret U.S.-alien underground bases throughout the country, the products of our govern-ment's illegal treaties and arrangements with the leaders of some alien nation whose ultimate goal is total control of our world. These were things we heard about and read about, all at rather a far remove from our own mysterious experiences.

But there was one rumor, at least, which was more available for us to check out, and our findings were disturbing. Part of the U.S.-alien alliance story says that there has been a falling out between us and them. As a result, and faced with the imminent mass confrontation between aliens and humanity, the government is now working feverishly in two directions. On the one hand, an immense effort is under way to develop superweaponry capable of defending us against alien technology. The aliens had promised early on to give us their technical expertise, but they had reneged.

And the second effort is the rapid education of the public, through the media, about the coming alien presence. Apparently, the rumor says, the aliens who are here now are just the forerunners for a much larger group, and that group's arrival is expected within the next four years. The government hopes to avoid worldwide panic by preparing us through advertising and the entertainment media for our encounter with alien beings.

Thinking back over the past two years, we began to see that there had indeed been an upsurge in UFO-related interests. The Gulf Breeze sightings got wide television coverage; Strieber's book was a best-seller, as were Hopkins's two accounts of abduction experiences. Abduction researchers and victims had been interviewed on all the talk shows and on a few prime-time programs: Oprah Winfrey, Phil Donahue, Gary Collins, even Morton Downey, Jr. presented Budd Hopkins, Whitley Strieber, Bruce Maccabbee, Stanton Friedman, and many other researchers to the public. "Unsolved Mysteries" devoted over half a show to the abduction phenomenon, and Ross Shaffer's "Late Show" gave it the entire hour. There had even been a one-hour pilot movie in July, "Why On Earth," which, strangely enough, had as its premise a joint U.S. alien secret base from which an idealistic young alien agent would make forays into the bewilderingly irrational world of humans.

And then there were the alien movies in the works, not to mention the classic ET stories of the past decades, when, rumor tells us, the government felt more kindly disposed toward their alien allies and wanted us to view them with affection. When the rift took place—a shoot-out of sorts at an underground base, in which the humans got the worst of it all—the government attitude changed, and we were presented malevolent reptilian aliens in the miniseries "V." And now we had a new series, "War of the Worlds," which we watched anxiously each week. In every episode, we saw some fact or detail which we recognized from actual cases, mixed in with the more creative aspects of the show, and as we watched we did feel as if a deliberate effort were being made to acquaint the public with at least part of the truth.

We read about current movie projects with alien subjects, such as Alien Nation and They Live, and more immediate was talk of an upcoming TV special, "UFO Cover-Up Live," about which little detail was known. I couldn't remember a similar time frame in which so much UFO interest had been evident, and like the rest of the group, I began to wonder if there truly was an effort going on, real preparations for a coming invasion. It seemed unthinkable, yet we had another reason to wonder about this rumor. James, we remembered, had been told by the interdimensional woman that his big task would come within five years and that we would all be involved in it. And he'd been told that we had every reason to fear the gray aliens, who had no concern for our welfare or wishes.

Strange marks continued to appear on our bodies, and we wondered who or what was causing them. Neither Casey nor I was aware of anything going on in the night, yet we checked our bodies upon going to bed and upon getting up, and new marks were frequently found. Stress and anxiety ran high quite a lot of the time, and I thought it would be good to have a trained therapist on hand. If things really were happening to us which we had no memory of, then hypnotic regression could help us discover it. Yet none of us was in need of traditional therapy—we were adequately coping with the demands of our lives so far—and we did not want or need the feeling of being a patient. So I contacted several counselors listed in the phone book and at last found one who agreed to see me.

We met in his office, and I was impressed with the man, an interning counselor just finishing up his work at the local university. As calmly as I could, I explained to him about the abduction phenomenon and about the need for a volunteer hypnotist who could work in complete confidentiality with abductees. His response seemed to show an open mind, and although he admitted his lack of familiarity with UFOs, he did say he would be happy and intrigued to work with abductees. But, at the time, no one in our group was having any overt situations to deal with.

In fact, aside from a bruise or puncture mark every few days, the only unusual event had been a conversation between Megan and the ROTC sergeant on campus. As a freshman, Megan had joined the Air Force officers' program and reported to a local detachment. Although she was planning to resign from the program (as she has since done, on medical grounds), the sergeant insisted that Megan make plans for the duty she wanted after graduation. Since Megan's major was physics, the sergeant assumed that she would want to work in Research and Development. But instead, Megan signed up for Meteorology, hoping that such an assignment would, should she have to stay in the service, keep her near to home.

When the sergeant saw the Meteorology listing, she tried to change Megan's mind. "You don't want to work in Meteorology," she told Megan. "Don't you want to get into R & D? That way, you'll get to find out the truth about UFOs and aliens. You might even get to do tests and research on them."

Stunned by the remarks, Megan was unable to answer.

She had told no one, outside our small group, about any of the UFO activity we'd been experiencing, and it frightened her to be confronted with it by a military official, in such an open way. It could have been a pure coincidence, we tried to assure her, but we didn't think so. The official Air Force reply to UFO inquiries is that they aren't in the business of dealing with the subject. Why, then, would the sergeant talk about Air Force research into UFOs and aliens? Was it a test of Megan, we wondered, or was it a warning that they knew all about us? Our phones had acted very funny on several occasions, and after having been followed twice during the summer, we wondered just exactly who was interested in us, and why.

Toward the end of September a few other strange things happened. I had two different spells of sudden exhaustion, which seemed to have nothing to do with my health, and one morning I woke up with a very painful left wrist, arm, and shoulder, as if I'd been wrestling all night, but the soreness was gone by the evening. On the twenty-ninth, Casey woke up with a long, bloody scraped gash down his right shin. It was obvious that getting such an injury would be noticeable—and painful—but Casey hadn't injured himself the previous day, nor did the gash hurt when he found it. We checked the bedsheets for blood and didn't find any there, so we were left with one more unexplained injury.

And none of these things was severe enough to require a doctor's attention. Besides, what could we say if we had gone to the doctor? "Look at this scratch, Doc—or this scabbed puncture—can you tell me where it came from?" Without pain or infection, without serious trauma to our bodies, what could we expect a doctor to do for us?

October 1988

Two mornings later, on the first of October, Casey woke up with a small triangular scar above the scraped shin area. It looked as if a triangle patch of skin had neatly been cut away, and already the wound was healing over. Checking our bodies became a daily ritual, but so far, except for Fred's and James's triangular wounds, Casey and I were the only ones with marks. That changed, however, on October 3, when David came over to show me a puncture he'd just found. It was a single mark, in the vein of his right arm, and it looked just like he'd given blood.

All the fears and paranoia I'd felt changed at that moment, and I became outraged. I wanted to protect my son, I wanted to protect us all from whatever was invading our lives, using our bodies without our permission or knowledge, and I felt helpless and angry. There was no one to go to and demand relief, or even answers. I knew from the few people I'd talked with that the subject of UFOs and aliens was not well received. Even my own parents didn't want us to talk about it, and they certainly didn't believe anything was actually happening to us.

And what could we tell people? That we'd seen a UFO, that we wake up with strange marks on our bodies, that impossible things go on in our homes? It was still easier, as it had been in the beginning, to avoid our friends than to tell them about our situation. The only people we could trust to believe us were the others who were being abducted, too. Our emotional stability depended upon mutual support, but all we could give each other was sympathy.

CHAPTER 6

Scratches and bruises and needle-like puncture marks are infuriating. As evidence of alien contact, they are useless if there is no memory of an event to go with them. We were the only ones who could truly know that a bruise or scratch had not been on our body the night before, that it wasn't the result of accidental, self-inflicted clumsiness during the day. We checked our bodies regularly and made mental note of any bump or scratch from known sources. Still, marks appeared on random mornings, after nights of apparently undisturbed sleep.

More than once we wondered if there were any way we could be doing these things to ourselves, in our sleep, but the evidence didn't fit. At times we'd find injuries on our bodies but no blood on the bed, and at other times there was plenty of blood on the sheets, although we could find no new cut or scratch. And once, after falling asleep only a couple of hours while staying up late studying, David awoke with blood drying in his ear. When he cleaned it out, fresh blood was also found. Yet there was no sign of a scratch or other lesion, and he remembered nothing out of the ordinary.

For James, things got even stranger at the farm. He was often alone there at night, and throughout the autumn the house was alive with bizarre activity. The couch had shaken, the entire house once shook violently, the lights didn't always behave.

"I was in the living room the other night," James told us, "and when I got up to get a drink in the kitchen, I saw that there was a light on in my bedroom. I went back there, and all the lamps were on, so I turned them off. A little bit later I was back in the kitchen and noticed the bedroom lights were on again. So I turned them off again, but it just kept happening. Four times!"

"Nobody else was home?" I asked.

"Nope," he insisted. "And the last time when I was going back to the kitchen after turning off the bedroom lights, I heard a noise outside, by the driveway. I flicked on the back porch light and looked out, but I didn't see anything. And I swear, I turned off the porch light and walked away. But I turned around, and the porch light was shining!

"And then," he continued, "when I went to the bathroom later to take a leak, I was standing there, and I heard a metallic sort of jingling sound. I looked around, and the hook-and-eye latch was moving! It lifted up and dropped into the lock, all by itself!"

"What did you do?" I asked, thinking how I might feel if such a thing had happened to me.

"I just stood there," he said. "I mean, I couldn't move, I was scared to death. I thought, there's something else in here with me, and I couldn't even move. And then I thought, 'I better get out of here,' so I forced myself to unlock the door. And I got out of there right away, drove over to my folks' house for the night."

"Are you still staying there?" I asked.

"Not anymore, but I stayed for a few days," he replied. "And it was real strange when I finally went back to the farm. Two or three times in the next days, or nights, rather, I kept hearing this voice. It said that 'they' were glad I'd come back, so they could help me."

"Did they ever show up, then?" I wanted to know.

"No," he admitted, "but once I heard this girl's voice, crying like she was in trouble. I went outside to see what was going on, but I couldn't find anyone out there."

James had been going through repeated, frequent intrusions for months, so it isn't surprising that by October his nerves were thin. He still found it difficult to discuss his experiences, although he usually came and told us when anything happened. There were many parts of the events which he couldn't remember, and he admitted he hadn't told us all the details of any of the experiences. He was twenty-three years old by then, entitled to whatever privacy he desired, but we thought he should at least let his parents in on the situation. They knew something was wrong, and they wanted very much to be able to help their son, no matter what the problem.

James was adamant, however, that we keep his secret. And we hoped that having us to talk to was enough for him, so we respected his wishes and tried to keep in close contact. Later in October we planned to go to a MUFON meeting to hear newswoman and author Linda M. Howe speak on the topic of cattle mutilations, and James planned to go with us. Primarily we hoped to see the woman again, the one who looked like the interdimensional female who'd been visiting the farm uninvited. When we arrived at the meeting, however, James wasn't there. After the speech, I phoned to check on him, and he sounded very shaken, so we went directly to the farm when we reached town late that night.

James was exhausted and seemed more visibly afraid than he usually did after an experience. He told us, in a quick, jerky manner, that he'd changed his mind about going to Oklahoma to work with Barbara, that he just wasn't ready. He'd been having horrible dreams and flashes of memories the past two nights, and what he saw frightened him. The worst was a memory of himself as a young child, pinned helpless against a wall and watching as alien beings dissected a human man on a table. The man screamed in agony as they cut parts of him away, and then the action stopped momentarily. The tortured man raised up his head, looked at James, and then he spoke.

"Don't worry about me," he said, "I'm going to die now, there's nothing to be done about that. But you're not going to die yet." Instead, he said, James would someday have to battle against these beings, but that was all James would tell us.

And he was shown images of the two farmhouse cats, mutilated in the yard, and a warning, reminding him of what the woman in St. Louis had told him: the Grays are coming down to earth, trying to hold back our evolution and keep us down; they regard us as little more than insects; their home planet had been destroyed at a past crisis point, and they don't want us to survive the current crisis in our own world.

He remembered the woman's claim that her group hoped to precipitate the crisis in such a way as to help us survive. Whatever the case, a crisis seemed unavoidable, and James clearly felt frightened and depressed.

We worried about his mental health and finally persuaded him to let us tell his parents a little about the situation by restricting our discussion to our own experiences. With the ground broken, we hoped James would have enough courage to go to them with his story. So we invited his parents to visit and little by little revealed what we'd been going through. To our relief and surprise, they seemed open-minded and inclined to believe rather than doubt our honesty. In fact, while talking about unusual experiences, James's mother, Sandy (pseudonym), recounted an early-childhood memory with all the traits of a screened abduction episode.

Before the evening was over, however, Sandy began asking questions that led to James, via David's experiences, and all I could tell her was that she should discuss any questions she had with James. Despite the very late hour, James's parents went to the farm and offered him their support, urging him to talk more with them the next day. He was surprised by their responses, but once the barrier had been broken, he admitted that his life became much easier.

The end of October came, and we prepared for trick-or-treaters on Halloween, with bowls of candy and spooky decorations at the door. Once or twice we joked about the real spooks in our lives, but the evening was uneventful. The night, however, must have been much more active, both in our home and at the farm. When we got up the next morning, I found three new punctures in my neck, still bright red. They formed a small triangle and were positioned over my jugular vein. But as usual I remembered nothing during the night.

November 1988

Later in the day, November first, David came by with a strange tale from the previous night, too. He and Megan had been alone at the farm when they went to bed around 10:30, and then a little before 2 A.M. he awoke with a headache.

"So I got up," he said, "and went through the house. I got a glass of water in the kitchen, then I went to the bathroom for aspirin. James was in bed by then, asleep. That's why I couldn't understand why all the lights were on."

"What do you mean?" I interrupted. "James still had his light on?"

"No," David explained, "every light in the whole house was on, except for the one in my bedroom. And the radio was playing in the living room."

"Has James ever left everything turned on like that before?" I asked.

"No, he's real good about turning off stuff," David answered. "I thought he must have been really wasted to be that careless. But the next morning, James said he had turned out everything as usual. He swore he didn't leave the radio and lights on."

After getting back in bed, David woke again a while later, feeling, he said, as if he were oscillating violently, as if his body were about to explode or disintegrate into its atomic particles.

"It felt really scary," he said, "like if that sensation went on much longer, I was literally going to come apart. I was just getting ready to scream, I was so scared, and then the sensation suddenly stopped.

"I think I turned over and said something to Megan," he continued. "I said, 'It's okay, it's stopped'."

"Was she awake?" I asked. "Did she know what was going on?"

"I don't think she even moved," he replied. "After that, I just fell right back to sleep. At least I think I was asleep some of the time."

He thought he woke again, though he didn't open his eyes or even seem to be aware of his surroundings, and lay there thinking about the sensation he'd felt earlier. Then, without any volition, he started seeing, or recalling seeing, a scene in which two separate images were superimposed on each other, like two different slides being projected at the same time.

"One scene was of a desert place, in the middle of a huge sandstorm," he described. "The whole world was a desert, tan, and the only way I could tell the sky from the ground was that the sky was a lighter shade of tan.

"The second scene," he went on, "was in an outside area at night, pitch-black. But I could see something in front of me. It looked like a fifteen-foot-tall tree trunk or irregular column, and it was covered with thick, dark brown fur."

"What was it?" I asked.

"I don't know," he said. "I could see some sort of appendage near the top of the column, but I have no idea what it was."

Throughout the strange night, David felt as if he never really got back to sleep after waking up the second time, yet he couldn't recall doing or even seeing anything around him all that time. When morning came, he woke up feeling that the night had been very exhausting, and Megan also felt that she didn't get much rest. They were both extremely tired that day. When we discussed the incident, David said that the only time he's felt anything similar was in the summer, recalling the night his head had been filled with a pressure-explosive sensation. At the time he said he was afraid he was about to be taken, in some way, out of his body.

A strange correlation to David's experience turned up well over a year later, and, since the similarity was so astounding, I think it worth mentioning here. After two successful nonfiction works dealing with his own alien experiences, Whitley Strieber published a novel in 1989, Majestic, which he described as "a work of fiction that is based on fact." While reading this book,

I was shocked to find a scene almost identical to the two scenes David recalled seeing. Chapter Twenty-Six of Majestic describes an experience in a desert setting, matching David's description right down to the "brown sky." Moving through this scene, the fictional character then tells of finding himself in a nighttime setting, and as I read those words, a sense of sickening uneasiness overcame me:

"There seemed to be a forest of thin trees all around me," the character says. "It took me time to understand that I was looking at tall, black legs, many of them.

"It took every ounce of my composure not to scream. I was under what appeared to be a gigantic insect of some kind, perhaps a spider. The rattling noise started again. I could see sharp mouth parts working.

"Jumping, twisting, turning to avoid the legs I made a dash to get away from the thing."

Setting the book down, I could read no farther. My son had been shown a tan world, with a tan sky, and then he found himself looking up at those tall, dark, fur-covered columns that had no reference to the reality he'd always known. Was it mere coincidence that Strieber had included such scenes in his novel? Had he invented the material, I wondered, or had it come from someone's actual recollections? And what, in the name of God, did it mean for my son? It was an ominous beginning for November, and I began to despair that the phenomenon would ever stop. The following evening after we went to bed, the phone rang precisely at midnight. I answered it and said, "Hello," waiting for a reply. At first there was nothing but very distant-sounding static, and then a bizarre voice said, "Hal-loo." Surprised by the voice, I merely repeated, "Hello?"

There was another pause, and then I heard "Hal-loo" once again. The voice frightened me in its strangeness, and I sat silently listening, but nothing further was said. I hung up and lay back uneasily, wondering who had been on the other end of the line. The voice kept repeating itself in my mind, but I couldn't recognize the accent, and I couldn't reproduce the sound of that "Hal-loo" when I tried to tell Casey about the call.

The next day, November third, the phone rang again just before noon, and when I picked it up there was nobody on the line. In fact, there was no sound at all, no background static, just absolute blank silence. Fearful that I might hear the strange voice from the night before, however, I wouldn't listen, yet I couldn't bring myself to hang up. Putting the receiver down on the cabinet, I walked away, wondering what I should do. A minute or so later when I went back to hang up, I heard a recorded voice repeating, "Please hang up and dial again. We are unable to complete your call as dialed." But of course, I wasn't the one who had dialed the phone in the first place.

Later that same day, I heard about a disturbing rumor that was making its way through the UFO community with all the speed of a highly contagious virus. Such rumors abounded in the ufological community. This one held that a recent public speaker had supposedly confided to a MUFON member that the Air Force was greatly concerned about a large unidentified object in space, apparently heading for earth. When others had tried to track down the source of this rumor, the trail finally led back to some unnamed and retired Air Force officer who kept in contact with his friends still in the service.

They had told him that the large object was emitting a lot of radiation and was following an unusual trajectory which seemed to show intelligent control. The military, so the rumor went, was concerned that the object was an artificial base of some sort and that it might be connected with the current upsurge in ET activity—the same kind of activity which was intruding into my family. There was even speculation that whoever was controlling the object might be involved in some sort of conflict, that the object was a battle station, and that they could be preparing to use the earth as a staging ground in the conflict.

It's no wonder we often felt as if we were unwitting characters thrust into a science-fiction movie. Casey's revelations of his past experiences had been shocking enough, and then there were the horrific stories of John Lear—the government's deal with aliens, the underground installations with vats of human body parts and prenatal nurseries for stolen fetuses. And now rumors of alien battle stations heading for earth? A year ago I would have laughed at anyone foolish enough to consider such things seriously, but now I was listening. And I wondered how we could ever hope to sort out the rumors from the facts.

Fighting off the feelings of anger and fear and disorientation that now accompanied every new twist in this phenomenon, I told myself, "Humans can lie, and so can aliens." My own research showed that different abductees had been told different things by their captors, and not all the information could be true. There were too many contradictions.

"Yes, some humans lie, but not all," another part of my mind responded, "so does that mean that perhaps some aliens are telling the truth?" It was important to know which humans—and which aliens—to believe, yet it was impossible. I relegated the battle-station report to the "rumor" file somewhere in the back of my mind, but it must have disturbed me more deeply than I realized. That night, or rather in the early hours of the morning, I awoke from a frightening dream that the "Night of Lights" had finally come. That was what we called the rumored event of the aliens' mass arrival on earth, taking the title from another abductee's account of what she was told by a golden-colored, humanoid alien.

I saw thousands of small spacecraft descending to earth in my dream, and all I could remember upon waking was the mass confusion as my family and I tried to prepare a way to survive. The dream left me shaken and fearful, and for the next two days I was preoccupied with the need to communicate with the aliens. No matter how frightening a conscious confrontation with them might be, I was desperate for more information, and so mentally I kept calling out for them to come.

On the night of November 5, Casey and I went to bed rather late, sometime after midnight, and quickly fell asleep. There was a noise in the room, three series of loud metallic clicks, that startled me awake, and I turned on the bedside lamp, looking around anxiously and feeling the adrenaline rush through my body.

"Did you hear that?" I asked Casey as he sat up in the bed, eyes wide open, and he nodded. I glanced at the clock and saw that it was 3:03 A.M.

"It sounded like clicking," he said. "Did you see anything?"

"No," I replied, "but we can't just go back to sleep as if nothing happened! Something made that noise, and I want to know what it was."

Casey got up and searched the room thoroughly, but he found nothing out of the ordinary. The sound had come from my side of the room, about a foot from my head, yet I insisted he search the entire house. Then he turned on the outside lights and peered through all the windows, but everything inside and out seemed normal.

"Maybe if we turn off the light and lie back down," I said when he returned to the bedroom, "we might hear the noise again and could catch whatever's doing it."

Casey agreed, and we got back into bed, lying face up under the covers. And since the noise had come from my side of the room, Casey and I switched places so that he could be nearest to the sound if it happened again. He turned out the light, and I noticed that it was now 3:09. Casey took my hand and held it tightly as we lay there. My heart was still pounding hard, and our eyes were open as we watched the room, anxiously searching for any movement or sound. At first there was nothing, and then after a minute or so we heard a low, deep rumbling noise in the distance. The railroad track runs a few blocks from our house, and Casey mentioned that it must be a train coming through town. We listened for the familiar whistle at the crossing, but it never came, even though the rumble continued.

After no more than four or five minutes, I turned to Casey and said, "This isn't getting us anywhere. The sound hasn't come back, so maybe we should just try to go to sleep again. What else can we do?"

"All right," he agreed, letting go of my hand for the first time. I rolled over on my side to relax, but then I suddenly sat up with a shock. "What's wrong?" Casey asked anxiously.

"Look at the clock!" I pointed. "It says it's 3:43, but it can't be!"

He glanced over at the clock and shook his head. "That's not right," he said. "It can't be! We've only been lying here a few minutes."

I turned the light on, and Casey got up to check his wrist watch on the bureau, but it also said 3:43. Yet we knew it shouldn't have been any later than 3:13 or 3:14. Half an hour had passed, apparently, without our being aware of it, and that didn't make sense. We had both been awake, our eyes had been open, and both our hearts were still pounding from the initial rush of fear we'd felt when the clicking noise woke us.

Eventually we fell back asleep, in spite of the strange time loss, and when we searched our bodies for new marks the next morning, we didn't find any. But both Casey and I were utterly exhausted throughout the day, and we were very concerned to know what had happened to us during the night. We felt certain that something had occurred, but if it was blocked in our memory, our only hope of finding out would be through hypnotic regression. I wished that Barbara didn't live so far away, and we began planning a visit to her as soon as possible. The loss of time was the most consciously jarring, most "immediate" episode we'd been through, wrecking our sense of reality, and leaving us in greater need than ever of answers.

A few days later, David called in the middle of the morning to tell me there were new marks on his body, and I asked him to come by for us to examine them. When he arrived and showed us the numerous long scratches and welts that covered his right thigh, I was shocked. All any of us had previously experienced were a few punctures and single scratches, but David's leg looked mauled. Several of the scratches formed inverted V-shaped patterns on the front of his thigh, and along the outside there were almost a dozen red welts running from the top of the thigh down to just above his knee. A bloody, curving scratch stretched along the hip, with a deep puncture between it and the welts below.

"Do you have any idea where you might have gotten these scratches?" I asked David.

He shook his head and then shrugged. "Maybe there was a sticker in the bed," he said doubtfully, "I don't know. I didn't find a sticker when I looked this morning, but who knows? And the scratches weren't there when I went to bed, so it must have been a sticker or something." He said the scratches didn't hurt, which was very unusual considering how many there were and how deeply some of them had broken the skin. Yet he did his best to dismiss the strangeness of the experience, since there was no obvious explanation. I decided, however, that if the chance ever came for him to work with Barbara, I would encourage him to do it. I hated the fact that he was involved in this phenomenon, but I knew that ignoring it wouldn't make it go away. The numerous scratches, however, healed quickly and without infection, as did all of our unexplained body marks.

The following week, Casey had a nighttime experience that upset him enough to tell me about it in great detail. He tried to call it a dream, but he admitted that the memory seemed much more real than that. He remembered standing outside in the dark, watching a very large, boiling black cloud rolling in quickly above him.

"I heard something that sounded like a helicopter," he told me, "and I thought it was coming from the cloud. And just as the cloud got almost directly over me, I looked up to watch what I thought would be a helicopter come out of the cloud. But instead of a helicopter, a late model white pickup came flying out of a 'portal' which opened up in the cloud. The truck flew downward steadily, still sounding like a 'copter. I don't remember it landing."

"The next thing I remember was seeing copies of myself trailing off into the distance, like I was seeing myself move through time, with images being left in place instead of dissipating." It was an unnerving memory, but one for which he could find no rational explanation. And the final part of the dream was just as puzzling. Casey felt himself falling down a narrow tunnel into a vast underground area, and then he was in a saloon, reminiscent of old western settings from movies and television. All he recalled here was sitting at a table in the saloon with David and a close male friend and wondering if they were going to play poker. It seemed to have nothing to do with the first parts of the dream, yet somehow they were all related.

The only portion of Casey's dream that we thought might have been triggered by our experiences was the helicopter. After living in the same location for five years with no noticeable helicopter activity, we had begun to see numerous craft flying over our house. They were of every variety—sleek blue and silver models, dark military types, even huge transport craft—and they came in groups or singly at any hour of the day. Once near midnight a helicopter flew so low over the house that all the windows shook with great force. During 1988, the number of helicopters at any one time was never more than three, but later that number increased. Once I counted nine flying over, in three groups of three different models, about an hour to two hours apart.

Sandy, James's mother, also began to have helicopters over their house frequently, and when I watched one fly directly above us and then circle around for a second sweep, I tried to find out where they were coming from. Contacting the local airport, I was told that there was no record of these craft in the area, and that the only military helicopter flights were twice a year when the National Guard carried out exercises far to the north of us.

It would have been wonderful to have some intelligent, insightful, open-minded and uninvolved person with whom to discuss our situation, but there was no one. On impulse, however, and also from a sense of desperation, I phoned Dr. Riley, my former therapist, again and asked if he would meet me informally, over a cup of coffee. He was the one I'd called back in May, when Casey first remembered the face of the Old One and the huge space-craft, and his response had been immediately negative. "Whatever it is," he'd told me, "it isn't flying saucers and little green men," and I was in too much shock to question his declaration.

But now, armed with much more information and more personal experience, I wanted a chance to find out exactly why he was so sure there was nothing extraterrestrial about the phenomenon. There was a remote chance, I told myself, that the therapist knew of some syndrome, mental aberration or condition, that produced hallucinations of alien beings. Yet I had read two different articles that reported, upon checking with mental health institutes, no relationship between mental imbalance and abduction scenarios. Still, if the therapist had any new information, it was worth my while to find out.

We met a few days later, and I wasted no time in questioning him about that negative response. Why, I asked, was he so sure?

"Do you remember when I called you about my husband?" I asked, and he nodded. "Why did you tell me that you were certain Casey's memories weren't real? How could you be so sure? You didn't even talk to him. Have you read studies on this subject, or anything? What do you know that makes you certain?"

"Oh, I don't have any evidence," he admitted, smiling. "It's just my own personal bias. I don't believe in flying saucers."

I was shocked that he would have offered mere opinion and then try to pass it off as fact without any logical basis.

I mentioned the strange marks that we had found on our bodies, and Dr. Riley reached across the table to take my hand momentarily.

"A piece of advice," he said, shaking his head. "Don't go around telling people that you have marks on your body."

"Why?" I asked. "The marks are there, and we don't know where they come from."

"I wouldn't mention them, though," he replied. "If you do, people will know that you've been abusing yourselves." And then he went on to explain that the only reason Casey thought he'd been abducted was obviously because he'd been abused as a child!

When I told him that Casey had certainly not been abused, Dr. Riley said that there are many forms of abuse. "He might have fallen down one time and hurt his knee, and then when he went running to his parents for comfort, they might have ignored it. That would be enough to traumatize a child," the therapist said, but I couldn't see the logic in such a statement. If all children experience such abuse, as the therapist implied, then why didn't everyone feel as if they'd been abducted?

"So you think these memories stem from some mental problem?" I asked, remembering what I'd read about the lack of such symptoms among the mentally ill, "Do people in institutions also have these experiences?"

The therapist admitted that there was no clinical evidence to connect the two things, but he still thought the real answer could be explained in purely psychological terms. So I challenged him to investigate the reports of abductions, as a mental health professional, but he refused.

"No serious professional would touch this subject," he said. "They'd be afraid of the ridicule."

So I was left with a psychologist—and, apparently, the entire field of psychology—who would have nothing to do with what was declared to be a psychological situation. It seemed they began with the assumption that reported abduction experiences were simply not real. It didn't matter that they couldn't find anything psychologically wrong with us. Once again I realized that all we really had were each other.

(An interesting note: when I was preparing this story for publication, I contacted the therapist again and asked for permission to use his real name in my account. Reviewing what he had told me in both of our conversations, the therapist refused to let me name him. "It's awfully embarrassing, professionally embarrassing, for anyone to know I said those things," he told me. "I wouldn't have responded to you that way now, believe me. So please don't use my real name. Just refer to me as 'the stupid therapist' or give me a pseudonym.")

CHAPTER 7

December 1988

The approaching Christmas holidays and the end of 1988 kept us all busy, and, as if respecting our need for diversion, the strange episodes temporarily left us alone. We still found punctures and other unexplained marks on our bodies, though. But without any remembered event connected to them, we were able to put the phenomenon out of our minds and enjoy visits with our family and friends.

In mid-December I received a phone call from my sister-in-law, Tanya (pseudonym), which brought us right back to dealing with ET intrusions. My brother, Paul (pseudonym), and his family had been in California for over ten years, and during that time we had little contact with them at all. In fact, it had been over two years since I'd spoken with any of them, so when I picked up the phone and heard Tanya on the other end, I was extremely surprised. And what she had to say was even more surprising. She had overheard a phone conversation between Paul and my father in which Dad had mentioned our claims of UFO sightings and alien abductions.

Tanya wanted to tell me that she and Paul were involved in the very same situation, that they had been abducted more than once in the past years, and that the ETs were active in their lives again now. It was because of the strange events they had experienced that they had decided to stay away from the rest of the family, since they feared their stories wouldn't be believed. I could hear the relief in her voice as we talked, and for once I felt that something positive was coming from these events. My family is important to me, and I was grateful that we were once again in touch with each other, no matter what the motivation.

January 1989

After the holidays passed without any overt activity, Casey and I hoped that the phenomenon was diminishing, at least in our lives, although we knew from other friends that there was still quite a lot of strangeness continuing with many of them. We also still wanted to meet with Barbara again and go through more hypnotic regression, hopeful of discovering what had happened to us in the past few months and the source of the many scratches and punctures we'd received. But as there was no immediate opportunity for us to visit with her, we decided once again to attempt a regression ourselves, for the first time since last May. We were both much more familiar with the process now and trusted ourselves to carry it through competently.

The foremost mystery we were intent on investigating was that of the missing thirty minutes on November 5. So in the first week of January I put Casey into a hypnotic trance and moved him back to that date for a look at the events of that night. The session was not so successful as before, however, and Casey had a very hard time relaxing and going deeply into trance. What he did recall was unsettling, enough to let us know that an intrusion had indeed occurred, but not enough to give us any thorough explanation.

The first thing he remembered was seeing a bright light shining through a diagonal vent or slash in the dark room, as if a rip had been made through the air itself. He also saw that he was lying face up on the bed, because he could see his feet pushing up the covers. The next specific thing he recalled was a light near the foot of the bed and a clawed, webbed hand reaching out to grab his ankle. At that point, Casey's courage weakened, and I was unable to help him continue looking at the event. His last memory was very unclear: a glimpse of some coppery metallic surface whose form he was unable to perceive. Neither of us felt that the regression had been very successful, for obviously much was still missing from his recall, and we decided that a trip to visit Barbara would be our first priority.

After more than a month without overt activity, we were both lulled into a sense of security and relief, but it didn't last long. On the morning of Friday, January 13, Casey woke up covered with long scratches on his back, very similar to the marks David had found back in November. There was also a large triangular patch of bright red rash covering Casey's left side, and as usual he had no memory of anything occurring during the night.

On Saturday, when David and Megan stopped by, I asked if they had experienced any strangeness in the past couple of days. David just grinned in confusion and glanced over quickly at Megan.

"Yeah!" she exclaimed, staring back at him. "David's been acting really strange. For the past two nights, he's gotten out of bed and gone out of the room, and he won't tell me where he went."

Knowing how frightened Megan had been at the farm since all the ET activity had begun, I asked her why she didn't follow after him.

"I couldn't move," she said. "I tried to ask him where he was going, but I was too tired. I couldn't even talk, or move."

"How long was he gone, then?" I asked.

"I don't really know," she told me. "I just fell back asleep when he left."

This in itself was unusual, because Megan's uneasiness at being alone in the spooky old farmhouse had gotten worse with the advent of the strange experiences, and she never let David out of her sight. It was also hard to believe that he could have spent any time out of bed without his clothes on at that time of year. The farmhouse was frigid in the winter, with no insulation and only small gas heaters that warmed a very limited area.

"So, what were you doing?" I asked, turning to David. "Where on earth were you going in the middle of the night?"

"I don't know," he told me. "I don't remember getting up at all." And he playfully accused Megan of making up the whole thing, which she vehemently denied. So we were left with two new mysteries: David's disappearances and the scratches on Casey's back.

When I told Roger, the local researcher, about these events, he suggested that we might try to get some evidence of nocturnal visits by setting up a sound-activated recorder in our bedroom. I doubted that whatever or whoever had been bothering us would let such evidence be acquired, but we had nothing to lose by trying it. So we began putting a small recorder on the bureau opposite our bed and turning it on when we retired each night.

For the first two nights, the tape recorded only the usual sounds we could expect: creaks in the house as it settled, an occasional cough, and the small noises I made when I'd get up to go to the bathroom. But on the third night, something much more noisy was recorded. When I played it back the next morning, I couldn't imagine what the sounds were. After the noises of our coughing, turning out the lights, and saying good night, there was a series of eighty-five almost identical sounds, the likes of which I had never heard before. The best description I can give is the noise a six-foot-tall can of hair spray might make: short, breathy aspirations that were more mechanical-sounding than organic.

For the next week, we recorded every conceivable sound in our house, trying to duplicate the eighty-five noises, but to no avail. We recorded the central heating unit turning on, our own coughs, even Casey's occasional snores, but nothing reproduced the original sounds. Finally, we hired a sound-studio technician to analyze the tape and see if he could identify the noises, but after more than an hour of working with the tape, he was as mystified as we were. And although we kept the recorder going nightly for a while longer, the sounds never came back.

The rest of January was uneventful, but in the first week of February we found yet more scratches and punctures. By mid-month we made plans to visit Barbara for a weekend, and while we were in Tulsa, Casey and I both went through another regression. Barbara always recorded these sessions, but the machine didn't work properly during Casey's regression, so there is no transcript of the entire session. Barbara and Casey remembered most of what transpired, however, when she took him back to the night of January 12 and the scratches on his back.

Casey recalled being wakened as several aliens were trying to turn him over, facedown, in our bed. When he saw them, he tried to resist their manipulations, but they proceeded to turn him over, pulling hard at his side and back in the process. The result was the pattern of claw marks we'd found the next morning, for these aliens, unlike the small Grays, were the reptilian type, with webbed, clawed hands and vertically slit eyes.

He also remembered that they examined his back with an instrument that left no marks. He described it as a small bar with two "light-pen" points on the curved end, and he said the alien held it to the base of his spine. Casey's impression was that the instrument in some way was able to check on his entire biological system, although he had no real way of knowing exactly what was being done to him.

This was all he recalled, and it made a sketchy story at best. But that was typical of most people's experiences under regression, we knew, finding gaps in the chain of events that even hypnosis couldn't fill. Casey admitted later that the session was a difficult one for him this time. He wanted to know what had happened, of course, but at the same time he was afraid to look at it too closely.

In my regression, I had the same mixed feelings when Barbara took me back to Halloween night, in hopes of discovering the cause of the three punctures in my jugular vein. Once I was finally relaxed enough to let myself focus in the trance state, however, the memories began to return, and I saw myself in bed.

"I'm feeling heavy, my head, neck, real heavy," I said. "Feel strange across my face, like gravity is pushing on it. I feel real tingly, my hands, my arms, and my ears ring. Feels like my arm's hurting, a little, in my vein, had a real sharp pain, left arm. It's still hurting a little bit. My eyes close. I'm tingling all over now."

"Describe your surroundings," Barbara instructed.

"The bed's flat open and there's not any cover, and I can see me. I don't want . . . it's making my heart beat. It's like I'm the only thing on the bed."

"Look around," Barbara said. "Are you alone in the room? Is anyone else there?"

"There's, umm, I think"—I hesitated— "it looks like people around the bed. There's heads around the bed: one, two, three, four, maybe four. There's one by my head, there's one at the side of the foot of the bed. There's one at the other corner, one behind me on the other side. I just see little round heads, and it's dark."

"What is happening, Karla?" Barbara asked, moving me forward.

"It's like they have got all the covers off me," I replied. "I'm still on my side. Barbara, I don't even know if I want to see this. It makes me shake. I'm really not moving. My legs and body are uncovered. There's one about six inches from my head, and there's another one. I don't see them moving. Nothing is moving right now, but I feel like it's looking at me. My eyes are closed, my arm's not hurting now."

"Where is Casey?" Barbara asked. "Isn't he there with you?"

"Casey isn't here," I told her. "I'm in bed by myself."

"How is your body positioned on the bed?"

"My legs are straightened out now. I'm on my back. I don't know how I got there, I didn't see me move. I'm afraid they are going to touch me. The one on the left is holding my left arm. He's touching, I'm not moving, I'm not even awake. I just see his arm, and the top of his head, and his arm's out touching mine.

"My arms and legs are a little apart now, I can't open my eyes. I don't know what the bottom ones are doing, but my legs are spread apart about a foot and a half. My arms are spread out. I think I'm afraid to see.

"There's a light flash, overhead, above my body on the bed. Maybe they have rolled me over. I'm real limp, they have to move me. I can start to see the other one by my head, and my arm hurts. I don't see him doing anything to it. Now it's like afterwards, while before it was burning, a little burning spot. Now it's just sort of tender."

"Move forward to the next thing you can recall," Barbara said.

"Oh, Barbara," I replied, uneasy, "I feel like they are standing up right there. I'm in the bed, in the center, and they are moving, but they don't make any noise. I'm on my back, and I feel them moving right here." My eyes grew wet. "I don't know if this is all real, but it's making me cry. I'm trying not to, but it does make me cry. I'm afraid they are going to touch me again."

Barbara paused to reassure me that everything was all right, that I had survived the experience and could look at it now without fear.

"There's a hand right here," I continued. "I don't want to look at them. I don't want to see their faces. I see they have big, round heads. I don't want to look. These things touch me, but I'm not going to feel it. I don't feel it, it doesn't hurt. I can see something reach out to me on this side," I pointed left, "by my head. There's a sensation on my neck, but it doesn't hurt. It feels like a cold burn, something so cold it feels like it's burning. It's like it's frozen, like feeling skin that's asleep."

"How is this happening?" Barbara pressed. "Tell me exactly what you see."

"Something is touching it real lightly," I explained. "I don't know if it's a thing or a hand. It's very still, and the one on the left has something in his hand that's reaching out. It's a stiff arm straight out, not bent like ours, and there's a point touching my neck. It's just resting there very lightly."

"Can you describe the thing itself?"

"I can see it's in his hand, almost covered by the hand," I said. "It may be round. It's smaller than a saucer, the hand's not real big, and just a little bit is showing on either side of the palm. It's held stiff over that spot. The others aren't moving."

"How long does this take?" Barbara wondered.

"I can't tell how long it's there. I did feel a frozen burn, but I'm not feeling anything now. I'm just looking at the bed, and I see all the covers are down at the foot of the bed. Now I'm no longer in the middle of the bed, I'm closer to the right side, because the one on the left has to reach across. They all look bald.

"I feel pressure on my neck, and it does hurt a little bit. And I don't feel afraid, and I keep my eyes closed. And it feels real tingling still and real tired. I just don't want to look at them. I can't move myself, so it's just like I surrender. I've just given it up, and now I'm ready to go to sleep. It's okay, it doesn't hurt, he took it all away."

"Did anything else happen?" Barbara asked. "Was anything else done?"

"There may have been something running over the top of my body without touching it," I remembered, "over both legs, over my belly. It's like something goes above this leg and goes above that leg and up over my belly, but I don't feel it going any higher. Checking, or scanning. They're still holding still while this thing moves over me. They seem like robots, they seem so stiff I hardly see any movement, and I don't hear any sound. That may be because I'm so out of it."

"What do these beings look like?" Barbara probed. "Describe them to me."

"They look just the same as each other," I answered. "My bed is tall, and the heads of them about a foot taller, and they are real close to me, maybe four feet tall. They look a darkish gray in this light. The arms sticking out seem a light color, probably wearing something on them. They might be wearing a covering. They look like ghosts, they look so hollow, they don't have any real feelings. That's why they are so scary, they just look dead, but they're not. They don't even look mean. They're really hardly there. I don't know where they came from. I don't even feel surprised, I don't even feel curious. I don't feel anything like that. I just feel real sedated."

So sedated, in fact, that I found it too hard to continue and asked Barbara to end the session. I wasn't satisfied that I had recalled everything that had happened on Halloween night, but what I had seen was more than enough to deal with. This was the first time I had remembered being face-to-face with such beings, and the fear I experienced under hypnosis was heavy and real. It had been one thing to see flashing colored lights on a UFO up in the sky, but it was much more disturbing to recall how the gray alien beside my bed reached out his stiff arm and touched my neck.

At least, however, this time both Casey and I remembered the instruments used by the aliens, which we hadn't seen in previous regressions. Up to this time we just had no idea what sort of devices were being used on our bodies, except for the teardrop-shaped metallic instrument Casey had recalled from his 1947 abduction.

The regression sessions were very draining, on Barbara as well as us, so we left off further attempts until our next visit and returned home. Before we left, however, plans were made for Barbara to visit us in March, to attend a talk given by Budd Hopkins in Dallas. At that time we planned to undergo more hypnosis, and both Casey and I felt that we were really beginning to discover at least part of what was happening to us. We were also anxious for Barbara to work with David and Megan, and we even hoped that James would agree to hypnosis, although he found it difficult to deal with his frightening experiences.

March 1989

In the week before Barbara's arrival, there was one more unsettling incident. One Monday morning while changing the bedclothes, I found several splotches and smears of blood. A smallish smear was on my pillowcase, and there was blood on my right thigh, although I couldn't find a puncture or cut. But most of the blood was on Casey's side of the bed. There the spots ranged from tiny flicks of blood, some smeared and some not, to large areas about the size of a fingerprint. We looked all over Casey's body, trying to find an injury to account for the blood, but we found nothing.

And then, a few days before Barbara was scheduled to come, James and David came over, telling us about a series of nightmares James had been having. They started on Saturday night and recurred on Sunday. During both nights, James said he woke repeatedly, sometimes after only half an hour's sleep, frightened by the same nightmare. He saw himself spread out on a table with tubes coming out of his arms and body. A large screenlike mirror was above him, and in it he could see what looked like a thick plastic blue washer in the middle of his forehead, with a hole in the center of it. Although he felt no pain and saw no beings in the dreams, they left him terrified and afraid to sleep. It was clear that he couldn't simply dismiss them as normal dreams, or he wouldn't have been so affected.

On the third night, Monday, the nightmares were different. This time he awoke again and again, from recurrent dreams of some member of his family or of his friends, including David, dying a violent death. One dream showed his father dying of a heart attack, another showed his mother and sister falling from a tall building, and he saw David crushed in a car wreck. These dreams, James said, were much more frightening than the first two nights, and he begged us not to tell his parents.

We agreed reluctantly, not liking to keep secrets from such good friends. It would be especially difficult, we thought, since James's parents were planning to attend the Hopkins talk with us. They were anxious to learn anything they could about these experiences since their son was being so often affected, and a second motive was to look for the woman we'd seen the previous summer, the one who looked like the interdimensional woman who'd visited James repeatedly at the farm. James hadn't had any visits from her since September, but we still hoped to find the woman and question her about any connection she had to James.

By the time Barbara arrived, we had planned several sessions of hypnosis with David, Megan, James, and Fred, besides hoping to work with her again ourselves. On the way home from the airport, we caught up with the latest findings from her work with people in the Tulsa area, including new abduction cases and several reports of people being taken to some sort of underground facility.

Over and over, Barbara said, she was getting reports of huge vats in these underground areas, vats filled with parts of human bodies, and there were also repeated experiences where people found themselves taken by aliens into bathroom or stall areas and experiencing exams and manipulations of their sexual organs. Such accounts sounded familiar now, after having heard John Lear's talk about the government-alien underground bases, but word of his revelations was by no means readily available to the general public. Yet somehow, without any knowledge of Lear's tales, many people were telling the same, or similar, stories.

But what it all meant, we really had no idea. The only thing Barbara could be sure of was that more and more people were undergoing or remembering abductions, and that many of their reports confirmed each other. She had been dealing with cases in which children as young as two years old were reporting strange beings in their bedrooms, as well as older men and women, most of whom had previously had no interest at all in UFOs or "little green men." Listening to Barbara's accounts, we felt very sympathetic, because we too had been entirely uninterested in UFOs before our own experiences forced us into this fringe reality.

And it made us feel worse, somehow, knowing that so many people were involved. So long as we thought the phenomenon was a limited one, we could still tell ourselves that it might all be some sort of hallucination or psychosis, involving only a few people. The idea that such experiences were widespread, and apparently on the increase, sank our spirits. What on earth, we wondered, was really happening? From my own research, I had learned of hundreds of abductions, but the numbers were now well into the thousands. Barbara was in contact with researchers on the East and West coasts, and they too were finding more and more cases turning up, begging for help in trying to understand their strange and frightening experiences. All we could do for the time being, however, was to concentrate on the events involving our immediate family and circle of friends, and so, less than two hours after Barbara's arrival in our home, she was conducting her first regression.

CHAPTER 8

David was the first to undergo regression. He had been through several disturbing episodes that puzzled him—vivid UFO dreams, strange physical sensations, punctures, and scratches—but Barbara decided to take him back to the night in August when he first heard James's story about alien visitors. When we had phoned Barbara to tell her about that night and about David's strange behavior, his not remembering how he'd frightened Megan, Barbara felt there was something serious going on with him. As we were to learn, she had come across other abduction cases in which the victim sometimes acted in similar ways, doing or saying things which were later unremembered.

In the first part of the regression, David recalled the conversation with James at the bar, having several drinks, and then riding home to the farm with Megan. He told how upset Megan became when they arrived before James and of her reluctance to stay there.

"I start to get out because we're home," he said. "She's yelling at me not to get out. She's scared. Now she's real scared. But that's stupid. So I get out, and I walk up the side of the car, around the front by the tree. She's close to the tree, so that was tricky. Her lights are still on. And I'm looking towards the satellite dish. Left turn, front. Nice and cool, it's real dark. There's no light on outside, we left early. The [car] door slammed. Megan goes out and comes and grabs me."

"What is she saying?" Barbara asked.

"'Let's go inside. Let's go inside now!'" David replied. "But I'm pointing toward the satellite dish. I don't want to go inside. It's nice and cool."

"Why are you pointing toward the satellite dish?"

"I don't know," David said. "I mumble, but Megan's really freaked out. She wants to leave."

"You mean she wants to leave the farm? Get away?" Barbara asked.

"Uh-huh," David nodded, pausing. "I'm just kind of standing there."

His reference to the satellite dish was a surprise, since neither David nor Megan had mentioned the dish when they originally told us about the night. The satellite dish belonged to a neighbor on the street behind the farm, and it was clearly visible from the farm's backyard. But at that point Barbara had no idea of its significance, so she moved David on in his account.

"She's getting more and more skittish, scared," David told her, "so I turn and I walk around the bee tree because the car's too close. Probably fall if I went that way, but there's lots of branches. So I walk far around it. Yeah. Something behind the tree."

"Something behind the tree?" Barbara repeated.

"I can't see, the fir tree, I cannot see behind it," he replied. "It's real dark over there. I'm pointing again."

"What direction?"

"At the fir tree. No, I'm in the car," he suddenly said in surprise. "I'm by the car. Megan wants to go in the house, but James might not get the beer. He must. But that's silly, we don't need beer."

"How is Megan acting now?" Barbara asked, trying to learn why David had been surprised to see himself suddenly shifted from one location to another.

"I can't see her," David replied. "She must be quiet."

Prodding him further, Barbara said, "Let's go back. You were looking at the satellite dish, and then you were looking at the fir tree."

"Yeah," David went on. "How'd I get . . . ? I'm over in the back near the plum trees."

The change of location puzzled David, so Barbara asked him to retrace the entire sequence of events after the arrival at the farm. He went through the drive up the long driveway, feeling rather tired and drunk, and Megan's fears about getting out of the car before James had arrived.

"So I pull out and slam the door," he said. "I'm leaning against the car for a second. Megan gets out. She's stopped the car now. I'm looking at her across the car. I walk up to the bee tree. Hmm." He paused, puzzled by something.

"'Hmm'?" Barbara urged. "What do you mean, 'hmm'? Did you remember something you'd forgotten?"

"Well," he answered, "walking towards the back porch. And I'm almost to the back porch, and I turn real quick. Jerk around, and I walk toward the satellite dish real thump, thump, thump, thump. Like a, uh, soldier. But Megan's yelling to stop. 'Stop going over there!'"

Barbara asked David to explain what he meant, why he was walking strangely. "My feet seemed, 'thump,' on the ground, real hard. Stiff legs. Rocking, like a penguin," he said, and then he mumbled something about the metal plate that covers a water line just before the porch.

"What's the flat metal plate?" Barbara wanted to know.

"By the pack porch," David told her. "And I cut across the corner of the porch, and out into the back. I'm rocking, and I'm not thinking at all. I can see the satellite dish."

"Where is Megan?" Barbara asked. "Do you see her behind you, feel her, are you aware that she's right behind you?"

"Well, she caught up, and grabbed my shoulder," David explained, "and I stopped. Hmm, that's strange. 'Just look at the satellite dish'."

"Did you say that?" Barbara asked.

"Yeah."

"Did you say it to her?"

"Yeah," he answered, with a note of wonder in his voice.

"Why did you tell her to look at the satellite dish?"

"I don't know," he said. "I was just pointing at it."

"What was in your mind?" Barbara inquired. "How did you feel then?"

"Confused!" David replied emphatically. "Megan's really tugging on me to come back. She's yelling, screeching. And I'm pointing at the satellite dish. So I stop. She's upset. She wants to go back to the car? So I follow her. Kind of slow, hard to walk here. Now I want some beer. She can't get it, so I have to go, because I'm old enough. She won't go."

He paused for a moment and then asked, "How did I get here?"

"Where are you?" Barbara wanted to know.

"I'm in the car," he told her.

"What makes you wonder how you got in the car? You wondered that before, when I took you through the story the first time."

"I was standing by the tree, not thinking," he said. "Looking. Pomegranate tree [beside fir tree]. I can't see it very well. And now I'm in the car."

Something was obviously missing in David's recollection of events, so

Barbara asked him more about what he had seen by the fir tree.

"I'm looking at a shadow," he replied. "Maybe it's the cat, he likes that tree. Rustling, pomegranate tree. At the bottom? But how? This, there's something moving, but I can't see it. It's a dark spot, a black spot, moving around the tree. And it's gone."

Barbara asked him to expand his description, so David continued.

"I saw, it looks irregular. Is it a shadow? It's black. It's on the ground. It's moving around and away, quickly, rustling. Like walking on leaves. And it's very faint with a whisper, snwww, snwww, a snake sound, real faint. But it's gone quick, quick. Around the tree." His speech, throughout the regression, slurred and stumbled a bit, as if he still felt the effects of the alcohol he'd drunk at the bar that night.

Since nothing identifiable had come from David's description, Barbara asked him instead about the satellite dish. "Now that you're in a deep state of hypnosis," she said, "what was taking your focus over to the satellite dish? Why were you looking over there?"

"I always look over there," he replied, "because it's white, and it stands out at night. But it's pointing down! It's pointing down! Never pointed down. Megan's mad. She's crying. 'What? "Shhhh!' Oh, I see, upside down. Sort of."

"The satellite dish is upside down?" Barbara interrupted.

"Sort of," he told her. "Hanging over the fence. It's almost, it should be on the other side of the fence. Some of it is, but some of it's upside down. Well, that's interesting."

"What?" Barbara asked. "What did you see?"

"The end of it's stuck in the ground," he replied. "That's gonna break it. Megan can't see it. It's got a pipe coming out from the center of it, with a box on the end, or something. No. Yeah. It didn't have that box before, but the box is pushing into the ground. And one end of it on the fence. And it's just kind of sitting there. And it used to have a cone. It should have a white cone, but it's got a zinc box. It shouldn't work that way, it should fall! Unless it's tied down. It's not stable. Maybe that's what the box is for. No, it should fall. I want to go look at it. It's dark underneath it. The back is bright, but the bottom is real dark."

Puzzled by David's obsession with the dish, Barbara asked, "Have you ever seen anything like it before?"

"Looks like a satellite dish," David told her again. "It's got an upturned rim, curly." And then he said he was walking back, after Megan grabbed him and turned him around. "She's hysterical," David said.

"She's hysterical now?" Barbara asked. "Like crying?"

"Uh huh," he replied. "I'm confused."

"Why are you confused?"

"I don't know anything that's going on!" he exclaimed. "Just tell me the thoughts that are coming into your mind," Barbara urged him.

"Now I'm just following Megan," he said. "That's the only thing I could do. Because I can't know anything."

"What do you mean?" Barbara asked.

"My brain's not working," he said. "I'm just tramping behind her to the car. Ah, ah. 'But I want to go look at that.' I heard a noise."

"What did the noise sound like?"

"A rope, pulled real fast," he replied. "Whooooo, kind of like a top. But soft, so it was muted. And that's when I see the thing. The black. It's just blackness, on the ground. Very quick. Something, hit me, before."

"Where?" Barbara inquired.

"Shocked me," he answered. "In the back. In my hip, at the bottom of my spine, but it's all over, just zzzzz."

"How do you feel after that?"

"I'm bouncing, mechanically, towards the satellite dish, I think," he said.

"Take yourself back to when you felt that shock," Barbara told him.

"It's big," he replied. "It hurt, all over, the shock. Tingles real loud. All over my bones it's tingling, shaking. I just turned! Nothing touches me, I don't think. Just all of a sudden I felt a shock. I turned, quick! A little to the left. I started marching! Now I'm looking at the satellite dish."

"Did anything happen to Megan?" Barbara wanted to know. "Do you think she felt that shock, too?"

"I can't see her," he said. "I'm walking off. I'm just walking, until she starts screaming."

"Are you marching?"

"Yeah, stiff. Robots. Toy soldiers. That's totally stiff. Jarred. Jolts every time I step. Like a thud on each foot. But I can hear Megan, so I sort of ease up, slow down, relax."

"What about the satellite dish?" Barbara asked, returning his focus to the sequence of events.

"It's upside down," David repeated. "It's very strange. And the box is square. I can't understand it at all. I want to go look at it."

"Did you go look?"

"No," he answered. "Megan made me forget about it. Because I turned around a little, I couldn't see it anymore. Just forgot about it. Just walking away now. And I bang a little into the post, not bad. Walking around the car, and then shhhwwww"

"What happens when you're there?"

"I'm walking around the tree, and I hear a noise. Like a top, a spinning top. It starts high-pitched and goes lower, and goes away pretty fast. So I look towards it. I can't see very well."

"Describe it to me again," Barbara instructed.

"It's like a blot on the ground," he said. "A black towel? Or garbage bag? Kind of odd-shaped. It's flat, flat-flat. It, it is on the ground. It is the ground, it's no different than the ground, but it's just black and moving fast. And it's making a little noise."

"What's Megan doing now?" Barbara asked.

"I don't know."

"Can't you see her from where you are?"

"No."

"You're not aware of her now?"

"Huh-uh."

"Look carefully," Barbara said. "Where are you?"

"I'm a little beyond the tree."

"Well, where's Megan?"

"I don't know," he insisted.

"Can you look to the car and see if she got in the car? She wouldn't be too far from you, would she?"

"She's not in the car," he said.

"Do you hear her at all, screaming or crying?" Barbara asked.

"Huh-uh," he replied.

"Where is she?" Barbara asked again.

"The thing's gone quick," David said. "So ... now I hear her."

"Let's go back to where you couldn't hear her," Barbara told him.

"I'm looking at the thing," David responded. "A blackness. A 'not.' Like a 'not-there.' "

"Give me a better description," Barbara said, "so I can understand."

"Like a moving oil puddle on the ground," David told her. "And it's moving, but changing, too. Not much, just the edges, not very stable. And it's gone quick."

Barbara made one more attempt to figure out the events, taking David through everything again from the moment he got the shock.

"I'm looking at the back porch," he began. "I'm going into the door in a minute. I see the motorcycle there. I'm just looking straight into the porch, just walking. I never got there. I was just walking toward the house, and then I'm shocked, all over. It hurt. Just real sudden. Quick turn. And I start to march. And Megan shouts. She grabs me and says, 'Slow down, stop.' Pretty quick. Don't know what that was, the shock. And Megan gets to me. I'm confused now."

"Do you remember trying to take Megan to look at the trees?" Barbara asked, recalling Megan's story that David had dragged her off in that direction.

"Well," he replied, "I was going over towards that satellite dish, but she came along and I just forgot about her."

"You saw the satellite dish before you got the shock?" Barbara wanted to know.

"No, after," he replied. "Because I wasn't even looking there, till then. I'm trying to show her the thing. And then I'm, just forget it. I just go. Huh. Wonder, I feel strange."

"How do you feel strange?" Barbara asked.

"I'm just, not me," he said. "I'm disconnected."

"Do you feel like you're not David?" Barbara pushed, "is that what you're saying?"

"David's not here," he replied, laughing a little.

"What?" Barbara asked, surprised by his answer.

"Where's David?"

"He's unplugged," David told her. "I feel blank, but I can't feel."

"David's unplugged?" Barbara echoed.

"He's just, not there."

"What is walking David's body around, if you want to put it that way?" she asked.

"I can't, all I see, nothing, just going," he replied. "Very strange. Like a remote unit."

"Who is guiding that remote unit?" Barbara wanted to know.

"I don't know," he told her, as if pausing to think harder. "Quite quick, it's like a trance, an empty trance."

"How do you get reconnected?" Barbara asked. "How does David plug in again?"

"When Megan comes up to me, she grabs my shoulder," David said, "and I melt in. And that's why I'm confused. Because I'm pointing at this thing. I don't know why I'm pointing at it. I'm just pointing at the thing, and she comes up. Now I don't know what I'm doing."

Convinced that David had given all the information he could, Barbara ended the regression and returned David to full consciousness. A debriefing session followed, in which David drew a picture of the satellite dish, as it had looked to him that night. And she asked him to promise not to talk about his regression with Megan, at least until Barbara was able to question Megan separately about the same events.

But we were able to listen to the tape recording of the regression after David's departure, and we wondered at the strange events, the shock, the noises, the black "not-there," and the odd description he'd given of the satellite dish, none of which David had consciously recalled before the regression. We hoped that perhaps part of his confusion came from the amount of alcohol he'd drunk with James that night, and we waited anxiously for Megan's turn at regression. Unlike David and James, Megan had not been drinking, so we hoped she would have a more coherent recall of the events and could explain away some of the strange things David had remembered.

CHAPTER 9

"How did I get here? I'm confused! Something shocked me, all over. I can't know anything. David's unplugged."

For the two days between David's and Megan's regressions, such remarks kept running through my thoughts. What did he mean, "David's unplugged"? And why hadn't he been able to remember, the next day, anything that happened between his arrival at the farm and James's arrival some time later? What worried me the most was wondering just who or what had been controlling David that night when he felt as if he were a "remote unit" or in "an empty trance."

Barbara had been right, we realized, when she said that something important had happened to the two young people, and we looked forward with great anticipation to Megan's revelations when she and Barbara disappeared into the back room for regression.

Two hours later, they came back into the living room, and the look on Barbara's face told us that she had indeed learned much more about the events of that August evening.

David had kept his promise not to discuss his memories with Megan before the regression, but now they both insisted on knowing everything the other had said. At the time of David's regression, Barbara's video camera was broken and an audio recorder was used instead. But we were able to borrow a camcorder in the meantime, which she used thereafter. So we settled back to watch a replay of the video Barbara had made.

At first, Megan's recollections matched David's. She went over the conversation at the bar, David's description of the woman James had seen and his immediate denial that he'd given such a description, and then the drive home. During this first foray through her memory, Megan recalled only the details she'd told us originally, but Barbara patiently guided her back through the whole thing, occasionally deepening the trance and reminding Megan to sharpen her focus whenever necessary. In her first retelling of the story, Megan experienced a skip in her memory, just after arriving at the farm.

"And I don't know what happened right then," she said. "It skips. Uh, we're standing over towards where the driveway curves. And David starts pointing at the trees, one of them's an evergreen. And he points at it, then he started to pull me over there first, grabbed my arm and started walking over there. And I started pulling back because I was scared. And he said, hmmm, he said something over there wanted to see me. And I started getting very, very upset. My arms were flying all over, and I was pulling back and crying and screaming. And, and, I couldn't figure it out. Because it wasn't David, it wasn't like David.

"Then we started going up toward the house. We got over to the other end of the shed, and we walked through it, and just as we got on to the other side, where the bees are, he pointed over toward that little line of [plum] trees. And he pointed towards those and tried to take me over there. And I started pulling back again, and telling him no because there was, I was, there was something over there."

"What was he saying to get you over there?" Barbara asked.

"He was pulling on my arm and saying we had to go over there. I was pulling back and I was crying and saying, 'No, we can't go over there.' And so David just . . . something happened, he looked different. You could see the change, kind of a shift."

She described David's desire to go for beer and his insistence on taking the wheel, and then James's headlights coming up the long driveway. So far, her story was essentially the same as it had been the morning after the incident: when James went with them into the house, David insisted he hadn't done any of the things Megan described, and he didn't even remember arriving at the farm.

Barbara asked Megan to go through the events once more, taking care to calm Megan's emotions and to give her a more objective point of view, since during the first description Megan had become very upset, crying and showing all the fear she'd felt the first time. With her feelings more under control, Megan started telling the story again.

"We pulled into the driveway," she said, "and I stopped the car because James wasn't there, something was wrong. And I turned over and looked at David, and he was sitting there. He kind of had his eyes half closed because it was late at night and he'd had so much to drink. So he was just laying back. He looked at me and said, 'He's probably just gone to 7-Eleven to get some beer.' And then it was kind of like, it shimmered."

"What shimmered?" Barbara asked.

"Not everything," Megan answered. "Just like when it's hot and you can see the shimmery coming up from the ground, the heat waves. They were in between us. They were just there. They didn't really come from anything, they were just there. All of a sudden."

"Did you feel any temperature change at that time?" Barbara wanted to know, trying to figure out what Megan was describing.

"No," Megan replied. "They were really on David. And they were surrounding, no, they weren't surrounding. It was like there was a quarter circle of it. It stopped at the boundaries of the farm and the road. And David was just on the other side of it. It went through the car. It was like a shimmery sheet between us. And then it was kind of all on him."

"Was there a color to the shimmer?" Barbara asked.

"I can't see a color," Megan said. "Just a heat wave was like what it was, just shimmery. And then it was on him. And then he was different. His eyes and his whole being was different."

"How did you feel about this change?" Barbara inquired.

"It scared me," Megan admitted.

"Did you like what you were sitting next to?"

"No," Megan replied, "but I knew he was still there, but he was hidden. They'd covered him up, he was still there, but he was surrounded. But he was still there, it was, it was doing it. I was scared because of David. David was, they . . . I didn't want him to get hurt."

"What's happening?" Barbara asked, trying to move the regression forward.

"He's, I don't, something's . . . wait," Megan hesitated in confusion. "I don't know if this is. . . David is sitting there. We had just stopped, and David just did this thing, shimmery had just stopped shimmering. That's when he started talking, but David was just still sitting there. It was like it wasn't actually there. David was there, but this other was on top of him. And David just sat there, but it was on top of him. It opened the door! David just sat there? It was something else. And it looked like David, like a hologram, but it opened the door and said he was gonna walk up to the house and I'd be sitting there by myself. But David was there, but I couldn't see him. It was like a hologram. It wasn't him. It was something else. David was sitting there the whole time."

"What did that hologram do?" Barbara asked.

"What I told you," Megan responded. "It walked around to me and tried to pull me to the tree. Something wanted to see me on the other side of the tree. That's what he said: 'something.'"

"Did the voice sound like David?"

"Not really," Megan said. "Like it was somebody else trying to sound like him, a recording would sound like it, but it's not. David was in the car."

"Was it walking like David?" Barbara asked. "Did it feel like David?"

"I couldn't, I knew David was still in the car, but this was, I couldn't see him. This got up, but I couldn't see David, but David was there. And what I saw moved, and got out of the car, and looked like David did, but it wasn't. David was in the car still."

"What was the feeling you were getting from this hologram?" Barbara wanted to know.

"Not anger," Megan told her, "but something. Like it had to hurry. Speed, anticipation? When you've got to do something really fast, you don't have much time, that's the feeling. You have to hurry, but have to do it right. But I don't know what, but trying quickly. Tried to pull me toward the trees. I couldn't see anything different, but I knew I couldn't go over there. There was something wrong.

"And then I could feel a change, but I couldn't really see. And it pointed up at the sky and talked, looked at the moon and the stars and pointed up at the sky. Kind of went around and talked about how pretty the sky was. And then we turned around and started like we were going into the house. And as soon as we got under the roof of the shed, I wanted to stay by the car. It tried to pull me to the line of trees on the other side, on the back side of the house."

"How much force was it using to pull you?" Barbara asked.

"Not any more than David could have used, but not physically hurting me."

"Was it talking to you then?"

"Just, 'Something wants to see you over there.' He said, 'You've got to go.' It tried to pull. . . . Where did David go? It tried to pull me, but where did David go? Where's David? He was in the car, but, I wanted to go back to the car, but it changed again. I could feel the change but I couldn't see it. He said he wanted to go to 7-Eleven for some beer. And he wanted to drive, and so I got in the car, but David. . . . I got in the car, and he wanted to drive, and he grabbed the keys. And I climbed over into the passenger seat where David was, but David wasn't there. He'd been there the whole time, but now he wasn't. He was there when I was pulled back to the car, and then when it tried to pull me over to the trees he wasn't there anymore, not in the car.

"But it was just a minute or two! It got in the car, and started the car, and then I looked over and I could see James's headlights coming up the drive. And it was like David was back again, but it was still there. David was in the driver's seat, but it was there, too. And then it was gone when James got there. And it was David, but he didn't remember anything, because he wasn't there. He was just sitting there before, but he was gone for a minute or two."

Watching the video, we could see how concerned Megan became when she realized David was missing. And then I remembered that David had said, during his regression, that for a few moments he had no idea what had become of Megan. Apparently neither of them could account for the other's whereabouts during that time, and we listened anxiously as Barbara questioned Megan about the disappearance.

"Remember that part when you noticed he wasn't there in the car?" Barbara asked. "Go back there."

"Yeah," Megan nodded. "I pulled over to the car because, this was when we started going back into the house. When it stopped trying to pull me toward the trees. And right when it got back to the little shed, David was in the car then, and I was pulling towards the car. And then it tried to pull me toward those other trees. And that's when David was gone."

"Look around now," Barbara told her. "You're aware that David isn't in the car. You become alarmed. Where is he? See if you can see anything in that area."

"They were trying to separate us for something," Megan replied. "They couldn't let me see. That's why they didn't take him out when it was trying to pull me to the trees, because I kept looking back. But they didn't have time. They had to stop. That's why they changed."

Who was this "they," we wondered, and then on the video Barbara asked, "They didn't have time?"

"I couldn't see them, but I know they're there."

"How many are you feeling now?" Barbara asked.

"Aside from the one that I was with, there were three. They were waiting to take David out of the car, but they couldn't while I was looking. They didn't want me to see them. They were behind something, I don't know what, because there's nothing there. They were behind something, though, because I couldn't see them. They couldn't let me see them pulling David out of the car because I wasn't supposed to know. That's why it was trying to get me over there behind the trees so I couldn't see."

"You mean you were being distracted by that one?" Barbara offered.

"Right," Megan said. "That's why it was trying to hurry, so it could get David out. But I don't know what for. That's why I wanted to go back to the car."

"Where was David when he wasn't in the car?" Barbara pressed. "Can you see the three that were with him?"

"He was behind the thing," Megan told her. "It wasn't there, but you couldn't see behind it."

"The thing?" Barbara echoed. "What are you talking about?"

"It was something . . . you couldn't," Megan hesitated, "they were behind it but you couldn't see that it was there. It projected something, but they just had him for a second because then James started coming up and they had to put him back in the car."

"Can you remember what they looked like?" Barbara asked.

"I didn't see them," Megan said. "They did it when I was looking at James's car. They stayed behind." She paused for a moment and then exclaimed, "They moved it! They moved the thing! I didn't know they could do that!"

"Where was the thing?" Barbara asked. "Where was it being projected?"

"It was like, kind of like it was a screen," Megan explained. "And it projected what was supposed to be behind it on that screen, so it looked like there wasn't anything there. They were just on the other side. Like a thin metal thing. It was just a square except it bowed a little bit. But you couldn't see any equipment, it just looked like a thin, metal sheet, and it had a stand thing on it so it wouldn't fall. It kind of curved a bit. It was a square metal thing, but it could project what was supposed to be on the other side. They moved around, but you could kind of tell along the edges that it was there. But otherwise you couldn't. And they moved around over there, and the one that looked like David got David into the car. I didn't see the others. I don't know how I knew there were three, but I did."

"What was your feeling about these guys?" Barbara wanted to know. "How did you feel about them? Did you feel like they were nice, or what?"

"It's kind of like they weren't there, like mechanical. No feeling. The one that looked like David, at least a sense of it had to hurry. But I couldn't get any feeling from the three."

"Did they come back again?" Barbara asked.

"Not that night," Megan replied. "I don't know when they've been, but they didn't come back that night."

"Did you feel like these energies, whatever they were, did they seem familiar to you? Had you met them before?"

"The one that tried to distract me seemed like it knew me or something," Megan admitted. "The others were just not important."

Barbara continued the regression a while longer, but Megan had nothing further to add about the events of that night. After she was out of the hypnotic trance, Megan drew a picture of the screen device, and we were surprised to see how closely her drawing matched that of David's satellite dish. By now, of course, we realized that whatever he had seen had certainly not been the neighbor's dish. Given his description of the dish—curly edges, square, with a pipe supporting it on the ground—and his description of the black thing on the ground—a 'not-there' with unstable, changing movements along the edges—it seemed that David had seen something unusual and had tried to make sense of it in terms of the familiar satellite dish. But could it have been the same machine, the invisibility screen, that Megan described?

Just to make certain that the neighbor's dish had not been the object, I phoned a few days later and asked the neighbor if anything had happened to move the dish during the previous August. She assured me that the satellite dish had never moved from its original location, and that there had been nothing like a pipe and zinc box attached to it at any time. Whatever had been in the yard that night, it was nothing we could identify.

And that wasn't the only puzzle we had to consider. How could we make sense of the "hologram" Megan described, the double of David? Had his image actually been duplicated in some way? Or had his body somehow been borrowed by an outside intelligence, with his consciousness, his psyche, unplugged?

We had strong relationships with both David and Megan, and we felt certain that they weren't deliberately lying to us about their memories. Neither of them had consciously recalled these events, and David had not told Megan about his regression before she underwent hers. Yet their strange stories confirmed each other's accounts, and we were left with many worrying questions. What had happened to them during that time when they lost sight of each other? And who on earth was responsible for the entire incident? Neither recalled anything like a UFO, nor had they described aliens. Megan insisted she didn't know what the beings really looked like, so it was possible that they had been human. But who had been at the farm that night, and why?

CHAPTER 10

For several months, James had talked about visiting Barbara, but on the only weekend he'd actually planned to go, he had been frightened, by memories of seeing a human mutilation, enough to change his mind. Now, with Barbara's presence and his parents' support, James decided to go through a regression. It was a real act of courage, we all realized, considering his decidedly unobtrusive and private nature. Telling his parents, whom he loved and wanted to protect, about the alien encounters was the hardest thing he'd ever done, I believe, and I silently congratulated his strength of will when he asked Barbara to help him with hypnotic regression.

A few months before, it was all he could do to talk about his experiences even with us, and by this time I knew that part of his reluctance was fear of being thought crazy. For too long, that had been the only explanation he could accept—such thing just weren't real—and he worried that others would naturally make that assumption, too. Casey and I hoped that reclaiming his lost memories would help him as it had helped us, by relieving the isolation and the faceless fears abductees develop.

Barbara and James began his regression one evening after dinner, with his mother, Sandy, waiting for the results with us. From the first, she had been emotionally supportive of James, which surprised me. Until, that is, I learned that other members of her family had had their own strange stories to tell in the past, including her father and sister. Most intriguing was her story of a night long ago when her sister encountered a small floating ball of light, about the size of a basketball. We immediately remembered James and the basketball-sized light that had come into his room and told him he couldn't understand any more than the interdimensional woman had already told him.

When the regression was over, we listened to the tape of the session together. Barbara asked James to choose which experience he wanted to look at, and he went back to the series of nightmares he'd had just prior to Barbara's visit here. He knew, at the time of the terrible dreams, that they were more than just dreams, but it was hard for him to accept that they revealed a real event until he'd gone through the whole thing under hypnosis.

"I'm lying down on my back," James said, beginning to relive the experience. "I see my head, about here, there's no hair. Hurt. Lots and lots of holes in my head. Holes around my head, in a line. Makes your heart speed."

"How do you feel about this?" Barbara asked. "Are you scared?"

"Yes."

"Can you see if there are any other presences in the room? Where are you?" she questioned. "Is there a color to the room?"

"Mostly white," James told her. "Shadowlike. Different colored lights. Red, yellow. It's like, five lights. Five flash. I saw a hand, reach out to the lights."

"What are those lights?" Barbara asked. "Do they have any purpose?"

"A hand touched the lights, five lights," he replied. "Something hurt my arm."

"What part of the arm hurts?"

"My wrist. Wires in my wrist, through the wrist, like threads."

"Do you know what their purpose is?" Barbara prodded him.

"No."

"How many are in your wrist?"

"One," James said, "just one in the wrist. It hurts, the wire."

"Is this the dream you wanted to look at?" Barbara interrupted. "The dream that happened a few nights ago?"

"Yes," James affirmed.

"Have you seen those wires before?"

"Yes," he admitted, "a long, long time ago. I'm lying down, with my arms and legs spread out."

"Is this room unusual in any way?" Barbara asked. "Can you give me more description?"

"It's busy," James told her. "Lots and lots of things going on. Lots of things moving."

But when Barbara tried to question him for more details, James mumbled unclearly that he couldn't move his head or see out of his left eye. He became disturbed by his immobility, and Barbara calmed him down.

"Relax," she told him, "there's a reason why you can't move. I understand it, it's okay. Just feel good about it. With the eye you can see through, tell me what else you see in the room. Are you aware of any presence in the room other than yourself? Other than that hand that went up to the light?"

"Just the hand that touched the light," James answered. "It hurts, my head hurts, my left ear."

Barbara, sensing James's discomfort, asked him to move ahead to the next time he was able to move and be free of pain. "Where are you now?" she asked.

"It's different," James said. "It's dark here."

"What do you feel like this room might be related to?"

"Healing," he replied.

"Is it like a recovery room?" Barbara suggested.

"Yes."

"You feel much better now, don't you?" she soothed him. "What are your other feelings? Can you think about where you are, or are you just drugged from this experience?"

"Clear," he mumbled. "Curious. Something has my hand, right hand. I'm walking."

"Are you wearing anything?" Barbara wanted to know.

"No," he answered.

"What does it look like around you?"

"It's big. Lots of things. The things walk around. It's big."

"What kind of things?"

"Lots of bodies."

"Are they human bodies?" Barbara asked.

"They're something else," James told her. "Not very tall. They're short, about as short as chest-high."

"Are there any distinguishing features about this big place you're walking through?"

"It's like a bowl. There's nothing on top," he said. "It's like the inside of a bowl."

"Have you been there before?" Barbara queried.

"I think so," James answered. "I'm not scared."

But his voice was barely audible, and Barbara saw that he was not at ease. "Can you tell me why it's difficult for you to talk about it?" she asked.

"It's hard to latch on, to see something," he finally replied. "There's something over, opening, a little taller, and something pulls me, my hand, says something."

"How do you receive this? Do you hear him audibly speaking to you?"

"Not with words," James tried to explain. "It says something. It's, I can't tell, I don't know. It seems . . . he's sorry. 'Poor James, poor James.'"

"Like he's apologizing to you?" Barbara asked.

"Yes, for hurting me. He's nice. He's more gentle with me."

"Do you feel he's a male?" Barbara continued. "You said that they're not wearing clothes. Do you see any distinguishing sexual parts that would make you think he's a man?"

"No," James responded, "he just looks like a man. We're stopped. I'm at the wall."

"What's happening now?" Barbara asked. "He said he's sorry? You get the impression he's apologizing for hurting you?"

"Yes. He says to walk through the hole."

"Tell me what happens now," Barbara instructed, and as we listened we were surprised by James's reply.

"I'm in bed," he announced. "It's hot." Barbara questioned him again, going back through descriptions of the bowl-like room, the colored lights, and the area where James saw hundreds of beings at work, moving from counter to counter in a crowded space. But James was ready for the regression to be over, so she soon brought him out of the trance and then questioned him a while longer in the debriefing session.

Describing the initial scene, James told her about the wire in his wrist. "It's like when the hand touched the lights," he said, "the wire just came down out of the ceiling, straight down, and got me. It was thin, thinner than piano wire, and it shone. It looked like metal. There were other wires, I could see the tops of them, but I couldn't see or feel where they were touching me."

"Could they have been acting like some kind of acupuncture?" Barbara suggested, "a healing process?"

"No," James replied, "I think they were, like at the end when he said he was sorry, he was saying they were monitoring, testing things out to see how things worked. Just monitoring, how I worked on the inside. He said he was sorry my head hurt. It was a way to find out what he needed to know. And then we walked through this hole."

"Could you pick up anything about that one that seemed to be nice?" Barbara asked. "Was he showing you the ship or taking you from the recovery room to your exit point?"

"Yeah," James answered, "but I could have gotten from the recovery room straight to the exit point, but they propped me up and walked me through. Things were just walking around ignoring me."

"Were you the only human you could see?" Barbara wanted to know.

"Uh-huh," he nodded. "The things were just walking around doing stuff."

Barbara asked him then more about the creatures, which he consistently referred to as "things," as well as about the bowl-shaped area.

"It was black on some of it," he said, describing the large area, "but there was a front and a back, a definite front. You could see, coming up over this part of it, you could see stars, and then all the rest of this top was black. It was just one level, sloping, and I looked all around. It was gently sloping, and then all of a sudden I just walked up and there was a wall."

"Did you feel this place was up in the sky?" Barbara asked.

"Yeah," he said. "Standing over here you could see that it was curved, because you could look down and see it all. All over and curving down to the walls. It was all real flat [beneath] except for these counters coming up about this wide, and then they made a maze of these things. And the little 'things' are standing around them, and they were all walking around, with all these lights on top [of the counters]. They were different colors, flashing, and they were looking at them, not touching them or anything, just standing over there." As he described the place, he pointed to various parts of a sketch he was making.

"It was just a maze," he said. "It didn't look like there was any kind of order to it. Just lights. They'd stop and look down at the lights, and then they'd walk to another counter and look at the lights over here, and they were all just walking around looking at lights."

Next he sketched a rough picture of the being who escorted him. "The one that was leading me around," he said, "his head came out further in the back than mine does. They all looked pretty much identical. The head was flat in front. They were colored kind of muddy-brown, or gray mud color."

When he finished the drawing and the description, Barbara asked one more question, remembering something else she'd heard earlier about James's experience.

"And then it seemed that you were walked through a little bit and taken to that opening, where you were transported back down to your bed," she reiterated. "Was that the night you found blood?"

"Yeah," James recalled, "that was the first night. It was in the middle of the sheet."

"When the being apologized to you," Barbara finished up, "how did you feel about him?"

"I believed him," James said quietly. "He seemed, he didn't say like 'I'm sorry,' it was like, an overwhelming feeling. I came out with the words to match whatever it was, the feeling I got. He was sorry for hurting me, but there wasn't any other way. I got the impression I was part of what they were trying to find out. The pain, they were monitoring some of that as well. As to how it registered with me, how I perceived it. Or how I worked."

"Maybe the holes were just put in your mind to see how you would react to holes in your head," Barbara suggested. "They could have projected it into your mind, and then you get afraid, and they register your fear. Does that make sense? There aren't any holes in your head, and your hair hasn't been shaved."

James shrugged, and Barbara asked, "How do you feel now?"

"Spooked," he said.

"You know," she told him, "this is happening to other people, but often the most intelligent ones."

"Small consolation," James replied. We nodded sympathetically, listening to the end of the tape. We had been going through the experiences for almost a year, and so far we had learned nothing that offered any consolation at all.

That night, exhausted after working through two regressions, Barbara slept as soundly as we did, yet the next morning both she and I had new marks on our bodies. She had two deep, round bruises on her upper arm, and I had a strange, red, V-shaped mark in the bend of my elbow, with a puncture mark about an inch below it. The V-shaped mark quickly faded, but the puncture scabbed and disappeared more slowly in the next few days.

On Friday, my best friend Bonnie came by to meet Barbara and was soon being interrogated about her own strange experiences. Barbara was very interested in one particular occasion, about eleven years earlier, when Bonnie and her husband had been on vacation in South Carolina. Visiting an old country church, Bonnie had encountered a Siamese cat, which led her from tombstone to tombstone, while her husband disappeared into the thick woods nearby to relieve himself. When he returned, quite a while after leaving the area, he said he'd seen a spooky light, but Bonnie didn't recall anything but the cat. Yet when she went to get the cat and take it with them, it was nowhere to be found.

Barbara suggested that there might be more to the event than Bonnie consciously remembered and wondered if she might like to go through a regression to explore it. But Bonnie laughed away the suggestion and assured Barbara that there was nothing strange about it or about anything else in her life. (Later, however, Bonnie did decide to explore the incident under hypnosis. Without including the entire regression, which didn't take place during the year covered by my journal, it's interesting to note that the Siamese cat proved to be a screen memory of an apparent double abduction involving Bonnie and her husband. The beautiful cat she'd remembered turned out to look very different, as Bonnie described some sort of being "three feet tall, about two feet wide, covered with metallic shavings.")

Before Barbara could pursue the idea of working with Bonnie, Fred arrived, ready for his regression. More than anyone else in our small group, except perhaps James, Fred's life had been frequently disturbed by bizarre experiences during the past year.

In the beginning, the occurrences usually involved missing-time episodes when he worked the night shift at his job, alone. Often there would be some sort of signal that an abduction was about to take place, such as wind blowing through his closed office room or a low horn sounding, and once he heard a voice commanding, "Don't turn around, Fred." But lately the overt signs of contact were gone, and the only reason he suspected that abductions might still be occurring was that he so often found puncture marks, subcutaneous red or purple streaks, bruises, and cuts, frequently forming triangles on his body.

Like the rest of us, Fred also had "dream" experiences that were frightening and confusing, and, like us, he had no sure way of deciding for himself which experiences were truly just dreams, which were replays of past actual events, and which were screen memories of recent abductions. It was his lack of certainty about the phenomenon that was most frustrating for Fred, the utter lack of knowledge about who or what was responsible, as well as the frightening things he recalled from the experiences. When we first met him, he said that he'd somehow been led to believe these things were "growing new bodies for us" and also that he felt there was something he was supposed to do, related to the aliens, within the next few years. This, too, was a piece of information that had come from his encounters, yet he couldn't remember the context or even the specific event in which it occurred.

He felt angry and scared and cheated, and his sense of almost desperate urgency to know more was at a peak. Regression with Barbara was something he'd been anxious for, in hopes of getting answers, and he proved to be a good subject for hypnosis. Fortunately, Barbara had borrowed a video recorder again, so she was able to tape Fred's entire regression. And as we viewed it later that evening, we saw once again that the difference between actually watching someone's face as he goes through such emotional recollections and merely listening to the voice on an audio-tape was astonishing.

The focus of the session was on two disturbing dream memories Fred had recently been having. After putting him into a trance, Barbara began by asking him about the dreams.

"One, I was in a pool of water," Fred told her, "and I thought I was going to drown. I did not have any way out, so I tried to relax and began breathing through my nose and found I could breathe underwater. I was shocked and didn't know what I was doing there. The second dream was early this morning," he finished. "Had something to do with animal and human crossbreeding." His face showed increasing stress as he talked about the second dream, so Barbara took his lead and pressed him about it.

"You are upset, Fred," she said. "Can you explain why you are feeling this way?"

"I feel like they are doing something to me with the animal," he replied. "They are doing something with me, my blood, my sperm, and my genes. They are injecting my fluids into this animal. I think it's stupid, and I don't like it. Why are they doing this?" His expression became even more disturbed, yet he forced himself to continue as Barbara questioned him.

"I think I was lying down, and they were doing something to the animal," he told her. "Taking something from me and putting it into the animal. Then I remember seeing another type of animal running around. I can't remember what the animal looked like, but it was bizarre. Seems like the animal is part human, part animal. Like a small child around two years old. The one animal that appears to be part human seems to be real hairy.

"I remember feeling angry," he said, mentally watching as the aliens injected fluids into the apparently female animal. "I am trying to sit up in a state of anger. I must be sitting down or lying down. They have the animal next to me. The thing appears to be flat, not like a walking animal."

"You expressed trying to sit up and protest in anger," Barbara commented. "Let's go back, right before that time, and see what happened to cause this anger."

Instead of answering, however, Fred suddenly began to shake all over in wrenching spasms. We watched apprehensively as the spasms continued for long, silent minutes, and then at last he was sobbing and moaning in distress, his face still contorted from the tension.

I watched with great concern, wondering why Barbara hadn't intervened to relieve this stress. With previous subjects she had always calmed them whenever their fears upset them, and I asked her why she hadn't helped Fred.

"He had to have the release of getting it all out," Barbara explained, stopping the video momentarily. "All of that emotion you just saw has been inside Fred for a long time, building up and getting worse. But now that he's been back through it and let go of it, he'll feel much more at ease with himself." Later, watching Fred's evolution through subsequent episodes, I saw that Barbara had been correct, for he never again was at such a point of intensity after the regression.

The video started up again, with Barbara soothing Fred and bringing him back to his account. When he was ready to go on, she asked, "What are your impressions, Fred? Look now and tell me what you see."

"I just see light, a lot of light," he began. "It's last night, and I can see them coming into my bedroom, but I want to block it out." Fred began shaking again, silently straining against the violent spasms, but through gritted teeth he kept talking.

"I see flashes of faces coming towards me," he shuddered. "Seems like whoever it is is holding a big tube. It has a blue base. I can see three inches of the tube, but I can't see all of it."

"Is the animal feeling upset like you are?" Barbara asked.

"The animal is sedated. It's about two feet away. I'm on one and it's on another table."

"What are you on?"

"I'm on a singular bed," Fred explained. "It's in a curved position. The animal is next to me on a table. I vaguely see computers."

"You said there was another animal," Barbara interrupted. "Can you describe it?"

"I can't see it clearly," Fred replied. "It doesn't have a shirt on. It has some hair, but not a lot. It seems like it has skin, pink or white, on the top and hair on the bottom. Brown hair. My logic is blocking a good description."

Barbara then suggested a protective mental viewing device for Fred, removing him from the immediacy of reliving the events, and took him back through the entire experience again, searching for new details.

"I can see me in a chair," Fred said, relaxing at last and becoming more objective in his description. "I don't think I'm wearing anything. This is a chair with a curvature, in the middle of the room. There is a table beside me. There are computers around the walls, and medical equipment. The room is yellow in color, and I can only see part of the room."

"Can you move your head?" Barbara suggested.

"A little bit," he responded, "but I can't move my arms or legs."

"What do you see now?"

"Two little men are bringing in another tray, sliding in a little table, and it's got medical equipment on it."

"What do the men look like?"

"Grays," Fred said.

"So they brought in the tray," Barbara repeated, "and what happens next?"

"It's a stand-up table. There are two Grays, one on each end. They roll it in, and it stands a little lower than the height of the table. The animal isn't on the table as yet." Once again, Fred began to shake and shudder, but this time Barbara calmed him back down until he was more easily able to continue.

"They are levitating this animal," he told her, "and now there are two Grays on each side, and she is spread-eagled on her back. There is one now that is sticking the needle device up her groin or vaginal area. Or whatever it is. It has hooves, like a cow. I'm not seeing the body too clearly. He pulls the needle out and looks at what they have collected in the tube."

"You mean they collected, extracted, fluid from the animal?" Barbara asked.

"Yes, they were extracting fluid from the animal."

"Fred, what were they doing with you?"

His face visibly changed, sagging and smoothing out as if he were suddenly sedated. "I'm strapped down," he mumbled.

"What parts of your body are secured?"

"My upper arms and chest. My legs are strapped."

"Are you wearing clothes?"

"No."

"Are you embarrassed?"

"No, I'm too frightened to care."

"Has anything been done to relieve your fright?" Barbara asked.

"I haven't been in there that long," Fred answered. "Now they bring the animal in, but they don't talk to me. They don't do anything to relieve my fright."

"Have you been in this place before?"

"I think so."

"It's all right, you may continue."

"I remember, last night," he said suddenly, "they did something to me in my bed. There were two of them. They touched me with something on my forehead. It looked like a circular object, and when it opened it splits down the center, and it might form a triangle shape. It looks like a gold-type metal. After they do this, I can't move, and I feel like I'm sort of being dematerialized.

"I'm not aware of standing up," Fred continued. "I don't have any clothes on, and there are three Grays standing around me wearing red uniforms.

"There are two of them in front of me. Now one moves out of the way. The other one takes me by the hand and guides me to the curved chair. I know to sit down."

"Are you resisting?" Barbara suggested. "What is your mood?"

"No," he replied. "It's as if I don't have a mood."

"Continue, please," she said.

"They are sticking something into my penis. He's holding something like a tube with a slender metal object on the end. He gets it and pushes it in. I tried to raise my head to see what he is doing."

"Do you feel pain?" Barbara questioned. "Discomfort? Or sexually aroused?"

"No," Fred shook his head. "He keeps sticking this thing in me."

"How many times?"

"Just once, it's still in there. Now I lay my head back down, it's still in there. He's doing something with the tube."

"What are the others doing?" Barbara wanted to know.

"One is standing over by the computer. It looks like a computer with a light on top of it. He's doing something there while the other one is behind me. They aren't saying anything to me. He's pulling the tube out, and it's like a suction device. I feel no pain, no feelings. But it's like it's happened before."

"Can you see the contents of the tube?"

"It may be sperm," Fred guessed, "I don't know. Seems like there is a nude woman. I see a corridor, and she is in another room. There is a circular room with a long corridor going into the room. Now they have her on a table, and they are rolling her into this room."

"Is she human?" Barbara asked.

"I can't see her clearly," Fred replied, "but she is human. They leave her on the table. On the opposite side of the room. She is now about fifteen to twenty feet from me. The table is near the doorway that opens into the corridor."

"Is she moving?" Barbara wanted to know.

"No," Fred shook his head. "They are removing the animal. The animal was floated away. I'm just there. They have taken the tube out and taken the tube and contents over to one of the computers. Before they removed the animal, they put part of the fluid into the animal. The rest is taken to the computer."

"What can you tell me about the woman?" Barbara asked, directing his focus back to the subject.

"She's been opened up and has a vertical incision from the top of her chest straight down to her groin area," Fred replied. "They have moved her close to me, about five feet from me. The one that had my stuff in the tube, over by the computer, is going over to her. He's putting his hand inside her."

"Did his hand enter her body through the incision," Barbara interrupted, "or vaginally?"

"Through the incision," Fred said. "His hand entered through the chest opening and was directed down towards the reproductive area." He stopped talking and his brow furrowed deeply as he concentrated on the mental picture. "God," he whispered at last, "what's he doing?"

"Give me a description," Barbara prompted.

"He is doing something with her insides. He's got his hand stuck in the lower portion of her body, and his other hand is up under her hips. He lifts her hips up so he can do some kind of manipulation with the reproductive region. Her legs are up in the air. Some kind of clamps around her ankles are used to secure her legs to keep them raised. She is spread-eagled, and even though her legs are up, she is still being supported on the table. It looks like he's got a long, tube-like instrument going in through her vagina."

"Is she still cut open?" Barbara asked.

"Yes," he nodded. "Now another one is approaching with an object with a light or laser on it. What he is doing to the skin, as he pulls it together, it's just sealing it up as if there wasn't any cut." His voice is filled with amazement as he studies the mental image. "He uses the light, pulls the skin together, and you can't tell she was ever cut."

"Did you ever have any physical contact with the woman?"

"No, this was strictly surgical."

"Do you think the contents of your tube were injected into her?"

"I think it went into the animal or a combination of both, the woman and the animal." He began to be upset again, agitated and gritting his teeth, shaking his head.

"How do you feel, Fred?" Barbara asked, wondering what brought on the tension.

"They are getting ready to do something to me," he answered, still so agitated that Barbara had to remind him of the protective viewing device before he could continue.

"He's going into my eyeball," he told her. "He's doing something to my eye. He's going into the corner of my left eye. He has a long, thin rod, probing between skin and the eyeball."

"Is he hurting you?"

"No."

"What is happening now?"

"He has this long needle-tube device, and he's putting it into my navel, and he's going up under my skin to the left side of my chest." Fred's agitation turned to obvious distress as he fought to keep control.

"What's he doing?" Barbara asked, "what is the purpose of this procedure?"

"He's scraping tissue from the inside," Fred replied, still very disturbed. "I don't know why they want to get inside tissues. Hell, they could have gotten that from the girl when they had her opened up!" His expression changed then, from fright to anger.

"They've got a vial of something, clear fluid. I don't know if they are going to make me drink it or what. No, they are going to inject it right in through the cut into the navel."

"How large is this vial?"

"About three inches." He indicated with his fingers.

Concerned about his angry mood, Barbara asked if he wanted to stop the session, but Fred refused. "I want to see them clearly," he told her, and Barbara gave him instructions to sharpen his mental vision.

"As you leave this event," she said, "walk behind the thick curtain and close it. Then quickly pull it apart just enough so you can take a quick peek at them. You will be able to see them clearly."

There was a pause as Fred implemented her instructions, and then, becoming extremely upset, he told her, "They are the Grays."

Once the vivid experience was behind him, Barbara asked a few more questions and let Fred express whatever opinions he might have about the things he'd seen.

"They are regenerating from animal to human, from human to animal," he surmised. "Regenerating DNA. I think it has something to do with the immune system. Either they are testing our immune system, or doing something with it, what it is I don't know, but they did implant something into the woman. They seem to be crossbreeding, too. Between animal and human."

"Fred," Barbara asked, bringing the session to a close, "do you like them?"

He shook his head silently in the negative.

"Are you being taken against your will?"

"Yes."

"Do you think you are genetically linked to them in any way?"

"Yeah," he answered, "in a way."

"Does that give them a right to do what they are doing to you?"

"Nobody has the right to do or mess with my body," he insisted, "unless I want them to."

CHAPTER 11

With all of the scheduled regressions taken care of, we were now able to go back through the material and try to make sense of what had been discovered. It was clear, from comparing David's and Megan's regressions, that they both recalled previously forgotten events and descriptions which supported each other's accounts. From Megan's point of view, David's image had somehow been duplicated and used to distract her while three beings took the real David out of the car and behind a screen which kept them from being seen. Yet David recalled walking to the places that the duplicate, in Megan's story, had walked. It seemed to us that perhaps David's volition had been somehow shut down— "unplugged," as he put it—so that some other intelligence could manipulate his actions.

We also noticed that both David and Megan gave descriptions of devices from angles that neither of them recalled being in positions to observe. And there was the matter of missing parts in their stories, for at a certain point neither of them was aware of the other's whereabouts.

Barbara hoped to explore the missing parts in later regressions, for she reasoned that they must each have been inside or behind the device in order to know what it looked like. Whatever had happened there, however, David and Megan could not recall.

Equally disturbing and frightening were the memories of painful physical experiences that Fred and James related. Yet Barbara said there were many such cases she had worked with, and in some instances other abductees had described identical procedures to the laser wound-closing and the probing into Fred's eye. We discussed the fact that James's experience seemed utterly real to him, even though there hadn't been any scars or other evidence, save the blood on his sheets, to indicate anything had been done to his head. What kind of intelligence, we wondered, could cause hallucinations that seemed so real? And why?

Barbara, through her research work with over two hundred cases, had learned enough to formulate her own interpretation of such experiences. She believed that at least a certain group of these beings in some way "feed" off our emotions, especially the strong ones that come from fear, pain, depression, and compulsive actions. It was no news to us that blood and fluid samples, as well as sperm, ova, and skin tissue, were reportedly taken during abductions.

But we hadn't seen anything in our research reading that mentioned aliens inflicting pain in order to "harvest" or otherwise use the abductee's emotional responses. Barbara was the first researcher I'd heard who presented such an idea, with case after case to back it up, and I wondered if her cases were particularly different in that way from the abductions studied by other investigators. Aliens as emotional vampires was a very strange thought, but no stranger, perhaps, than anything else we'd heard. And then I remembered my dream, of Casey and his black-garbed vampire friends sitting in a circular room, and wondered if it had indeed been an insight into the truth.

In looking back through the material from Fred, I also saw a few familiar elements. At one point, for instance, he described a circular object which he thought could be manipulated into a triangle shape. I immediately thought of the round device I'd seen in the alien's hand on Halloween night, which I recalled as the source for the triangle of punctures on my neck the next morning, and I wondered if it was the same device Fred saw.

And then he'd talked about feeling as if he were about to be "dematerialized." David, I remembered, had said much the same thing about an experience the previous August. It had begun with an invisible pressure-source seeming to penetrate into his head, and he said he felt as if he were about to be pulled out of his body. Another time, feeling a very similar sensation, David thought his body was about to disintegrate or explode into its atomic particles. If they had indeed felt the same thing, I wondered what experiences David might have gone through without any memory, hoping he had never felt the sort of pain and fear that Fred had recalled. But without more regressions, there was no way of knowing.

Barbara's time was limited, however, and the Budd Hopkins lecture was important enough, we hoped, to postpone further hypnosis sessions for another visit. James's parents decided to attend the lecture with us, but an hour before we were to leave, his father phoned to say they wouldn't be able to go. When I questioned him, he was vague, saying only that a family situation had come up which needed immediate attention. So our group consisted of Casey, Barbara, David, and me, with Fred meeting us at the lecture site.

We arrived early, but the hall was already crowded. From our seats in the middle of the room, we scanned the faces, hoping to sight the woman James had seen at the August meeting. Casey and I had both recalled seeing a woman standing where James described and matching his description; in fact, I had noticed her looking in our general direction several times that night, so I had a very good idea of who to look for. Of course, we had watched for her at all the other meetings since Lear's August lecture, without success, but Hopkins was the first widely known guest since Lear, so we assumed there was a chance she'd show up.

The hall filled up with so many people that we couldn't keep track, and then the lecture began. Having read both of Hopkins's books on abduction experiences, I was aware of how his views on the phenomenon had slowly changed. At first he'd dealt only with people recalling abductions from their past, and he thought such events must be one-time occurrences. Then, working with more people, he'd learned that abductions were sometimes repeated. But for a while, he assured himself and his cases that once the experience was relived under hypnosis, such experiences stopped in the abductee's life.

That idea, too, had gone by the wayside when he started working with the person known as "Kathie Davis." During a series of regressions, he found out that she was having current episodes of abduction, and the fact of her hypnosis did nothing to make the episodes stop. His ideas had changed as the material coming from the abductees had indicated, so I wondered what new ideas or discoveries he might have now. About halfway into the lecture, we found out that indeed his views had somewhat changed. Moreover, many of the things he said fitted very well with what we had learned through the regressions of the past days.

After going through the evolution of the abduction phenomenon, Hopkins related fascinating details from several of his own cases. But it was his conclusions that struck home to those of us who sat listening with very personal interest.

"I'll tell you two things I've learned that are new and disturbing, having to do with the purpose behind UFO abductions," he said, digressing for a moment to dismiss the idea of benevolent "space brothers" as well as the horror of creatures devouring us, flesh and blood, for nourishment.

"One of the things that has been very disturbing emerges in three cases," he continued, "which suggest that in an abduction experience a person is being deliberately subjected to pain. And they're being subjected to pain very much like we might do in an experiment with a laboratory animal. A pretty grim idea."

Immediately I thought of Barbara's theory of alien emotional vampires, and of James's regression, the pain he felt and his remarks about the alien's apology. "He was sorry for hurting me," James recalled, "but there wasn't any other way. I got the impression I was part of what they were trying to find out. The pain was, they were monitoring some of that as well. As to how it registered with me, how I perceived it." It seemed clear that Hopkins had heard the same story from other cases, to make such a specific statement. Here, then, was some sort of confirmation that James's story could be true, and the realization made me feel weak, almost nauseated. The same "thudding" sensation affected me every time I learned of any new supporting information, reminding me how desperately I wished the whole phenomenon were mere delusion.

Hopkins had more to say, though. "A second thing that seems to be extremely important and new, to me," he went on, "is the sense that they seem to be very interested in human sexuality, and I don't mean just the reproductive mechanisms and ova and sperm, but actually the whole physical range of sexuality itself. They seem to be very curious about it, and they seem to want to sense intuitively or however, telepathically, what sexuality feels like, as well as how the plumbing works, so to speak."

Here again, I thought of James. When he had been approached at his parents' house by aliens who wanted him to mate with one of their females, he'd been able to refuse, at least as far as he has remembered. And at the time of the event, I wondered why, if the aliens needed his sperm, they didn't simply take it mechanically as I'd read about in several cases. It didn't really make sense to attempt impregnating one of the aliens, since abductees often reported seeing fetuses growing in artificial wombs or nurseries. And Casey, too, had been made to have sex with an alien female.

The alien interest in sex, according to Barbara, also involved cases where abductees found themselves irrationally and sexually obsessed with some highly unlikely person. This had happened to three people I knew, so I didn't doubt that in Barbara's wide range of contact she'd found other cases. She thought that such obsessions were deliberately manipulated to stir up strong emotions, which in turn were "taken" by the alien intelligence in control. I also knew of one book on the abductions of five women in which the investigator concluded that homosexuality was an important factor, a curiosity, to the abductors.

"Pleasure and pain," I heard Hopkins remark, "they're interested in those two aspects."

There were other of his remarks that also seemed relevant to our group's experiences. He said, for instance, that there were credible cases in which normal-looking humans were encountered cooperating with the aliens, and I thought about the very human-looking woman who had appeared so many times in James's bedroom. He also described reports of various alien types, including the reptilian being with long, thin, webbed hands replete with claws or "talons" such as Casey had seen.

And when he began talking about the aliens' genetic experiments, his comments echoed Fred's own conclusions under hypnosis. "We know that they seem to need genetic material," Hopkins said, "that they're taking sperm, ova. We know they're doing these reproductive experiments in an attempt at hybridization. Too many cases have come to light, too many similar descriptions, for this to be eliminated as a possibility. It is very central."

I had to agree. The alien female who had sex with Casey had looked like a mixture, a hybrid with both human and alien features. Fred saw his sperm put into the woman and also into the strange animal and rationally concluded that crossbreeding was the reason. But Fred hadn't stopped with the idea of crossbreeding; he also surmised that the aliens were interested in "regenerating DNA," and that the work "'has something to do with the immune system."

And Hopkins, in his final remarks, hit upon the same subject. "More and more I am convinced," he concluded, "that they have evolved in some way or another past a certain point, so that they seem to need to come back again and revivify their own species, and not only in the physical sense of taking our genetic material." He came back to the emotion factor, too, saying, "They seem to want to feel telepathically what humans go through emotionally," when he described the "baby-presentation" abductions and the aliens' interest in the parent-child relationship.

"They look at us as being varied and rich and interesting," he told the audience, "because they're not. We are a resource for them, physically, emotionally, and spiritually."

The phrasing was clean and concise, depicting us as an abundant "resource" for a race that is pitiably lacking in such qualities. But, recalling the fear, the strong emotional costs to the abductee, remembering the frightened emotion of Megan's regression and the shattering spasms and pain that had torn through Fred, I wondered if Barbara's term, "emotional vampires," was not a more accurate way to put it.

During intermission, I looked around the crowded room again, scanning for the face of the woman we'd seen at the Lear lecture, and this time I saw her. At least I thought it was she, so I pointed out the woman to Casey for his opinion. He also thought she might be the one, as did David, but without James's verification we couldn't be sure. I bitterly regretted his and his parents' absence and wondered again what had changed their minds at the last moment. If James had been here, we could have approached the woman and questioned her, but I was too afraid of making a mistake to risk it then myself. Still, I reasoned that if she was here tonight, she would likely show up at later meetings. Surely James will want to come next time, I told myself, once he hears that she was present again.

When the lecture ended, some of the study group members invited us along for coffee and dessert with Hopkins at a nearby restaurant, and we accepted eagerly. By the time we arrived, more than a dozen people were already seated at a long table, but there were several vacant seats across from Hopkins. We sat and talked for a few minutes, and then more people arrived. Imagine our surprise when the woman we'd seen at the lecture was among them. And I was even more surprised when she took the chair next to me and began talking familiarly with Mr. Hopkins.

At first I was too shocked to speak to her, but I listened and learned that she had just been through her first regression with him and had discovered her own abduction experiences. A little later I managed to say hello and introduce myself. Ann (pseudonym) seemed to be a normal person, not at all what I expected from the woman who might have been at the farm with James.

Yet I was certain, upon closer inspection, that she was the woman I'd seen looking in our direction at the Lear lecture, so I tried a few innocent questions. I remarked that she looked familiar and asked if she'd been to any previous meetings. When she answered yes, I asked if she'd attended the Lear meeting, and again she answered that she had.

"That must be where I've seen you, then," I said. "Were you one of the ones who had to stand up?"

"Yes, I was," she confirmed, beginning to sense that my questions were leading somewhere. "Why?"

"Were you in the doorway, the front doorway near the podium?" I continued.

"Well, yes," she replied.

"And were you wearing a sort of blue sweater top?"

"This is very strange," she said, a little uncomfortably. "I don't remember what I was wearing, but I do have a blue top like you're describing and I could have been wearing it, I guess. What is this all about?"

"Nothing, really," I told her, afraid to go any further without James's positive identification that she was the one. "It's just that I remember seeing someone looking over in our direction several times, and I think it must have been you." And then, to change the subject, I asked if she'd ever been up to our town, since that's where the inter-dimensional woman had visited James.

She replied that she hadn't ever been there, though, so I quit trying to get relevant information from her. Instead, we talked about our respective backgrounds, marriages, children, and abduction experiences, although not in great detail. But when I heard that she was originally from St. Louis, an alarm went off in my head.

The only place James had ever seen the woman, other than the farm, was in the St. Louis area on his trip the previous summer. James and his entire family had come from there, and it seemed like a very big coincidence that this woman also was a St. Louis native. It now seemed extremely important to bring her and James together—I was certain she was the woman I'd seen at the Lear lecture—but I was still afraid to tell her that, much less to tell her why. It was clear that she was a victim of the abduction phenomenon, not a perpetrator, yet it was her image, I was convinced, that James's alien visitor had used. And his attendance at the Lear lecture, where he would spot this woman, had to be more than coincidence, too.

Facing a long drive back home, we finally left in the early morning hours, but we were too excited to go to bed right away. Still, the prospect of getting up early and driving back into the city for Mr. Hopkins's workshop was a good incentive, and the few hours of sleep we managed to get gave us new energy for the next day.

Ann was present at the workshop, again to our surprise, and it seemed fated that we should have more contact. After discussing it with Barbara and Casey, I decided to give Ann my phone number and ask her to call after she had finished with her regressions. I hoped she wouldn't question me about my motive, but she did, and my evasive answers probably made it seem that much more mysterious. I told her that it was important for us to talk, but that I didn't want anything I had to say to influence what she might find in her regressions, and finally she was satisfied enough to let the matter drop.

I hadn't had a chance to tell James about her yet, but at the workshop we managed to make a videotape which included her in the group. We couldn't wait to show it to James, and I had no doubt he'd identify her as the right person. But James wasn't easy to locate, and it was several days before the opportunity came up to have him view the video.

In fact, I saw Sandy, James's mother, before I could get in touch with him, and I told her excitedly about seeing the woman. She agreed that it was important for James to have a look at the videotape, and then, worriedly, she told Barbara and me about the reason her family hadn't come to the lecture. Just before time to leave, she said, James had called from the farm, very upset, so she asked him to come by. Once he arrived, he seemed almost desperate about something, refusing to go to the meeting, even implying self-destructive threats. Frantic to calm him down, his parents stayed home and talked with him and the other children about the situation.

Listening to Sandy's story, I wondered if James's actions hadn't been caused by fear, after the nightmares he had in which he saw his family violently destroyed. But I'd promised him I wouldn't tell anyone else, so there was no way I could offer an explanation to Sandy. Besides, I couldn't be sure that those dreams were responsible. James, from the beginning, was extremely reluctant to talk about his experiences. Even under hypnosis, he was slow to respond, frighteningly quiet, and his answers were frequently either monosyllabic or fragmented. I doubted that he would consider any more regressions for a long time, and I wondered if he had found it easier somehow, before breaking his long silence, to cope with the phenomenon when he assumed he was losing his mind. That, at least, was an understandable thing. It was a treatable condition. Alien abductions were not. If these encounters have taught us anything, it's simply this: Reality Isn't.

While Sandy was visiting with us, she and Barbara got to know each other a little better, and it came out that all of James's family were from the St. Louis area. Barbara was surprised and pleased, because she had grown up there herself. She was only two years older than Sandy, so their memories were of many similar places and things in St. Louis. And, as she is wont to do, Barbara managed to ask a few questions about Sandy's own experiences—missing time episodes, scars, health problems, recurrent dreams—and turned up an important new piece of information.

There was one dream, more a nightmare, Sandy told us, that had recurred throughout her life. The first time she'd dreamed it was when she was very young, perhaps five, and as she described the dream, I saw that Barbara's eyes got wider and wider. It was always the same dream: Sandy is standing very close to a dull gray surface, her face only inches away. The gray thing is an enormous sphere, so huge that in comparison Sandy is only a tiny dot. Something is drawing her into the sphere, but she is fighting against the urge, for she knows that if she ever enters the sphere, she will "never come back." This dream had first occurred when Sandy was seriously ill and there was a question of her surviving the illness.

She finished telling us about the dream, and Barbara's expression was very strange. "You are the first person I've ever met," she told Sandy, "who has seen the sphere."

"You've seen it, too?" Sandy asked in surprise.

"Yes, in St. Louis," Barbara replied, "when I was about five years old."

"What is it, do you know?" Sandy wondered.

"Well, no, I'm not sure," Barbara answered evasively and changed the subject. But it was clear that she knew more than she was willing to say. When we were alone, however, on our way to take her to the airport, I immediately asked her about the gray sphere. "I've never told anyone about this," she said. "That's why I couldn't believe it when Sandy started describing the thing! Our experiences must have been very similar."

"Why didn't you want to tell her about it, then?" I asked.

"I didn't want to frighten her," Barbara explained. "When I was taken to the sphere, I was told that it was 'a repository for souls,' where human souls are somehow recycled. If that's the same thing Sandy saw, I guess she wouldn't have come out of that sphere alive."

I agreed that there was no need to worry Sandy with this information, but we both hoped that at some future time she would decide to undergo regression. There were several unusual experiences Sandy had remembered, all indicative of alien encounters. But that would have to wait for a later visit. Meantime, I finally tracked down James and played the videotape from the Hopkins workshop.

"You have to remember," I warned him, "that she doesn't look exactly the same as she did the first time we saw her. Her hair is different, and she looked really worn out at the lecture, so her face isn't quite the same, either."

I fast-forwarded the tape until Ann appeared, and then I stopped it. "That's her, isn't it?" I asked confidently, watching James's face for the spark of recognition I was sure would come.

His eyes seemed to glaze over as he stared momentarily at the screen, and then he looked away.

"Isn't it?" I repeated.

He shook his head faintly. "I'm not sure," he mumbled softly, and then, "It's not her."

"She looks different, I told you," I said. "Watch it again. I'm sure she's the woman I saw at the Lear lecture." I played the tape again, but James wouldn't look at the television screen.

"It's not her," he said.

"Well, she was standing in the doorway, I know for a fact," I argued. "Did you see any other woman who looked similar standing in the same doorway?"

James was silent.

"She even told me she has a sweater like the one you said David described!" I kept on. "How can you be so certain it's not her?"

"It's not her," was all he said, and I left in frustration.

Everything pointed to this woman as the right one, I knew, and I couldn't understand how James could say she wasn't. David, Casey, and I had all been fairly sure, even though we'd only noticed her casually. And there hadn't been another woman who even came close to the description of the figure in the doorway, only this one.

To be honest, I just didn't believe that James was telling the truth. It was understandable that he might deny her identity as a way of pushing the phenomenon out of his life. It had been six months, after all, since he had last encountered the inter-dimensional woman, and he must have hoped it would never happen again.

Barbara, however, thought it might be that James's denial was a manipulated reaction rather than his deliberate choice. She had worked with cases in which abductees showed sudden and unprecedented personality changes during times of frequent alien contact. And, even more disturbing were the cases where abductees seemed to be under direct outside control of their speech and actions. In these cases, the abductee's own personality or consciousness is "put on hold" and a separate intelligence takes over. Such things had happened to James in the past, we knew, as on the hill near St. Louis when he couldn't physically control the direction he drove, or take his camera and recorder out of the car trunk. And it had certainly happened to David that August night at the farm when the change in his demeanor had frightened Megan.

Whatever the reason, James denied the woman's identity. But a few days later, when a few people, including Ann, were planning to visit, I begged James to at least drop by and meet her face-to-face, and he reluctantly agreed. Both cars arrived at the same time, and I watched out the window to see his first response to her. He never looked up at the three women who walked to the door ahead of him, however, and once he was inside, the woman had already disappeared into the bathroom.

James was noticeably nervous. He asked for a glass of water and took a couple of hasty sips, staying in the kitchen while the other two women and I talked. When Ann returned to the living room, I introduced her to James. She looked directly at him and smiled as she said, "Hello. I guess we really ought to talk."

James mumbled something in return, but again he refused to look at her. His uneasiness was so clear that I began talking to Ann and the others about something different, and James went back into the kitchen. A moment later I followed him and asked if he still thought she wasn't the right one.

"It's not her," he said, shaking his head emphatically. "I can't stay, I have to go somewhere." And before I could respond he hurried past the women and out the door.

It didn't make sense. If Ann really didn't look like the inter-dimensional woman, James should have been very relieved. He should have relaxed, yet he was extremely uncomfortable the whole time and seemed almost in a panic by the time he left. As it turned out, James didn't come back to our home for a long time after that day. In the fall and winter, we'd had frequent contact, so his prolonged absence was noticeable, and regretted.

A few days after Barbara left, David got a strange phone call at the farm. From his description of the sounds on the other end, the call was very much like the one I got on May 2, 1988, while Casey was under hypnosis. At first, he said, he could hear only a distant static, and then an unrecognizable "voice" made a series of screeching and hacking-cough sounds. David said he was sure the noise wasn't electronically produced, but he had no idea what it was.

As March drew to a close, things seemed relatively calm, and except for a few new small punctures, we noticed nothing out of the ordinary. On the night of the thirtieth, we decided rather late to drive out north of town and look at the stars. The weather wasn't too chilly, and the sky was clear, so we meandered through a sparsely populated area where low hills blocked the lights of town, giving us a much clearer sky for gazing. After a short while, however, we drove back home and went to bed.

The next morning, Casey got up for work but let me sleep in late. I woke up momentarily to tell him good-bye, and when I fell back asleep I had a very strange dream. The setting was a familiar large house, divided into various sizes of suites, and I had several times in the past had memorable dreams that occurred in this same structure. But in this dream, the house had been expanded, with a new motel-like row of rooms connected to the original building by a long, spacious hallway. The manager, a short, stocky man in a tight-fitting blue suit, guided me down the hallway, but I stopped to go into a restroom along the way. I sat down on the toilet and then saw that the manager had followed me into the room. I was flustered, wondering why he didn't know enough to stay out of the ladies' room, and then I saw we weren't alone.

Beside the toilet was a small alcove with a seat and a tiny white table, and sitting there were two women. I was startled, but the women made no move to leave or even to speak to me. They talked to each other very softly, their heads close together, in a quiet chirping sound, and I thought they seemed Oriental, wearing long black wigs. I was ready to get up from the toilet, so I asked the manager to leave the room. Before he could move, however, the door swung open violently and a tall, thin man stepped through, glaring at me.

I was terrified, unable to move, and then the tall man suddenly bent his body in half, unnaturally, bringing his head down to the level of my feet. He peered up at me, saying nothing, but I saw that he'd stuck two of his fingers into the fiery jets burning in a gas space heater.

"Get him out! Get him out!" I screamed at the manager, but the man stayed bent down, heating his two fingers. Suddenly I knew that he was going to plunge those burning fingers into my brain, through my temple, and I went crazy with fear. His hand left the heater as he moved up to grab my head, but I cried out, "I want to wake up now!" The dream vanished, and I woke up in bed trembling.

Barbara had told me months before about the numerous "bathroom" dreams turning up among her cases, but I'd never had one before. I didn't know what it meant, and I certainly hoped I would never have another one. When I undressed and went to take a shower, I found a new scratch on my lower left abdomen, below my waist, about an inch long and horizontal, perfectly straight. By now, I'd had so many anomalous scratches, bruises, cuts, and punctures that I didn't give this new mark much thought. But when Casey came home from work, he told me he'd also found a new mark in the shower. His right shin was scraped horizontally in a one-and-a-half-inch broken line, almost an eighth of an inch wide.

"It was still really bloody when I first found it," Casey told me, "but I don't remember hitting it or scraping it at all."

From the size of the scrape it was clear that he'd have surely felt quite a bit of pain from the injury, certainly enough to remember doing it. The sheets were still on the bed, so we drew back the cover and searched for any spots of blood, to see if his leg somehow might have been injured while he was still in bed, but the sheets were clean. And later, looking back through the journal I was keeping I noticed that this was the third time Casey had gotten out of bed with a raw, bloody scrape on his right shin and no known explanation.

CHAPTER 12

In April, the occurrence of physical marks on our bodies dropped off drastically. On the fifth, I found a small scratch on my left kneecap that I couldn't account for, but for almost the next three weeks neither Casey nor I found any anomalous marks. Strange things continued to happen, however, and we wondered if they were in some way related to the UFO-ET phenomenon.

One of the incidents in particular captured my imagination, and now, over a year later, having learned a bit more about possible UFO technology, I believe it may indeed be important. After going to bed as usual on the sixth of April, I awoke sometime later in the night, and I soon began to hear music in my head.

I wondered momentarily if I were generating the music myself, but it was so unfamiliar and such a surprise that I didn't think so. Besides, the music had a very concrete quality about it, as clearly heard as music coming through perfectly balanced headphones would be. It was possible, then, that something might be sending the sounds into my thoughts, either by accident or design. I do know that I was not asleep, as I tested my reality several times, opening my eyes, sitting up and moving around.

I heard the music very clearly, for a sustained period of time. It was like synthesized music, light and airy and beautiful, with a strange rhythm and quick succession of notes. As I listened in amazement to this music, I began to "see" a rectangular shape, like a piece of paper, on which the notes traced out ephemeral designs in various colors. The rectangular image and the note designs, like the music itself, I experienced internally rather than through sensory input, yet I saw them clearly.

Then I began to hear other things. As if a radio dial were being moved up and down the frequency bands, I picked up bits and pieces of various voices, none of which I recognized. The words made no real sense, just snippets like, "Hey, brother!" in one instance, and another voice that sounded like someone trying to talk in a computerized voice. That was followed by more music, and then the voices started up again, and finally the music returned for a little while longer. It stopped quite suddenly, and before long I fell asleep again.

At the time, I could make no sense of the experience. But through another researcher I've since learned that military intelligence and research may well have a way to monitor information transmitted by alien technology directly into the human mind. Alien communication with humans has traditionally been telepathic, and in the past few years there has been a steady increase in the number of people claiming to receive telepathic or "channeled" information from beings who identify themselves as ETs.

If this is the case, then I can think of at least one situation which might explain the music and voices I heard that night. Perhaps the music was transmitted to me by aliens, for whatever reason, and then the military monitoring of such transmissions could have targeted that particular communication. With its own equipment tuning to the same frequency used by the ETs, the military's own broadcast could also have been received by me, at least partially, accounting for the succession of excerpted conversations I heard. Whatever the case, at the time I was simply intrigued by the experience, by the beautiful music and the designs it made.

A second event in the middle of April was much less pleasant but just as intriguing. Friends arrived from England to visit us for a few days, with their thirteen-year-old son Tim (pseudonym). It was Dan and Kay's (pseudonyms) first visit to Texas, so we showed them the most interesting places around. We also told them a little about our ongoing involvement with alien intruders, being careful to avoid such talk whenever Tim was present.

On the third night of their visit, Tim asked if he could sleep with the overhead light on in my stained-glass workroom, where we made his bed each night. When Kay asked him why, he was reluctant to answer any more specifically than that he had felt frightened the night before. We turned on a small lamp, said good night, and closed the door. Our home is rather small, with all three bedrooms connected by a single small hallway, and Kay and Dan were sleeping in the corner room, with Tim to their north and our own bedroom to the east.

The next morning, Sunday, was hectic. Our friends planned to leave later in the day, so another friend dropped by early to visit with them. While they all sat in the living room talking, I went into the kitchen to clean up, and then I headed down the hall to make my bed. When I walked past the door to the workroom, I noticed that the lower half was covered with a brownish-red substance splattered and dripping from the knob all the way to the bottom of the door. I bent down for a better look and saw that there were also a series of smudges in a line down the white painted door, but I couldn't imagine what might have made them. They were larger and squarer than adult fingerprints, and there was nothing human about them, no patterns of ridges and whorls and lines. Instead, each smudge had wide, erratic globs of the substance in uneven horizontal rows.

To this day, I am amazed at what I did next. Instead of calling attention to the door, my mind quickly raced through the possible explanations. That someone might have spilled a drink was the first thought, but I knew that we hadn't served anything resembling this substance. Also, our guests were the sort who would immediately clean up any mess they made. Then I wondered if someone had accidentally been cut or injured. The brownish-red color and the thick consistency of the stuff most resembled blood, but surely, I realized, if anyone had been injured enough to bleed this much, I would have heard about it.

Ruling out those possibilities, I was left with a very bad feeling about the stains and smudges, and all I could think to do was to clean it all up before anyone else saw it. Most of all, I didn't want Tim to be frightened, especially after his uneasiness of the night before. So I grabbed a damp cloth and a can of scouring powder and quickly began washing the door. Just as I was almost finished, I suddenly realized that I was destroying evidence of some as yet unexplained event. I stopped, staring at the dirty rag in my hand and feeling extremely stupid. Now there was no chance to test and identify the substance, and I couldn't even take a photo of the stains. Down at the bottom of the door I noticed a few splatters that weren't entirely gone, so I left them, determined to tell Casey about the door after our guests had left. A few days later, when our friends phoned from Florida before flying back to England, I asked them if anyone had been injured while they were at our house. As I expected, the answer was no. With the possibilities of injury and spilled drinks ruled out, I was determined to find out exactly what had dripped down the door. I contacted a pathology lab and a forensics lab, hoping someone could test the residue on the rag, but I was told that the presence of the scouring powder and the minute quantity of the reddish substance still left on the rag would make testing a worthless effort. So the stains on the door still remain unexplained. They may have had nothing to do with our ET episodes, but they are part of a whole group of strange events, seemingly meaningless occurrences, that are as puzzling as the UFOs.

Twice in 1989, for instance, one of our dogs was inexplicably moved from an enclosed area during the night. In the first case, our thirteen-year-old dog Asha, who was mostly deaf and completely blind, was put in the far backyard behind a locked gate for the night, while our younger dog Honey slept in the garage to keep her barking from disturbing the neighbors. The garage door was closed securely, although not locked. When Casey went into the garage the next morning, the garage door was ajar and Asha was in the small storeroom on Honey's bed. Casey went out back and saw that the gate was still-latched, so he couldn't understand how Asha could have appeared in the garage. On another occasion, we were awakened by Honey barking in the backyard one Saturday morning, after she had been locked in the garage the night before, and once again the gate was still shut.

When Barbara came back in May to do more regressions, a series of odd events took place, involving the bathroom light. Whenever guests are sleeping in the house, we leave the front bathroom light on. But on the first two mornings of her visit, when I awoke I noticed that the bathroom light was turned out. I assumed Barbara had gone to the bathroom during the night and flicked out the light behind her, so I didn't mention it until the third morning. I asked her about the light, and Barbara assured me that she had not turned the light off any of the previous nights. In fact, when she had gotten up once to go to the bathroom and found the light off, she assumed one of us had turned it out after she'd gone to bed.

So that night we all three stood together in the bathroom, turned on the light, and agreed to leave it on until morning. We said goodnight and went into our bedrooms, closing both doors. Casey and I brushed and undressed for bed, and I inserted my ear plugs as usual, since I'd become a very light sleeper through the past stressful months. We turned out the bedroom light, and then a few minutes later Casey raised up and called out, "Good night, Barbara."

"Why did you say that?" I asked him, knowing that Barbara couldn't hear him in the guest bedroom. "She just yelled 'good night' to me," he explained, and we went to sleep shortly after that.

I was the first one up the next morning, and when I opened the bedroom door, I saw that the bathroom light was out once again. Knocking loudly on Barbara's door, I roused her long enough to ask if she'd turned out the light, but she said no. Casey was up by now, and he also denied touching the light switch or even getting out of bed during the night, and I knew that I hadn't, either.

A few minutes later, Barbara emerged from the bedroom. She said that after we all went to bed the night before, she'd gone back to the bathroom for a moment, and that the light was turned out then. So she called out from the hallway, "The light's out," hoping one of us would open the door and explain. Casey had misunderstood her, thinking she had simply said good night again, so he didn't bother to get up.

The light, apparently, had been turned off only minutes after we left the bathroom, and we had no idea what was doing it, or why.

We had little time to dwell on the mystery of the light, however, with people coming out daily for regressions. Barbara had also scheduled another session with David, hoping to find out what had left the multiple scratches and welts on his leg the previous November. She put him under and directed him back to look at "a significant experience" he had that month. David instead began talking about an earlier event, one that took place the night of October 31. The scratches hadn't turned up until November 8, but Barbara followed his choice to examine the October event since it seemed to be important to him.

David had told us about that night right after it happened, and I had noted it in my journal. What he consciously remembered was waking up around 2 A.M. with a headache and going to the bathroom for aspirin. He noticed that all the lights in the farmhouse were turned on, except in the two bedrooms, and that the radio was playing in the living room. James had been away when David and Megan went to bed, but David now saw that James was asleep in his own room by the bathroom, so he figured that James had been careless and forgotten to turn everything out when he went to bed.

David also remembered waking up again at some point, being unable to move in any way. He said he had seen some strange things with his eyes closed: a scene of a tan world, with tan sky, ground, and buildings; and a night scene when he was looking at some tall, thin structure covered with dark fur. After that, he couldn't remember going back to sleep, but he woke up the next morning feeling extremely drained. Megan also said she felt very tired, as if she hadn't gotten any rest, although she didn't remember waking up.

That was all David had recalled, but under hypnosis he remembered much more. After describing getting out of bed, going to the bathroom, and seeing all the lights on, David told Barbara that he was feeling pain at the base of his neck, but eventually he lay back down. Barbara took steps to deepen the trance and his ability to recall events, and then she moved him back slightly in time to a point before he woke up.

He described himself lying down on his back, unable to open his eyes but aware of a bright light in the room. "Can you tell where this light is coming from?" Barbara asked.

"I think it's from behind my head," David answered. "My head is tilted back. That's why it feels like it's behind me."

"Your head is tilted back, then. How far back?" Barbara asked. "You mean, you're not on a pillow?"

David's description of his bed was highly unusual and nothing like the bed he sleeps in at the farm. "There's something underneath my shoulders," he explained, "supporting underneath my shoulders, so my head's tilted back. My arms are kind of off to the side, hanging. My head is hurting, because my head is resting on my head. Or it's tilted back and resting on something hard, kind of on the back part of my head. And there's pressure on it."

"Are you wearing clothes?" Barbara asked.

"I don't know," he replied. "I don't have any socks on, because I can feel something, it feels like metal, almost smooth. Like in a doctor's office."

"Are you aware of any presences other than yourself?"

"I can't hear anything," David said, "but it's not like I'm in a room and there's no noise. It's just real distorted, shielded, or like underwater. I can hear something, barely. Just a kind of high-pitched whirring, like vents, or aspiration. And then every couple of seconds there's a zoooont sound." He laughed slightly. "I can't do it right," he apologized.

"What kind of temperature do you feel?" Barbara probed.

"It's cool. This thing under my shoulders is kind of soft but rigid, like a piece of plastic foam or something. It's not metallic. My feet are cold on this hard surface. I can feel my heels resting on it. My head is on it. Where my arms are touching it, it seems real sharp."

"Is it a solid plane?" Barbara continued.

"Except underneath my shoulders," he said. "I'm kind of lifted up off of it." His face changed momentarily before he continued. "I just got a prick on my forehead," he said then, "like a little scratchy something, pointed. It's right in the middle of my forehead, right above my eyes, between the eyebrows. And it's sitting there."

"What is it?" Barbara wanted to know.

"All I can picture is something that looks like, shaped like, a pair of headphones. There's some sharp thing coming, and it's placed on my forehead. I can't really focus on it. The sharp thing is coming down off this thing, the hoop thing—it's not a whole hoop—it's kind of fuzzy."

"Tell me what it's doing," Barbara urged. "Is it touching you now?"

"No," David answered, "the sharp line, thin blade type thing, is attached to it, so it's part of it."

"Does it touch your skin? Analyze it," Barbara directed him.

"It's gone," he told her. "Just pulled down. I can see some motion. Something's behind my head. Everything's very out of focus."

"Why are you blinking your eyes?" Barbara asked.

"It feels like my pupils are dilated. Like they do at the eye doctor's," he explained. "I wake up, and I'm tilted up like I said. Something is fiddling with my left wrist, and it's uncomfortable. Just feels like my hand is being held up a little, and it feels like maybe a needle or something is in my wrist. I can feel my hand resting on something real smooth but sticky, kind of."

"What do you think it is?"

"Feels like a snakeskin or an eel skin, like a belt," he said. "It's dropped. It's stopped doing whatever, but my arm, my forearm over there feels kind of tingly or like it's been Novocained, kind of burning, tingling, and it pretty much stops at my elbow."

"It's tingling from the elbow down?" Barbara echoed.

"Yeah," David told her, "and I don't like that. It didn't hurt so much, but it was uncomfortable."

"Do you know what's taking place when you're feeling that feeling?"

"Well, something pricked me for a few seconds, I guess. And then that started. Feels like getting a shot, or something."

"The needle would have penetrated specifically what area?" Barbara wanted to know.

"Right on the inside of my wrist, kind of off a little bit to the left of the center," he described.

"How long did that needle or whatever remain in your wrist?"

"Not long, maybe five seconds, less than ten seconds. That prick was kind of uncomfortable. It's just weird."

"How long does that remain that way?" Barbara asked.

"It's just going on and on. And then there's that pointy thing on my head. It's attached to a band. It was placed on my head, like a pair of headphones. Looks like a thin metal band that's bent in that shape, some kind of strange pad on the ends of it. And then from the middle comes out this wiry-looking thing that bends down to a real sharp point. And it kind of feels electrical or charged. And that's on there for, uh, it's still there. It doesn't hurt."

"David," Barbara interrupted, "can you mentally ask what this apparatus is for and why you feel the tingling in your arm?"

"They're connected," he answered. "I just felt a tap on my foot. Flat, like the back of a spoon or something like that. Just 'tap' against the bottom of my foot. It was kind of hard."

"What else is going on with your feet?"

"Nothing. But my arm, that shot in my arm is for this thing up here to work," he told her, gesturing toward his head. "Ooh."

"What?" Barbara inquired.

"Well," he began, "I don't know. It's like the pads on the side are recording something. This whole thing is attached to something else. And then the pointy thing in the middle. It's like one is taking something out, and the other is putting something in. I don't know how I'd know that," he admitted, puzzled.

"What are you experiencing as this thing is recording?"

"Let's see," David hesitated, "I'm, I think I'm focusing on this pointy thing, and it's kind of angering me, and then that's when I get tapped on the foot. That kind of distracts me, because I try to bend my head up. Ah, but I can't. Yeah. Hmm, okay, I see the. ... I was getting intent on this pointy thing, and then it wasn't working right. Or it was interfering, so then I was tapped on the foot, but I couldn't see what was going on down there. Then," he finished, "my mind was kind of blank."

Barbara asked David to look more carefully at the entire situation, encouraging his ability to see the details with a clearer vision.

"I can feel a burning," David told her, "or a hot spot on my left knee, right on the inside of it. It's real intense." He described the source of the sensation as coming from an instrument "like a screwdriver, sort of."

"What's happening?" Barbara asked.

"I feel like there's something in my left knee, or it just feels swollen. Some kind of little tube running off the inside of my knee, off to something long, and it's thicker. It's like, now wait, it feels like it's sucking something out, but my knee feels kind of like my arm still does." He described the tube as clear and "thin, very thin, like fishing line," and it was his impression that something was being taken out of him rather than put in.

As he went back through the entire situation, David once again reached the point where the headphone apparatus was removed from his head.

"What was taking these things off and putting them on you?" Barbara queried. Thus far in the regression, although David had mentioned seeing movement beyond his head, he hadn't described any other beings. Barbara questioned him carefully, letting his own recollections emerge rather than leading him toward any single point of view.

"Off to the left I can see some kind of little boxy cabinet thing on the corner of the bed," David replied. "And it just stays there. I guess there's things on it or in it. I see that when I first wake up, because my eyes fly open.

"I just wake up. Open my eyes real quick. I'm in this strange position. I can see it, and it's kind of white, and the background is kind of white. I can't really move," he continued, "but I can move a little bit, so I'm trying to lift my arms up."

"Why can't you move?" Barbara questioned. "Do you feel restraints?"

"No," he said, "I just can't move. I can't even shake my head back and forth. Because it's sort of hard to breathe. I mean, I can. That's all I can see from here. I look over to the right, and it seems darker over there, but not much. That's all I'm seeing now. And I feel kind of, oh, apprehensive, but I'm not very skittish. I mean, I can think a little," he finished with a short laugh.

"Evidentally you're a little bit awake," Barbara commented, "a little bit attuned to what's going on."

"I feel real dead-weightish, though," he said.

"Remember when you put your hand on top of the kind of stick thing?" Barbara asked, "that felt like snakeskin?"

"Well, I didn't put it up, it was. . . . " David paused. "Yeah, see, that's what happened next. It's like something lifted up my hand, maybe two inches. It's just resting there. Then kind of pulled the hand back a little. I guess it's a hand that's holding mine. Feels like a hand that's in a mitten. It's holding my hand from the side, and I can feel it pull back. It's lifted up a little, so it can stick something in my wrist."

Barbara questioned him about the description of "snakeskin" or "eel skin" he'd mentioned earlier.

"That's the texture of this thing," he explained, referring to the hand which was holding up his own. "I can feel the texture of it, kind of like eel skin. It's smooth but kind of got a stickiness to it."

Assuming there must be more of a being present than just the hand, Barbara pursued a better description. "Does it have any moisture to it?" she asked.

"No. I mean, it's hard to tell."

"Does it communicate with you in any way?"

"Huh-uh."

"Do you ever get to look at it?"

"No, I don't leave this position."

"Is there just one?" Barbara asked.

"No," David told her.

"How many?"

"That one," he replied, referring to the one holding his hand, "and one or two more, and then the other one, which is what puts the thing on my head."

"Does he look like the rest of them?" Barbara questioned, wondering why David had singled him out from the others.

"I can't see," David began hesitantly. "It walks over from right to left behind me, takes that thing off that, uh, boxy-looking thing, so I can see its body. Because I'm looking down towards the floor, sort of."

"What do you see?"

"I can kind of see it when it crosses. I can see its abdomen area, I guess. It's just, maybe, a foot across, or about that, maybe a little more. Seems real smooth and skinny. And then below that is some kind of, it looks kind of like a belt, but it's wide because it's, I can just see the top of it. It's dark-colored, kind of like an orangy-brown. And I can't see anything on it. I can only see the top edge, and it looks, I don't know, solid, not woven, and above that it's whitish."

"Is there a covering on the body?" Barbara asked.

"Well, it might be a covering, " David admitted, "because all I can really see is the top of this belt-looking thing. I just say it's a belt, I don't know what it is. It's in that region. And then just kind of a whitish color above that, but I can't see. I can see an arm when it brings over the thing. It's very, very thin, and it looks like it's got an oversized hand on it. It's pinching this thing between, like, two fingers, but one of them's big, and one of them's small."

When Barbara asked him if this being differed from the others, David replied, "It seems bigger, but it's an odd kind of view. It's hard to judge size, because it doesn't really touch me. It just places that thing on."

"How are your legs? Are they straight out?"

"I think they're straight out like they are now," David indicated. "And just the feet are up. They're spread apart a little, like that. I can tell that my feet are like this, because when that one—there's this one over here," he motioned, "and there's at least another one, because I can sense motion over that direction, too—and that's the one that taps me on the foot."

Barbara questioned him for other details about his surroundings. He mentioned once again his distorted sense of hearing; he described the room as having an "amorphous" shape and being ten to fifteen feet across; and he commented, rather sadly, "I don't know anyone else here."

"Are there humans?" Barbara asked.

"I don't think so," he answered. "I feel in the middle of it. Because this one behind me seems kind of hunched over, a little."

"Is that one behind you the same as the others?"

"I can't really tell. It seems big. I mean," he explained, "the one over here seems small."

Barbara asked him to describe the one behind him, to which he replied, "It's got extra-long arms for how tall it is. A very strange body shape. It looks like it's too thin, and it looks like it's wearing a mask."

"How tall is it?" Barbara wanted to know.

"Almost as tall as the room, six feet tall, maybe, over here, anyway," he said. "The room's probably taller in the middle. It seems darker down there. There's something blocking the light. Some kind of thing up towards the ceiling in the middle of the room. Seems flat."

Returning to his description of the being behind him, David added, "It's got a mask on, I think, because its bottom half of its face is smooth, like it had a handkerchief wrapped around it."

"What's the body shape like?" Barbara queried.

"Like a pencil," he told her. "It's sort of cylindrical. It kind of tapers off up towards the neck. It's got a real elongated mouth space, kind of pointy, and then round eye spaces, which are big. They're real big. The bottom part of its face seems to be covered with something, skin-type, and the eyes are kind of dark and round. I can't see all of them. They seem to wrap a little back, and there's some kind of bony, like a bony ridge, or just a little lip on top of the eyes.

"It's looking right at me," he went on, "and it's not really scary. Ah, I can't really tell any emotions right now, it's just kind of there, but it looks right at me when it reaches over. I could see it reach to pick up that thing, so I move my eyes over and watch that. It's got real spindly arms. It doesn't ever take its eyes off mine."

"This is when it's putting the band on your head?" Barbara asked. "Give me a better reading on those hands now."

"They're wider than the arm. The arm is like a thin tube, bigger than a broom handle but not much. They're kind of flat and wider than that, but still not as wide as my hands. And there's one long finger that I can see, and then a thumb-like thing which is not off to the side. Our thumbs are on the side of our hand," he explained. "It's like in the middle of the wrist it comes out [on the being]. I can't see any fingernails. One finger's kind of thick and big, and the thumb is stubby and pointy, so it might have a nail. But I'm not really looking at the hand. I'm looking at that thing that it's holding, the band."

Barbara asked David to go through his recollections one last time, noting the order of events. When David had awakened during his encounter, the tube was already in his knee. He then felt the burning sensation of the thin wire inserted into his wrist, and finally the headphone apparatus was placed on his head. As the band was being positioned, David looked directly into the face of the being behind him, but his attention was distracted by the sharp, bent wire on the headphone which came down to his forehead. At that point, he felt a sharp tap on the bottom of his foot and momentarily forgot what was going on. His last memory in that place was of the headphone being removed, and then he was aware of a pricking sensation in his abdomen and found himself in his own bed at the farm.

Although Barbara questioned him about how he got from the farm to the other room and back again, David couldn't remember anything helpful. So after a few questions about his feelings, Barbara brought him out of the regression and waited while he drew sketches of the strange bed and also of the being he'd seen behind him. It bore no resemblance to the usual image of the Grays, nor was it especially reptilian. Instead, more closely than anything else, the creature David drew looked like a tall, pale-white praying mantis.

As I stared at the drawing, a vivid, frightening image from my childhood came back to me. I recalled being in a strange dark place, standing beside a tall creature whose hand rested on my shoulder. I remember looking up at what seemed to be a giant grasshopper and insisting, "You're not my mother! You're not my mother!" This scene haunted my nightmares for several years when I was very young, and it crushed me to think of the fear my own son must have felt as he lay helpless before such a being.

CHAPTER 13

Thus ended the first year of our involvement with this intriguing, terrible world that drew us into and beyond reality's fringe. But the strangeness continued on, the familiar scratches and punctures showed up again and again, and there were new kinds of odd events, all of which combined to fragment our old, comfortable perception of reality.

Going on with our usual occupations had grown easier, though, and we managed to keep our wits and our humor, no longer so afraid of the phenomenon as we once were. Hardly a day passed without one of us talking to another member of our small support group, reporting the latest episode of strangeness to someone we trusted to be sympathetic. And although much of what we continued to experience was common to most cases of alien intrusion, each of us still had our own unique scenarios.

Once, when most of us were going through a time of very little ET activity, Fred reported a high frequency of physical marks and possible alien presences. As often as three or four times a week, he called to tell us of yet another set of punctures, or of long, wide swaths of purple bruising across his back, or of poltergeist-like occurrences in his apartment.

Even for those of us with our own eerie episodes, it was hard to believe that Fred really could be having so many intrusive events. At one point, I remarked, "Fred, there must be an entire ship full of aliens looking after you! I just don't see how it's possible for all of those marks to come from ETs. Surely you must be inflicting some of them accidentally yourself. Nobody can have encounters so often."

Aliens must have been listening to this conversation and laughing, because the next morning I found new marks on my body, the first I'd had in quite a while. On the side of my knee was a red scraped area about half an inch long, and below it three more smaller scrapes formed a triangle. Although I didn't realize it at the time, this was the beginning of a twelve-day period in which I would receive a total of twelve new physical marks that I couldn't explain. Besides a number of bruises, single punctures, and scratches, I also found the triangle described above, a group of four punctures arranged in an arch, and a small triangle composed of four punctures with a fifth puncture at the triangle's apex. By the end of the twelve days, I no longer doubted that Fred's frequent scars were as inexplicable to him as mine were to me. The theory that such scratches and bruises result from natural, unnoticed accidents was disproven to me then.

Now with over four years' experiences to evaluate, I am certain that the physical marks come from a source other than the victim. During this time, we have scanned our bodies twice a day, morning and evening, noting every bump and cut we inflict upon ourselves and comparing them with the marks we find. The unexplained marks have repetitious patterns, while the accidental ones are more random. Similar or identical odd marks have turned up on more than one person, in situations where there was no contact between them. And we've also seen that during periods of little or no alien intrusion the number of physical marks found on the abductee's body is greatly reduced or altogether eliminated, which shouldn't be the case if the marks were all the products of mere clumsiness.

There was also a time in 1989 when several people, both in and out of the support group, "heard voices" when no one was actually present. In two instances, people heard their names being called repeatedly, and a third acquaintance heard a man's voice shouting, "Stop!" while she was in her car. During this same period, some of us also began to "see things" that weren't there. Sandy glanced out the front window and saw two men standing in her driveway one day, but when she went back for a second look only moments later, there was no one in the yard or on the street.

And there were other cases where people kept "seeing" something move in their peripheral vision field, something that was often described as dark and the size of a rabbit or a large rat. No such animal, of course, was ever actually found. The incidents genuinely didn't seem merely to come from poor eyesight or vision problems, and, like the hearing of voices in the summer of 1989, the "invisible rabbits" were a transitory phenomenon.

It was also during this time that my brother and his family made their first visit back home in over a decade. They stayed at my parents' home, located on a private lake in a rural area, where their two teenaged sons took full advantage of the fishing. One night, when my brother was fishing with them until almost 1:30 A.M., the lake suddenly became completely calm. Paul said it was so still and mirrorlike that when he flipped a cigarette butt into the water, there was absolutely no ripple. Even the insects had stopped buzzing.

Paul told the boys to pack up their gear, since the fish had stopped biting, but as they stood up to leave, the oldest boy, Richard (pseudonym), pointed up to the sky and asked, "What kind of plane is that?"

Having been in the Air Force, Paul was familiar with most types of aircraft, but he couldn't identify the formation of lights that were flying low in the sky above them. All of the lights were orange-yellow, and a single light led an amorphous group of several others. The lights covered a relatively large patch of sky, so Paul assumed that the craft must have been flying quite low, yet there was no sound. The three of them watched the lights for a few moments and then left the lake. As far as any of them remembered, nothing else happened.

But two days later at a family reunion, I noticed that the older boy, Richard, had several V-shaped scratches on his chest. I asked him how he had gotten them.

"I don't know," he shrugged. "I didn't know they were there until I took off my shirt a while ago."

Intrigued, I asked my younger nephew if he also had found any strange scratches lately, and I was surprised by the look on his face and by the way he reached back instinctively to shield his rear end.

"How did you know?" he asked.

"I didn't know," I assured him. "I just wondered. Where did you get the scratches?"

"I don't know," he replied. "And don't ask if you can look at them, because you can't."

I agreed with a laugh and dropped the subject, but I wondered if there might have been more to their experience on the lake. The unexplained scratches on my nephew's chest were uneasily similar to the marks we'd seen before on Casey and David.

When the second year had passed, I wondered if our involvement would ever end. It seemed unlikely, as my contact with UFO researchers who studied abduction cases showed the phenomenon was spreading. And so was the media interest in UFOs and ETs, to judge by the increased number of reports in newspapers and, most noticeably, on television. In 1988, after we became aware of the phenomenon's presence in our lives, we began to pay attention to the media's references to UFOs and aliens.

It first struck me when I saw the Canon camera commercial televised during the summer Olympics coverage, where an alien who looks very much like a typical Gray uses the camera in his spacecraft. And then other advertisements began playing on the alien theme, from Tropicana Twister to Levi's Dockers and Tide detergent. Through 1988 and 1989, UFO sightings and abduction stories turned up in greater and greater numbers on the television talk shows, and the tabloid news programs such as "Inside Edition," "Hard Copy," and "Current Affair" aired reports on sightings and encounters around the country. Even children's television had its share of ETs. Gumby and Dennis the Menace were both abducted by Grays, and a Saturday morning special showed a cartoon version of the book Grinny, an evil alien android here to conquer and enslave humanity. It seemed as if the information and entertainment media decided to promote nationwide awareness of UFOs and alien presences, and we couldn't help but wonder why. Was there an urgency to our mass acceptance of ETs?

In 1990, although our personal direct encounters were rare, evidence of the phenomenon sometimes showed up. Both Casey and I woke with claw marks in January, for instance. And on Saturday, February third, I saw another UFO, viewing it from the same hill where Casey had been abducted in 1987. For eleven minutes I watched a brightly glowing ball of light bobbing along leisurely at a very low altitude from the west to the southeast, as easily identifiable aircraft passed overhead toward the metropolitan airport. The light was less than a mile away, for it passed between my vantage point and the buildings downtown, bobbing like a float on water but lower than the 19-story tower behind it. Unlike my response to the UFO I'd seen in Oklahoma in 1988, this time I wasn't afraid. In fact, I felt exhilarated and ready for a conscious encounter, and my hopes for a face-to-face meeting rose when the light began to move toward me. That movement lasted only a few moments, though, and then it returned to its original path and continued on to the southeast.

The following Saturday, James's parents pulled off the interstate at the edge of town to watch a triangular craft soar above them, unlighted but covered on the bottom with closely packed circular designs. And another swift-moving erratic light made sharp angular turns high in the sky above Casey and me in August as we watched the stars on a very clear night.

Nothing more personal interrupted our lives, however, until June. One morning we both discovered new punctures and bruises on our arms and legs, but the night had been peaceful as far as we consciously knew. A week later, though, we were awakened from a deep sleep by loud clicking sounds, yet we saw nothing in the room. The next day we discovered more marks on our bodies: two bruises and a pinpoint scab on my upper right arm, and a small, straight cut on Casey's inner thigh. The clicking sounds were all that seemed out of the ordinary, but the marks were inexplicable.

The intruders returned in late November. Sandy, James's mother, experienced an hour's missing time from 8:30 to 9:30 P.M. on the twenty-ninth, and then after going to bed that night she had a direct encounter. Waking around 3 A.M., she felt compelled to leave her husband and her bed to lie down on one of the couches in the den. Her dog, a large, protective animal, slept on the other couch as Sandy dimmed the light and covered herself with a knitted throw for warmth. She dozed off but was suddenly alerted by something tugging on the throw, both at her feet and also near her head.

Too afraid to open her eyes and look at whatever was beside her, Sandy found the courage to resist. She yelled, "Boo!" very loudly, and the tugging on the cover stopped momentarily. When it began again, she yelled, "Boo! Boo! Boo!" until the tugging ceased. Moments later, she opened her eyes and looked around the dimly lighted room, catching sight of a shadowy movement receding from her towards the kitchen. The dog still slept undisturbed nearby, oblivious to her shouts. Then suddenly he sprang up from the couch, as if released from some invisible restraint, and looked around in fright. He tucked his tail beneath his belly and darted from the den into the living room, burrowing under and behind the sofa. Whatever happened next was lost to Sandy's consciousness, but the next day her abdomen was extremely sore.

"It feels as if it's been stretched," she told me in puzzlement, "or inflated like a balloon."

I asked if there were any unusual marks on her body, and she nodded, showing me a circular mark at the base of her spine, with a straight cut inside the circle.

Sandy wasn't the only one. In her family to whom the experiences returned that winter. James had moved into a trailer park on the outskirts of town, and in January 1991, after months of no activity, he once again found himself under siege.

Barbara Bartholic came for a visit that month, and when I told James she would be in town he said he wanted to see her. This was quite a change in his attitude. Since late 1989 he had tried to put the whole series of incidents out of his mind and had steadfastly refused to discuss it with anyone, even his parents. Now, however, he was anxious to see Barbara.

When he arrived at our home, the two of them talked privately for over half an hour, and then he agreed to tell me about his recent experiences. It began with his awakening after midnight on January 3, jumping out of bed and throwing on his clothes, feeling a sense of great urgency. But he had no idea what had awakened him or what the emergency might be. In bewilderment, he undressed and went back to bed. The same thing happened again the following night, and for several nights thereafter, and each time he was compelled to go a little farther until he was actually rushing out into the street, frightened but unable to resist the urgent push.

"It was really scary," he told us, "and I never could figure out what I was rushing outside for. I'd get to the street like I was running from a fire or something, but I had no idea why."

These strange episodes stopped when he had a disturbing "dream" experience. "I was out in the street," he said, "and I saw this group of beings coming toward me real fast, maybe nine or ten of them. They shoved me down on the ground, and I tried to get away, but I couldn't. Then one of them took out this long tube and forced it into my mouth. It went down my throat and into my stomach. I was gagging and choking, and when they pulled it up it left an awful taste in my mouth, real bitter. Then another being came up and made those first ones leave me alone.

"But last night," James continued, "I had another dream, and it scared me more than that one did. This time I was outside again, and I saw a beautiful blond woman facing me. She was really pretty and looked totally human. And she was acting sort of sexy and alluring to me. She held out her arms like she wanted to hug me, so I went to her.

"I thought she was going to kiss me, but when we got really close together, it all changed. She wasn't pretty anymore, and she damn sure didn't look human. It was ugly, whatever it was."

"What did she look like?" Barbara asked.

"Terrible," James replied, "real dark and bumpy, like there were warts all over the body. And slimy."

"Do you remember what happened next?"

"Yeah. I was going to kiss her, and then I saw it was this warty-looking creature and I got scared. And instead of kissing me, all of a sudden it shoved another one of those long tubes down my throat. I don't remember anything after that."

"How did you feel the next morning?" Barbara asked.

"Not too good," James admitted. "My throat was sore, and I had that awful, bitter taste in my mouth, like bile."

He turned around slightly and pulled his collar away from his neck. "I found these marks this morning," he said, and we saw three parallel scratches running across the side of his neck. It may all indeed have been a dream, but the marks were real.

And it made me wonder if the dream Casey had had a few nights earlier might have been more than the usual nighttime fantasies. He, too, had seen a beautiful blond woman, in fact a whole group of handsome blond people who looked completely human.

Casey's dream episode happened one night after we'd made love and then gone to sleep. In the dream, he got up—also after making love—to go to the bathroom, when he had the distinct feeling that someone was watching him.

He turned around and saw that the window by our bed had somehow been replaced with a clear opening from floor to ceiling, and he could see out back where a group of blond people were standing and watching him in silence.

"I felt somewhat attracted," he said the next day, "but also a little repulsed because I didn't like them looking at me so obviously, like I was just something to be examined. I understood what they wanted, but at the same time I felt like I was just a specimen."

During Barbara's visit, Casey took the opportunity to look at that dream under hypnosis, wondering if both he and James had experienced more than mundane dreams. In the trance, he was able to recall more details, and when Barbara asked him what he thought it might have meant, Casey's reply was very telling.

"I think those blond people were watching me and reminding me that it's time to go, it's getting very close to time to go," he said. "What seems to be going on is that these beings who've been with me so long have let me see they're still here. I see them in a clear light, not dimly, and I'm welcome, and they are familiar. It's getting very close to the time to actually do something, to leave here, this place, and to begin something new.

"I'm taking Karla with me, she's part of it all," he continued. "But we'll leave behind everything comfortable and familiar. There's a lot of others involved. Part of me likes them, but another part dreads their coming. We'll have to change forms. I was beckoned by them. They were familiar to me. Very real." And, as it turned out, Casey's interpretation was at least partly accurate, because four months later he was offered a new job, which he accepted, that required us to move to another state.

While Barbara was with us in January, I also took advantage of her visit to undergo another regression, even though I had no recent puzzling experience to explore. It seemed useful to check for any hidden awareness I might have had that could shed light on Casey's dream of the blond people. That was our intended goal for the regression, but once I was in the relaxed trance state, my mind surprisingly skipped back instead to the encounter I'd had in 1980 with the four shadow beings at the farm who claimed to be my ancestors.

When we began working with Barbara in 1988, I had tried to find out more about that strange experience, but the regression hadn't uncovered any more than I'd always consciously remembered. This time, however, my subconscious was ready to let the hidden memories surface. I've already recounted that event in Chapter One, at least the part I remembered, but I had never been able to fill in the entire forty minutes that the episode occupied. With Barbara's help, this time I learned much more.

The first new information concerned something these beings did to me while I was still out in the yard and saw them standing beneath a large tree. I was already under some sort of influence or control, aware of a shimmering, heavy quality to my body and my surroundings.

"Things look funny," I told Barbara as she led me through the experience again. "The grass is shimmering, and I hear something. 'Welcome'."

"Do you hear the word spoken?" she asked.

"No," I replied, "coming from my head. 'Welcome. We're glad you're here.' Somebody's got a hand up. It's like they're greeting me. It's hard to move. I think I stop because it's so strange. Somehow I look up, and there's one with his hand raised, and then there's three and they look like cut-out paper dolls. I'm seeing things. The male says they love me, real warm."

My description continued, as I told of my persistent skepticism while talking telepathically with the four gray, shadowy figures.

"I ask who they are, and I think they say I belong there with them. He says something about ancestors. I feel a little tense," I told Barbara, "but it's hard to feel real tense. And I think he's lying. I think I just made it up. I want to laugh, sort of, or make a joke. But I'm out by the tree with them. They're saying something about pockets of stuff, all over, and I'm just doubting everything."

"Pockets of stuff?" Barbara questioned, for this was the first time such a thing had come into my memory.

"Something about pockets," I repeated. "Little pockets—not like pockets in clothes. There are pockets of things all around, in some places. And I say, 'You're kidding me.' But he's very sure. 'No, no, I'm not kidding,' he says.

"I'm just pretty skeptical. They look very gray, and I'm wondering where their faces are. Don't seem to have faces. I can almost see through them. They say I have pockets in me, that's what it was, secret little pockets of storage."

"What about the pockets?" Barbara questioned.

"It's like something right inside over here," I told her, gesturing in the air near my body. "I can almost see something reaching down, but I don't feel it. They're reaching down looking for something."

"Is it down near your ovary area?" Barbara asked, prompted by my gestures.

"No," I tried to explain, "just beside me, like I've got some extra part of me that's beside my body they can sort of touch. I see this other part of me."

"Like a field?" she interrupted, "electromagnetic?"

"Yeah," I agreed, "or something like that. It's extended out away from me, a few inches. Something can be gotten out of there."

"You're aware they're doing something to the field around your body?"

"They're trying to make me see how to get these things, this stuff out, this material or information," I said. "I don't understand, and they say, 'Look, we put this information in you a long time ago. Because we are your kin, your ancestors, and you've got this information. You carry it in these secret pockets.'

"I think they mean DNA stuff, and I ask them if it's DNA, my code. They say, 'No, it's more like knowledge.' But it's all the knowledge, all their knowledge, and they want me to know how to bring it out of the pockets. And that makes very little sense, and I just don't really believe them.

"They say, 'You know everything that we've put there, if you can just get it.' I think they said, 'Tap it, tap it open,' and that's frustrating. I tell them I have to go in and make dinner. 'Can I go in now?' But they still want to talk about something else.

"'Why don't I already have those knowledges open? Why don't I already know everything, then?' And they say, 'You can open it up when it's necessary.'"

From this part of the experience, I then described going into the farmhouse and cooking the pot roast, just as I'd always recalled. And once again, new information emerged from the regression.

"When I first pick up the meat," I said, "the two men are standing in the door of the kitchen near the stove, and the women are behind me. I pick up the meat—I don't remember getting it out of the refrigerator. But now I have it. And that's where the women are. The women are in my field, they're in here with me. That's why I can't see them.

"So we pick up the meat, and I watch my hands. I'm just amazed that I do this thing. Like I'm sitting back watching what I'm doing but I'm not doing it. There's a very spiritual feeling, like, my God, this gift of meat! And it's so moving. I almost want to cry."

I did begin to cry, in fact, and Barbara questioned me about this surprising surge of emotion. "Why do you feel this?" she asked.

"Because something died for that," I replied, unable to control the tears. "It's so important. I feel like I've got to pray or give something back. And it's very serious. I wonder if they want me to give something back to them, and then I cry. I know about doing the food and what it means. I know it, and I do it, and sometimes they talk to me over there, and sometimes they don't.

"They watch me do this, and I watch me do this because we're doing it together. Everything's on the stove after I've done it all, and I'm real satisfied. They felt very serious, but now the women are not in me anymore, and I feel sort of cut off."

I previously hadn't remembered the two females merging into my "field" and experiencing the cooking process with me. But I did recall the realization that they were no longer in the room when the cooking was completed. Barbara asked me to go back over this final part of the experience and try to explain where and when the beings left me.

"They're behind me, and I know they're there," I said. "I can almost see them now. Their hands are up here behind me, and they're making a noise, or something's making a noise like bees, like a hum that comes and goes in many sounds. That sort of bothers me. I asked them what that sound was. They said they were just talking to me, to this other pocket of my mind, and that it was okay, they were just instructing me. I wonder what they would be instructing me. And it isn't important that I know it right now, so it doesn't matter. I'm standing in front of the stove, and the humming gets louder. And now when I look up, the men are gone. I turn around, and the room is empty. It's sort of sad, and I just sit down."

Persisting, Barbara had me go through this part again, so I repeated, "I want to know why they're making that noise, and they won't tell me. And then I don't know where I am. And then the next thing I can see is I'm completely alone there. I don't know where they are, and I don't know when they went away, and I sit down. Something's hurting right here," I said, pointing to the middle of my forehead, "a pressure."

"Feel the pressure," Barbara told me, "and see its cause."

"I think that they came through my head," I answered, "from behind the head down at the base, is what I feel. It tingles and feels pushed on, real strong. I'm aware of it now, that something when I wasn't there pushed from inside my head up at that point."

"What do you mean, when you weren't there?"

"There was something that's missing," I tried to explain. "I wasn't there. I remember them making that sound, and it got loud, and then ... I don't know. Just nothing, nothing. I'm really alone."

"Look at the time gap," Barbara said. "What do you see?"

"I don't see," I insisted. "I'm not there."

"Is there an environment?" she asked.

"No. I'm not in a position. There's no noise now. I don't have a body, I don't have a feeling. It's just black."

No matter how hard Barbara tried to help me figure out this blankness, I couldn't, other than to feel that I was truly "out" of my body for some indeterminate period of time. So she asked me once again about the pockets.

"Something's been put into us that we don't know about," I replied. "That is prepared for opening up in the future. They're in the field around the body."

"What would be put into this field?" she asked again.

"It's a knowledge, sort of. Something is stored, it's a storage device. And we don't use it now, but something has to be opened up or set to open up. They were setting it. That's why they were rummaging around. But it wasn't ready yet to open up. They told me that these things would be opened up. They were getting me ready for using this stored thing, not yet, but getting me to know, showing me this secret."

For a long time after this regression, I wondered what the future might hold for me, for all of us, and what use this stored information would someday serve. The predictions made to James by the interdimensional woman echoed in my mind: we would all be used for some future tasks, participants in a battle yet to come, and I remembered that she had give a time frame of five years or less from 1988.

It was some consolation that the four "ancestors" had seemed so warm and loving toward me, but I was reluctant to trust them. How could I, without knowing more of their ultimate intentions? Throughout the experiences of many abductees, predictions have been made, many of which point to a coming time of great upheaval and destruction, but I kept telling myself that we would be foolish to believe the words of beings who take us without our permission and do things to us without explanation. If these experiences are for our benefit, I wondered, why can't they trust us enough to tell us what it all means? Deception and good intentions just don't seem to go together, at least in our human morality, and that was all I had to go on.

The lesson of human deception came home to us with great force later in 1991, when Barbara once again visited us. This time, however, it was Casey whose regression brought to light an even more surprising episode than those of alien abductions.

He and Barbara went into the regression with no specific event in mind to explore. By now we had learned that asking the subconscious to choose what to look at was usually quite productive, rather than trying to force a certain event into recall. But none of us, including Casey, expected his mind to focus on what had seemed, at the time, to be nothing more than a vivid and disturbing dream. It had occurred back in the winter of 1988, and he had already tried shortly afterward to look at it under hypnosis with no results.

In that dream, which had two apparently separate incidents, Casey was awakened in the night by the sound of a helicopter right over the house. He went outside and saw a dark cloud moving toward him as the whoop-whoop-whoop sound of the helicopter grew louder. Expecting to see the machine emerge from the cloud, Casey was shocked when a white Ford pickup showed up instead. The next part of the dream was of his moving down a narrow tunnel into a large underground opening. He found himself in what appeared to be an old western-type saloon, complete with a bar and several tables. He was sitting at one of the tables, along with several other men whom he knew, and he remembered thinking, "I guess maybe we're going to play poker." But somewhere in the dream he also recalled seeing large crates and boxes which looked to be of government or military origin.

Nothing about the dream made any sense, and when his first attempt to explore it in a regression didn't pan out, he forgot all about it. This time, in 1991, however, his subconscious opened everything up to him, and the results were shocking, even outrageous.

After reliving the initial encounter with the helicopter sound, the dark cloud, and the white pickup, Casey saw himself approaching a body of water. "The full expanse of my vision is of water with tall, marshy grass growing out of it in little tufted islands," he said. "You can see water rippling, agitated like wind's blowing across the top of the water. I'm looking down at a 45-degree angle, so I can only see water and grass and feel the wind. Like I'm coming in for a landing."

The next thing he recalled was entering a tunnel. "It felt like we went down into the ground," he told Barbara, "just falling. Such a narrow tube down into the ground. Real fast, standing on a little thing, falling down a circular shaft. And then stopping, outside of the cave, and then crossing over and walking back up part of the cave."

Inside this underground area, Casey saw "large, man-made storage tanks, with the building constructed into the side of the tunnel or the big cavern. Real sterile-feeling," he tried to explain, "but sort of musty and dusty. I can see lights really clear, and I'm right up next to a building. The wall that I'm next to is probably twelve feet high with narrow windows at the very top. I'm walking in through some doors, human doors, door knobs, like military stuff."

Barbara instructed him to proceed with the recall, once he felt certain that this was a real memory surfacing.

"Walking down a corridor," he continued, "guys with spongy boots on. We go into a room. Let's see if I can see what it's like," he paused. "Ah, my imagination just sees Mickey Mouse," he laughed. "That's Mickey Mouse. It's military, then," he explained, "because that's what I thought of the military."

"What does the place look like?" Barbara asked. "How does it feel and smell?"

"Kind of musty out in the cavern," he replied. "Dank, but this has a machine smell to it. On the inside it's very conditioned, very cleaned-up, though, filtered. There's something very significant about this waiting area. It was made up to look like a western saloon, but people are just sitting at tables, dumbfounded. Lots of people. What's going on? It seems like this is a human thing. I don't have any idea of any aliens in this place at all."

He described the "saloon" and its bar with no bartender and several little tables around which the people sat. "They're all just sitting there, sort of in a daze, like they've been drugged. Just waiting for somebody to come and take them away. The light is dim, and there's music playing. Not real loud, but it's like you're supposed to believe that this is not really happening, real dreamlike. But it's real solid."

Barbara asked if he recognized any of the others in the room, and he named David, our son, and a close friend, as well as others who seemed somehow familiar. But his next words were completely unexpected.

"I keep getting the feeling that there's a military officer there who's real angry," he said. "Real impatient. I don't have a face to connect with it, but there's a military officer that I'm not cooperating with. Yeah, I'm not cooperating, and they're real perplexed. Somewhat angry, but not authorized to be totally angry, holding himself back."

"I wonder what you're doing to antagonize him," Barbara replied.

"I'm not doing something that he wants," Casey said. "Maybe I'm coming out of it too fast. Because I'm seeing all this stuff, and I know it's not a dream." His memory began to clear so that the whole place was vivid.

"I remember coming in through the side of the wall on the other side of the cave," he continued. "Coming in through some sort of underground tunnel, and across the floor of this thing that's wide, maybe thirty or forty feet across, into these buildings that are in the side over here. I can see lights up high through the windows. I walk around some machines and into this building, and the bar is just inside of the saloon. It's a holding area where they put people when they first bring them in down here."

"What is going on with the officer?" Barbara asked.

"I'm not cooperating with them," he said, "I'm not in the state of mind they want me to be in. I was a little stunned, getting in there, and things are foggy. And then it gets clearer, too soon. I remember being real surprised. I sat in the holding area wondering what in the world's going on."

"Look around at the other people and see if they are accessible to you," Barbara instructed him. "Everybody's stunned," Casey said, "like zombies in a mental ward, just sitting there."

"How do you feel about this place and the officer?"

"I get the feeling they want to know, maybe they're trying to find out what it is we know," he answered. "And if you don't talk, they get real pissed."

"Who is this guy who is perturbed with you?" Barbara asked.

"I see a military dress uniform," Casey described. "Green military dress uniform. I can tell gray hair, clean-shaven, real quiet shoes."

"How many military types are there?"

"Just the guard and the officer," he said.

"What's the guard doing?"

"Just waiting. Never talks. He's there as the escort, somebody to guide people around, take them where they need to go because they're not in shape to talk or move of their own volition."

Casey described the fake saloon area in great detail, and then he told of being escorted by the guard out of the room. "We turn to the left, we turn right and go for some distance. There are doors, they aren't paneled, just steel doors."

"Proceed on through the door," Barbara told him, "and tell me what you see."

"A small room," Casey said, "about nine by twelve. I see only three pieces of furniture, just a metal chair, straight-backed, and I'm sitting in the chair. And a desk, plain military-type with nothing on top. With an officer standing behind it. He's got a chair, but he's not sitting in it. The guard stands outside and shuts the door. It's just me and this officer guy. Like he's in charge. And I don't like him, so I won't answer his questions.

"I'm fighting, I'm rebelling," Casey continued. "I can hear him yelling. 'Tell me!' Right now that's all I can get is 'Tell me.' What's he asking?"

"Have you ever seen him before?" Barbara wanted to know.

"No," Casey replied. "This man's trim, he's about five-ten, five-eleven, about my size, older than I am, and really upset."

"Just how upset does he get?"

"I'm supposed to tell him what he wants to know. That's the whole purpose, I get the feeling that's the whole purpose of the place."

"You mean, the other people, they're interrogated, too?" Barbara asked. "Like you are?"

"Yeah," Casey said, "like they're all there to be interrogated. The place, I never get a clue to location."

"What does this guy look like?"

"I would have to say he's about fifty-five, fifty to fifty-five maybe. He's not very old, but mature."

"Does he have very many feelings?"

"He's pretty emotional," Casey agreed with a short laugh.

"Okay," Barbara said. "How long does he rant and rave?"

"About fifteen minutes, and then he just yells at the guard to get me out of there."

"Do you think he's an American?"

"Definitely," Casey answered. "U.S. Army. A major. I hear myself thinking, 'What do you want from me?' Something about my family."

"What do they know about your family?" Barbara asked.

"They know that they've experienced something, that's my impression."

"You're clenching your teeth," Barbara noted. "What made you clench your teeth? Something must have made you real uptight at that point."

"I, oh, I'm confused," Casey said. "I don't know. I know that I'm feeling angry, and I don't like being here. And I don't like them threatening me."

"They're threatening you?"

"Yeah," he told her. "I mean, with promises of torture, you know, promises of pain or injury. 'We'll hurt your family if you don't tell us.' But they never touch me, the man never crosses his desk. He never gives me any medication or threatens to strike me or anything."

"But haven't you already had . . . ?" Barbara hesitated, uncertain what to say without leading Casey's answer. She assumed from his stunned condition that something had already been done to put him in that state.

"Yeah," Casey said, "somehow before I even got down. Everybody is stunned, we're all kind of foggy, but mine [my mind] kind of clears. I'm still not able to control my body that well. I can stand up and I can move."

"I want you to look at what might have happened to cause you to feel stunned," Barbara directed. "Retrace when that might have taken place."

"I'm working on that," Casey told her, "been working on how in the world we got into this place. It's nighttime. Where was it?"

"At the beginning," Barbara reminded him, "you saw the marsh and the water. And the dream of the white truck."

"Out of the cloud, yeah, sounding like a helicopter, looking like a Ford pickup truck. I see F-150 on the side. I see nothing, absolutely nothing but that cloud and the truck, no ground, no sky, no trees, nothing. And then it goes on over me, and I see this pickup. And I see nobody inside, no lights. It's got nice wheels, they don't look like military, cheap hubcaps.

"What's that got to do with the marsh?" Casey puzzled. "I can see everything I've described to you very clearly. But there's got to be more information. The man wanted to know. Why would they capture us and take us down there? Why take those people that he's got down there?"

"What do those people have in common?" Barbara asked.

"Well, some are my friends," Casey said, "and some look like they could be. As a matter of fact, they all look like they could be except for maybe a few. All of us that I know about in our group have had some sort of alien contact. That may be what he was talking about. What have I seen. What have they seen. 'If you don't tell us. . . .' But why would they do it that way?"

"Do you think you were injected?" Barbara asked.

"I don't ever recall being injected," Casey replied. "This felt more like the back of my neck, back in here," he gestured. "I was just being bombarded with something that sort of numbs you and takes away some of your will. I hesitate to say, but sort of like an electronic control. Sort of a numbing buzz, but I don't hear a sound. So I can't tell you what caused that state," he concluded, "and if it were an injection, I'm not aware of it happening."

"How much of your will is not there any longer?"

"I can't get up and move by myself," Casey admitted. "But I don't talk. I can't control where I am, and I cannot escape. At first I was totally confused. But it seemed like I sat there for a good while. And after a while it began to wear off, and I started looking around more. I remember wondering, trying to say out loud, 'What are we all doing here? Who's got a deck of cards? We need to play some cards.'" Casey laughed at the irony. "But when I get to the officer, I can talk, but I don't talk."

"I want to know more about those threats," Barbara said. "What are you experiencing now?"

"Oh, just trying to think of what that man was asking me. He can't read my mind, he can't read my mind!"

"Does he appear to be cruel?" Barbara asked. "Do you think he would follow through with those threats?"

"Nope," Casey said. "I think the military would, but I don't think he personally would. I know he would like for me to think that, but I don't."

"Okay, you're alone with the officer. . . . "

"Yeah, he's across the desk. He's standing up, and I can see the bottom of his full jacket. The black stripe on his arm, green jacket, some stuff up there. Don't see a name tag that I can recall. I see a spot for one, it's dull dark black, but I don't see his name. It's hard to focus. The whole scrambling of my head."

"Has your mind been scrambled to the extent that they're trying to block the memory of this?" Barbara asked.

"It's like they're trying to release it enough to let me talk," Casey said, "but not enough to do anything else."

"And you're being interrogated?"

"Like being debriefed," Casey agreed. "And my impression is they want to know what I know about the aliens, what I've done with them, what I know of their plans, what I've done to participate in anything, what I know about my family and their participation, my friends. But I'm not talking to them, I don't recall telling them anything. I try not to say anything but slip back into the stupor to get away from him. And he's getting really upset. I can't recall anything after the man getting extremely exasperated."

"That's where you go blank?"

"Yeah."

Unable to take him any farther, Barbara asked Casey to go back and describe more of the underground areas.

"I'm being led toward this area that has the office building to the side," he said, "office built into the side of this. We disappear off into the side of the mountain for the offices. And in the tunnel, on the sides of the tunnel were just big boxes. Some were boxes, some looked like diesel generators, large, very large, twenty feet high, maybe, almost that wide, with sort of a rounded top. Very long, forty feet or more. Large equipment, dark room.

"The guard, he's pushing me. We have to go through all this stuff to get into the interrogation areas, like a back door. Like we go through a back door to get into the back of this place. This is not like the front door of this area."

"Do you feel that in this facility there are only Americans?" Barbara wanted to know.

"Yeah, that's all I see."

Troubled by his inability to see clearly any more of the place, Casey was ready to end the session. Upset by the idea of his being taken by military people and questioned against his will, he tried to reject the whole scenario. But he couldn't; it had all been recalled with great clarity. And, to both of us it was even more disturbing than the memories of our encounters with the unknown beings.

We had often wondered just how much our government knew about the abduction phenomenon, and perhaps we'd hoped that those in positions of power had a better understanding of it all than we did. But if Casey's recollections were true, the government seemed to be as much in the dark as we were, maybe even more so. Otherwise, why would they—or whatever group this was—need to abduct their own people and interrogate them in this way?

A curious footnote to this event occurred after we moved out of state. I received a letter from Sandy, and she told of taking a leisurely drive around the outskirts of town with her husband.

"Remember the 'trip' over some water and entering the building through a back entrance?" she wrote, referring to Casey's recollection. "Well, the other day when we were driving on Hilltop Road traveling south, we passed [an underground federal facility] and just beyond it I saw a small pond or lake or whatever you want to call it. It definitely is not large. Interesting, as I have never noticed it before."

Very interesting indeed. Even though the federal facility was less than two miles from our old home, neither of us had ever seen the area behind it and the small lake Sandy described. We'll never know for certain just where Casey was taken for his interrogation, but the nearby underground site and the body of water seemed highly coincidental.

EPILOGUE

In May 1991, Casey accepted a new job, and we prepared to move to another state. It was difficult to leave our family and friends, but there was a stronger motivation than just a better position. For over a year we had felt an urge to get away from the large metropolitan area where we'd made our home, troubled by the thought of a coming time of upheaval and perhaps widespread catastrophe as so many abductees had been told or shown.

We didn't actually believe such a thing would happen— there were too many times in the past when one person or a small group of people were told of some imminent destruction, only to have the predictions prove false. Yet the urge to get away to a more rural environment grew stronger, and this new job offer would put us in a much less crowded place. So we arranged to sell our house and prepared to move.

A couple of weeks before our departure, James called and asked if he could meet with. Casey. We were surprised, having almost no contact with him since Barbara's visit in January, and Casey readily agreed. They met one evening at a small bar, and James was eager to talk.

He told Casey that nothing more had happened to him since the bizarre dream episodes of the winter, which had left him with physical aftereffects of the bile taste, a sore throat, and the scratches on his neck. Recently, however, he'd undergone an entirely new experience which he wanted to relate.

Although he saw no beings this time, he had been bombarded by messages coming from a chorus of voices. At first it was hard to hear anything clearly, but eventually he deciphered a warning of some sort. What follows is Casey's recollection of the things James told him, and James has since confirmed the correctness of Casey's recall.

The warning was about an impending "collective calamity," a sort of "psychic thunderclap" of great importance for the entire human race. "We have been controlled," James was told, "and we are still being controlled." And these controllers are planning a worldwide event which will be "staged, orchestrated, but not an invasion." As James understood the message, the entire world will be shown the presence and reality of the controllers. No one will be able to deny the existence of the UFO phenomenon any longer.

James reported that some people may think this is an invasion or a power play, but it won't be. They won't have to grab power because they already have the power and have had it all along.

What is to come is an "opportunity" for humans to demonstrate their worthiness to continue to exist. All of us must do this, collectively. It may be our only chance to prove we have something worthwhile and lasting to give to the future. James thinks the message told of a specific challenge to be presented to the planet, which we must meet in order to survive. And we won't have a choice of whether to participate. We will participate, and we will have a chance to win.

Could this message have been a fantasy? Perhaps. It would be nice to think so, to believe that the world will go on as it always has. Casey and I continue with the normal activities of work, caring for our family, visiting with friends, and making plans to build our home in the beautiful forested hills of our new location. We look forward to the grandchildren that David and Megan may someday give us, and to growing old together. But in light of the past few years' events—including all the global political changes and the "New World Order" which President Bush has been promoting with only the vaguest of definitions—it isn't that easy to dismiss the possibility that we truly are being warned of a reality to come.

Fred and James, among our group of friends, have been told or shown a nearing time of upheaval and change through their contacts with these unknown beings. They've been told that the aliens are somehow preparing "new bodies" for us, and they aren't alone. My research with abductions in our area brought me into contact with another man who has been shown a similar scenario. The beings told him he would have a task to perform at that time, helping a group of children, but that he would not survive beyond that task.

I have also read reports of four people in Britain who have been told of this coming catastrophe, and two of them were given a date only a year or two hence. And Barbara, as well as other researchers, have heard similar information from their contacts. In April 1991 at a UFO conference in Arkansas, Forest Crawford, a certified hypno-therapist from Illinois, recounted incidents of several of his cases working with abductees, and here again this upcoming date had surfaced time and again. Correlating the predictions from these cases, Mr. Crawford offers the following summary:

In early 1991 events will begin to happen that will culminate in mid-to-late 1992 with everyone knowing that there are intelligent beings from other worlds visiting earth.

October and November of 1992 were prevalent in many predictions. The events that may bring about this awareness include mass sightings, sustained landings near populated areas, government announcements of alien contact and/or open contact with the people of earth.

Many of Mr. Crawford's cases also discussed the aliens' understanding of such predictions, noting that they "are the probable future based on the present trend of events or energies. These trends can be changed by even minor events, thus affecting the future; therefore, predictions are always alterable. It seems," he concludes, "as though predictions and prophecies are warnings by other beings, or even our own higher selves, of what may come if we remain on our present path. We must realize that sometimes the best thing about a prediction is that our consciousness is able to change the outcome of events and render it false."

As I said earlier, there have been cases in the past when a single person was warned to prepare for a catastrophe: the end of the world; the evacuation of people from this planet; the coming of space beings who would destroy our world or, variously, who would save it. And in every past case, the predictions proved false.

They may certainly prove false this time, too. But there is a difference in these predictions from those previous ones. This time it isn't a single person who is receiving this warning, it is hundreds, maybe more, all over the planet. Many abductees feel they have been told of tasks they have been trained or programmed to perform in the near future, and most of them, like me, have no idea of what our instructions entail. Some abductees recall working on computerlike systems, some remember being shown how to operate the flying craft, but for the most part there is only the memory of training or instructions embedded in a part of the mind that our consciousness cannot penetrate.

We hope this is not going to happen. We hope with all our hearts that these beings are not telling us the truth. World problems are great—pollution and depletion of our resources, overpopulation and famine and plague—like diseases, war and destruction in many areas around the globe—but we want a chance to solve these crises through human means, for human purposes.

Still, all over the country, ordinary people are being exposed to the reality of UFOs, whatever reality that may be. In the first half of 1991, local newspapers carried reports of sightings and abductions in a wide variety of places. The February 28 edition of the Portland Oregonian, for instance, headlined a story, "UFOs Gain Notice," telling that "Scared Portland-area residents report increased inexplicable light activity in the area's night skies." The Gloucester (Massachusetts) Times (March 6) reported, "Strange Lights Spotted in Night Sky." And the February 19 edition of the Brown City (Michigan) Banner, in a story about five bright lights seen for half an hour, quoted one viewer who said, "They looked really close. They went off and on and every time they came back on they were in a different formation."

Other newspapers reported UFO sightings in Texas, Illinois, California, New Hampshire, New York, Pennsylvania, North Carolina, South Carolina, Virginia, West Virginia, Oklahoma, Minnesota, Connecticut, Ohio, Tennessee, Florida, Nevada, Maryland, and Indiana. In some places, such as Tennessee and Florida, the UFOs have been videotaped, and in many of these areas there are accompanying reports of close encounters, abductions, and physical traces left by the unexplained phenomena.

Great numbers of UFOs are also currently reported in all parts of the world, with perhaps the most extraordinary film footage, photographs and radar confirmations coming from Belgium. Since 1990, UFOs have been seen there by multiple reliable witnesses on the ground as well as by military pilots scrambled in response to sightings. The Wall Street Journal carried the story with the headline "Belgian Scientists Seriously Pursue A Triangular UFO" in their October 10, 1990, edition.

Another European phenomenon is the crop circle markings, which in 1990 and 1991 reached new levels of complexity and frequency in the British farmlands. Furthermore, news reports from Canada, Japan, Australia, New Zealand, and the United States indicate that the range of the circles is spreading globally. These circles and pictograms seem to have a connection to the UFOs sighted in the areas, but as yet no one knows the real cause or reason for the markings in the crops. Clearly, however, they are of deliberate design and may be a form of communication we have yet to decipher.

And more and more people are waking up to the fact that their lives have been punctuated by intrusive visitations of the unknown beings. Many of them who have kept their stories secret, as we did for so long, are now coming forward, ignoring the threat of ridicule because they know their experiences are real and they want an explanation.

I want an explanation. If there is no one on this planet who has one, at least I want to know what the powers of the world are doing to find one. Competent researchers, using the Freedom of Information Act, have obtained official documents verifying the existence of secret government involvement with UFOs, but all we have really learned from this is that there are many, many more secrets still kept from the public. Perhaps, as some researchers have said, all the media attention to UFOs is part of an orchestrated effort to prepare the public for the truth. But while TV ads and comical accounts of twelve-foot-tall ETs in Russia cajole us into thinking that UFOs aren't a serious problem, the real aliens are invading our lives in a very real, very threatening manner.

They are here. They are doing strange things to our bodies and our minds. These actions may be for humanity's benefit or for the aliens' own self-serving ends. And if we don't learn the purpose of their intrusions, we will never be more than their helpless victims.

BIBLIOGRAPHY

Farish, Lucius, Ed. UFO Newsclipping Service. Published monthly at Route 1, Box 220, Plumerville, AR, 72127.

Fowler, Raymond E. The Andreasson Affair. Englewood Cliffs, NJ: Prentice-Hall, 1979.

Holiday, Ted, and Colin Wilson. The Goblin Universe. Llewellyn, 1986.

Hopkins, Budd. Missing Time. New York: Ballantine, 1981. ————.

Speech to Metroplex MUFON, March 1989, Dallas, TX.

Strieber, Whitley. Communion. New York: Avon, 1987. ————. Majestic. New York: Putnam, 1989. ————. Transformation. New York: William Morrow, 1988.

Although there are scores of books and publications about UFOs and related phenomena, the following selections are highly recommended:

Fawcett, Lawrence, and Barry J. Greenwood. Clear Intent. Englewood Cliffs, NJ: Prentice-Hall, 1984.

Noyes, Ralph, Ed. The Crop Circle Enigma. San Francisco, CA: Gateway, 1990.

Randle, Captain Kevin D. The October Scenario. New York: Berkley, 1988.

Spencer, John, and Hilary Evans, Eds. Phenomenon: Forty Years of Flying Saucers. New York: Avon, 1988.

Stringfield, Leonard H. Situation Red: The UFO Siege. New York: Fawcett, 1977.

UFO Magazine. Published bimonthly by California UFO. Edited by Vicki Cooper and Sherie Stark.

Walters, Ed, and Frances Walters. The Gulf Breeze Sightings. New York: William Morrow, 1990.

The Not-So-Friendly Face of ET Encounters

By Tim R. Swartz

The galaxy is teaming with planets. In fact, it appears that there are more planets than suns in the Milky Way. Most astronomers now suggest that with so many planets, it is almost a certainty that intelligent life must exist somewhere in the vast cosmos. If there are intelligent creatures on other worlds, what can we expect of them? Would they be friendly or hostile?

Zhu Jin, director of the Beijing Planetarium, asserts that aliens wouldn't harm earthlings if they do pay us a visit someday.

"Extraterrestrial civilizations most likely exist. Personally, I don't think they would hurt earthlings because they have to travel countless light-years to get to here. The feat itself indicates that their civilization has developed to such a degree that violence has become almost impossible."

Many scientists agree that a civilization capable of interplanetary travel has evolved beyond the primitive emotions that create violent tendencies. As well, if these same scientists went to the trouble to examine the UFO phenomenon, they would conclude that whoever is piloting the UFOs must be friendly, or at least indifferent to the inhabitants of planet Earth.

However, a more detailed analysis of the interactions between humans, UFOs and the creatures associated with them, reveal a completely different, and very disturbing conclusion altogether.

EVIL EMPIRE OF THE ETS AND THE ULTRA - TERRESTRIALS

ANGELS FROM OUTER SPACE

Starting in the early 1950s, men such as George Adamski and Howard Menger claimed that they were in contact with benevolent extraterrestrials who allegedly were the pilots of the mysterious flying saucers. The so-called "Space Brothers" were almost indistinguishable from humans, and claimed to be visiting Earth because of their concern for the destructive spiritual path that humanity was taking. The UFOnauts wanted to save us from our war-like ways and guide us towards a galactic utopia shared by practically all intelligent interplanetary races.

For all intent and purposes, the Space Brothers were angels in physical form, preaching a new gospel of cosmic enlightenment and brotherhood. All humanity had to do was to stop fighting each other, dismantle our atomic weapons, and we would be welcomed into the loving arms of our brothers and sisters from outer space.

When you take into consideration the era, the whole concept of friendly, if not almost nurturing, aliens from outer space is surprising. The 1950s was a time of extreme mistrust and almost pathological paranoia. Both the United States and the Soviet Union were determined to eliminate each other at any cost, and this atmosphere of hatred spilled over into almost every aspect of life. Cold War paranoia was especially evident in popular culture such as movies and television.

1950s science fiction movies such as ***War of the Worlds, Invasion of the Body Snatchers, and Earth vs. the Flying Saucers*** popularized the notion that aliens from other planets had only one motive, to take over and destroy the Earth. You would think that the UFO phenomenon would have reflected popular culture. However, the alleged "real" contacts with space aliens were just the opposite from their mass-media counterparts.

Was this always the case, or did the "less-than-friendly" UFO encounters get swept under the rug by those who were advocating the "Happy Space Brothers" scenario?

EVIL EMPIRE OF THE ETS AND THE ULTRA - TERRESTRIALS

Visitors from Beyond Time and Space

Unidentified flying objects have been zipping through the skies of planet Earth as long as there have been people around to watch them. Ancient writings, folklore and religious texts are full of tales of unusual, glowing airships and the weird creatures contained within them, and much like the UFOs, the strange beings inside come in an amazing and prolific range of extraordinary shapes and sizes.

For someone whose only knowledge of UFOs comes from the popular media, this may seem perplexing. After all, anyone who has watched television or gone to the movies in the last twenty years knows flying saucers are spaceships carrying little gray men from outer space. The gray alien with large black eyes has seemingly supplanted the hundreds of other weird beings reported over the last sixty years by UFO witnesses. However, the gray alien stereotype is a relatively recent addition to the pantheon of "aliens" that have interacted with mankind throughout history.

What is strange is the almost complete disappearance of the friendly Space Brothers, replaced by the less-than-friendly grays. The Space Brothers interplanetary lectures on the path of universal spirituality had been replaced by frightening middle of the night abductions and painful surgical procedures.

Since the late 1970s, the abduction experience has captured the majority of attention in the field of UFO research. Much has been written about how to the abductees, these experiences seem to be purposely generating as much pain and fear as was possible. This seems to be an almost 360 degree turn around from the earlier reports of UFO occupants inviting witnesses onboard for tea and cookies and a quick tour around the solar system. It's not as if in the past the only interactions with UFO occupants were pleasant and harmonious. There were numerous cases all over the world where a UFO sighting ended up being an extremely dangerous experience.

According to the website ***Weird Australia***, during 1951 in the Gungal district of the Hunter Valley, NSW, prospector Graem Stout, was told by local Aboriginals that a "huge saucer" airship had descended upon six Aborigines setting up their campfire beside a local creek to cook their evening meal. Apparently, the UFO "sucked them all up through a big hole underneath it" then flew away with them. The six Aborigines had vanished from the face of the Earth.

In 1953, a lone bushwalker in the rugged Burragorang Valley in the Blue Mountains spotted a group of "man-like figures wearing shiny white "space suit-like outfits". Watching them from behind some bushes, the humanoids appeared to be "searching the ground with strange metallic devices, apparently collecting soil samples". This all sounds innocent enough, however soon after this event occurred, three young bushwalkers went missing in the same area...and according to researcher Rex Gilroy, were never located.

Beware the Little People

In 1979, researchers from MUFON's Humanoid Study Group compiled a long list of more than 1,600 different UFO entity incidents. Contrary to the popular belief that sightings of UFO beings are generally rare, researchers found that many of the reports are well-documented, firsthand investigations involving credible witnesses.

The most frequently reported of all the UFO occupant cases are dwarf-like creatures that average three to four feet in height. Their complexion ranged from dark and swarthy to very pale, often bordering on white, although reddish and bluish skin colors have also been mentioned. One of the more bizarre groups of UFO creatures seen, especially in the 1950's, was the animal-like hairy dwarves.

In the early morning hours of November 28, 1954 two truck drivers from Caracas, Venezuela, Jose Ponce, and Gustavo Gonzales were driving to Petare, about fifteen miles away from Caracas. Around 2:00AM, the men found their way blocked by a glowing disc-shaped object about ten feet in diameter, which was hovering about six feet above the street.

Gonzales brought his truck to a stop and both men got out and walked closer to the object. When they were about twenty-five feet from it, they discovered they were being approached by what appeared to be a very hairy dwarf-like man.

Gonzales impulsively grabbed the creature and lifted him off the ground, but the creature twisted out of the truck driver's grasp and gave Gonzales a shove that sent him sprawling backward.

Before Gonzales could regain his feet, the humanoid, whose eyes glowed in the headlights of the truck like yellow cats' eyes, leaped on the man and began to claw at him with webbed hands that had claws about an inch long. Gonzales later told police that he tried to fight back with a knife into the creature's shoulder . . . but the blade glanced off of the creatures shoulder as if it were made of steel. At this point Jose Ponce panicked and ran to seek help from a nearby police station.

As Gonzales tried to fight off his strange attacker, another hairy little man jumped out of the glowing craft and pointed a small shiny tube at the man. There was a brilliant beam of light that briefly blinded Gonzales. When he could see again, the object was rising above the trees and quickly shot away.

Gonzales ran for the police station and showed up a couple of minutes after Ponce. At first police thought the men were drunk or crazy. A doctor determined that both men were in a state of shock and that neither of them had been drinking. Gonzales was treated for a long deep scratch down his left side and later reports said that it eventually healed but left a permanent scar.

A few weeks later, on the night of December 16, 1954, three young men were driving on the outskirts of San Carlos, Venezuela, after a night out on the town. Jesus Paz asked his friends to stop the car so that he could relieve himself. Paz walked about 12 feet away from the parked car when he suddenly screamed and dropped down into the tall grass. His friends ran to his rescue and found him stunned and lying on the ground. A short distance away, a small, hairy, manlike creature was running toward a shiny disc-like craft that was resting on the ground. The hairy dwarf disappeared inside of the object which quickly rose off the ground with a loud buzzing sound and vanished into the night sky.

Paz was rushed back to the city to the hospital, where doctors found that he was in a state of shock. Furthermore, the man had long deep scratches on his right side and downward across his spine "like claw marks" the doctor said.

Paz told officials that he had walked around a bed of tall flowers when he almost stumbled over a short, hairy manlike creature that was examining the flowers. Paz tried to escape, but when he turned, the creature attacked him with its long talons, clawing and tearing his shirt, and striking Paz on the back of the neck.

Several weeks later, Paz told a local reporter that his scratches had still not healed properly, remaining red and inflamed as the day when he was injured. After his initial interview, Paz refused to discuss his encounter ever again.

They Might Be Giants

On the opposite end of the scale are the UFO giants. Even though their reports are not nearly as numerous as the small humanoids, the UFO giants certainly are the most bizarre of the UFO occupants.

The giants are the least humanlike of all reported entities - with sightings describing creatures seven to nine feet tall and an amazing diversity ranging from one-eyed Cyclops, beings with black-faces, bushy black hair, and in some instances, with three unblinking eyes and large, round heads.

One amazing giant story was the account of a truck driver named Eugenio Douglas who allegedly used a revolver to fight off three "shiny metal robots" some fifteen to twenty feet tall. This happened in Argentina on October 18, 1963.

Douglas told police that he drove his truck into a ditch after a brilliant white light engulfed it near the town of Monte Maix. The light, he said, came from a twenty-five-foot disk parked in the middle of the road.

When he got out of his truck, three "indescribable beings" approached Douglas and tried to grab him. He managed to draw his pistol and fire several shots at the giants, who seemed unfazed by the bullets. Nevertheless, Douglas managed to get away and run toward town as the saucer lifted off the road and made several passes at him. He said that each time he felt "a wave of terrible, suffocating heat." The police examiner later found that Douglas had suffered several unusual burns, unlike anything he had seen before.

What is Going On?

It is clear that we have no idea what is really going on with the UFO phenomenon. Good...evil...or both? Perhaps trying to place such human terms as Good and Evil to the situation is like saying a tornado that destroyed a town is evil. Such concepts simply do not apply to UFOs and the forces behind them.

Books such as Brad Steiger's "***Flying Saucers Are Hostile***" and Harold Wilkins "***Flying Saucers On The Attack***" prove at least some of the UFOs are evil. Steiger mentions an entire African village that was destroyed by a UFO Beam. Jerome Clark in his article "Why UFOs are Hostile" mentions the possibility of "hundreds, possibly thousands" of people being murdered around the world by UFOs."

Referring to Steiger's book, Clark says UFOs or their occupants have been responsible for aggravated assault, burnings by direct ray focus, radiation sickness, murders, abductions, pursuits of cars, assaults on homes, paralysis, cremations, disrupting power sources, etc. Clark says there is also "no objective evidence apart from contactee cases, that UFOs are friendly or from other planets."

The book, "***UFOs: What on Earth is Happening***" (1976, Bantam Books, by John Weldon with Zola Levitt) does an excellent job of listing why UFOs and their occupants are not something to be sought out.

"There are also dangerous physical effects resulting from close association with UFO beings or craft. These include blackouts, blindness, sexual assault, psychological disturbances, painful skin infections, chronic headaches, convulsive seizures and even cancer. In the case of those who claim personal contact with extraterrestrials (contactees), they have reported being programmed, deceived and made to look like fools. They have experienced the loss of jobs and experienced family disruptions. Reportedly, there are frequent cases of insanity, particularly paranoid schizophrenia, found among contactees and at times, they are commanded to murder others... There are a very large number of sudden or mysterious deaths, suicides and nervous breakdowns among UFO investigators."

A close examination of close encounters with UFO occupants indicates that the occupants seem to be habitual liars. They often contradict each other and espouse obviously false beliefs. The UFO pilots have said that their homes are Mars, Venus, Saturn, Jupiter, a hidden world behind the sun, the hollow Earth and various other places throughout the galaxy.

These are just a few of the thousands of unusual and hostile UFO cases that have been reported over the years. Many of these strange reports receive little attention because they do not fall within the boundaries that UFO researchers have imposed on what they consider acceptable cases.

The truth of the matter is that the witnesses did undergo something unusual, and their experiences are marginalized because the situations, as well as the creatures encountered, do not fit the current homogenized version of what an accepted UFO should be.

The incredible variety of UFO occupants should give serious researchers' pause to reconsider the popular theory that UFOs are interplanetary spaceships. For unless planet Earth is some sort of intergalactic truck stop, it is difficult to explain why each UFO occupant sighting tends to be unique. However, whatever their origins or purposes, one thing is clear, UFOs can be dangerous and the best course of action is to not seek them out, and to stay as far away from them as possible.

###

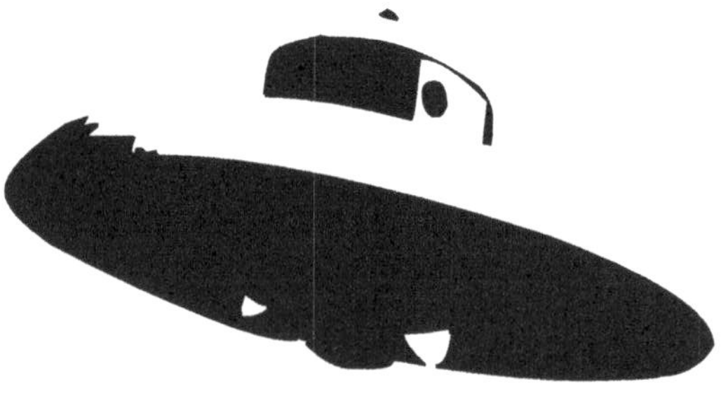

FROM THE FILES OF BRAD AND SHERRY STEIGER:

HOSTILE ENCOUNTERS WITH ALIEN INTELLIGENCES

Braniff Airways' Flight 542, a Lockheed Electra turboprop airliner, took off from Houston, Texas, en route to New York City at 10:37 P.M., September 29, 1959. Flight 542 carried 28 passengers and six crew members, and its flight plan called for it to travel over the Buffalo, Texas, area, 68 miles southeast of Waco. The sky was partly cloudy as Flight 542 neared Buffalo at an altitude of 15,000 feet and an air speed of 275 knots.

At the same time that Flight 542 was approaching Buffalo, Major R. O. Braswell was flying a C-47 at 6,500 feet between Shreveport, Louisiana, and Lufkin, Texas, which is east-northeast of Buffalo. It was there that Major Braswell first saw the "thing," colored "like a large red fire," looking like some kind of "atomic cloud," a "massive thing" at about 15,000 feet.

Billie Guyton of Centerville, Texas, was observing the aerial phenomenon from the ground at the same time as Major Braswell. Guyton reported that he watched an object emerge from the firey red cloud.

Jackie J. Cox, a thirty-nine-year-old schoolteacher, was driving toward Buffalo when he heard a noise overhead and looked up to see "a bright light in the sky that spread to cover the entire sky, as if phosphorus or magnesium were burning."

W. S. Webb of Buffalo had just gone to bed when he happened to glance out the window and see "a ball of fire, that looked like a star, shoot through the sky."

Farmer Richard White and his wife had just turned off the television set and gone to bed. White had decided to sleep on the breezeway that night in an effort to beat the summer heat. As he lay gazing at the summer stars, he noticed a brilliant light high in the southern sky: "The whole sky seemed to be lit up by a huge fireball passing overhead, only to be followed by a tremendous explosion, so violent it seemed to shake the ground itself. "

Seconds later the quiet countryside was shattered by the sound of shrill whistles as falling debris tore through the still summer night. The giant turboprop airliner had been torn into thousands of fragments.

A Braniff official investigating the wreckage of Flight 542 said that he had never seen a crash "where the plane was so thoroughly demolished, the wreckage so widely scattered, and the people so horribly mangled. And there was nothing among the wreckage to indicate a fire or a bomb aboard the plane."

An investigation and a thorough inquiry produced such uncomfortable facts as the following: (1) There had been no fire or explosion aboard the airliner while it was in flight or after it crashed. (2) Scorch marks found on glass window ports, the rear of the fuselage, and across the parting of the tail showed signs of having been exposed to tremendous exterior heat. (3) The force that caused the airliner to disintegrate had not come from within the plane.

The testimony of the residents of Buffalo, Texas—who saw a UFO launch a fireball at the airliner moments before it disintegrated—remains the only logical explanation for the disaster.

Attack on Police Helicopter Over Louisville

In another case of apparent UFO hostility toward humans attempting to share airspace with alien craft, two police officers on a helicopter patrol over Louisville, Kentucky, were attacked by fireballs from a UFO on a late spring night in 1993.

Officers Graham and Downs were already airborne when they received a call around midnight about a break-in. On their way to check out a possible theft, they spotted what they at first believed to be a large bonfire on the ground. But when Downs directed the powerful chopper spotlight down toward the alleged bonfire, he thought that what he now saw below them was more like a kind of balloon.

Perhaps activated in some way by the brilliant spotlight, the object now began drifting back and forth as it ascended.

The glowing object slowly rose until it hovered at an altitude of 500 feet, the same height as the police helicopter. As it hovered near them for a few seconds, the officers could see that they had engaged a strange, glowing, pear-shaped object.

Then the UFO took off at a speed that Officer Downs said he "had never seen before."

The object circled the police helicopter twice, then began to move up on it from behind.

Officer Graham was afraid that the thing was going to ram his tail rotor, so he pushed the chopper to 100 miles per hour in an attempt to evade their mysterious pursuer.

To Graham's complete astonishment, the UFO easily moved past them at an even faster speed, then shot hundreds of feet up into the air.

Baffled by the object's maneuvers—and by its apparent intent—the officers were horrified when the UFO blasted three fireballs at them.

Officer Graham expertly banked the chopper to avoid being struck by the fireballs, but by the time they circled and returned, the UFO had disappeared.

According to journalist Louise Milton, the extraordinary encounter of Officers Graham and Downs was confirmed by two other police officers who witnessed the aerial dogfight from the ground.

Officer Mike Smith said that he watched the UFO for about a minute and saw it shoot three fireballs at the police helicopter. Smith's partner, Joe Smolenski, said that the bizarre encounter over Louisville constituted "the closest I've come to something I couldn't explain."

A Swooping UFO Blistered His Arm and Automobile

On June 29, 1964, a Wellford, South Carolina, businessman was returning home from Atlanta, Georgia, when he claimed that a UFO swooped down over his automobile, burned his arm, and blistered the paint on the car roof.

"I saw the object so clearly, I believe that I could build one of the things," B. E. Parham said. "It came hissing down and stopped in the air right over my car [as he was traveling on the highway] ."

Parham said that he had been driving about sixty-five to seventy miles per hour, but when the UFO approached, the car's engine began to slow down. Parham, the district manager for a Spartanburg, South Carolina, firm, said the object made three passes at his vehicle. It had come from high in the sky, then swooshed over the top of the car, leaving behind an odor something like embalming fluid. Parham said the UFO gave off "terrific" heat and had a number of holes and openings in its sides.

When an Air Force analysis of the incident stated that Parham had been "frightened by ball lightning," the indignant businessman fumed that there was not a cloud in the sky when the object swooped down on him. In addition, he said, "Lightning wouldn't rotate at the top and the bottom, as this object did. Lightning would not stand still."

Parham also felt that he had more than adequate physical evidence to substantiate his claims: (1) His arm was badly burned. (2) The paint on the roof of his automobile was blistered and coated with an oily substance. (3) The radiator and other parts of his late-model car began to deteriorate as a result of the close approach of the UFO.

Struck by a Light from the Sky

Dead Within 6 Hours

In 1970, 40-year-old Joao Prestes, a healthy robust farmer near Sao Paulo, Brazil, was stunned and knocked to the ground by a mysterious beam of light from the sky. He managed to struggle in pain to the home of his sister, where numerous friends and neighbors came to his aid.

Eyewitnesses later told authorities that Prestes showed no trace whatever of burns, but within a matter of hours, the once vigorous farmer literally began to deteriorate before the eyes of his startled friends and family.

Although at no time did he appear to feel any pain, according the French journal Phenomenes Satiaux, "Prestes' insides began to show, and the flesh started to look as though it had been cooked for many hours in boiling water. The flesh began to come away from the bones, falling in lumps from his jaws, his chest, his arms, his hands, his fingers .... Soon every part of Prestes had reached a state of deterioration beyond imagination. His teeth and his bones ... stood revealed, utterly bare of flesh ... his nose and ears fell off. .."

Six hours after Prestes had been struck by the terrible beam of light, he was dead. The rapidly disintegrating man had not even been able to reach a hospital before he was nothing more than a grotesque skeleton. He died attempting to communicate details of his awful experience.

Paralyzed by a UFO

On February 7,1969, hundreds of people in the area of Pirassununga, Brazil, watched a strange, circular aerial vehicle swoop low over the town, then settle in a nearby valley on tripod legs. Nineteen-year-old Tiago Machado was nearest the mysterious craft when it landed, and he began cautiously walking toward the object.

As he later explained his terrifying experience to the press, Tiago said that the craft "seemed made of a material similar to aluminum, but it was luminous." The teenager described the UFO's rim as "spinning around the center." According to him, "It never stopped whirling."

Tiago said that the center section of the vehicle was stationary and appeared to be constructed of a transparent substance. "I could see what seemed to be shadowy figures in the cabin, gathering around what looked like an instrument panel."

The teenager said that he crept to within thirty feet of the UFO. He was aware that dozens of people had gathered on the distant hills to watch him approach the craft.

The next thing Tiago knew, a bright beam of light shot out from the disc and struck him in the legs. He toppled over, partially stunned and paralyzed, as the UFO suddenly rose into the air and soared into the sky at an incredible rate of speed. Within moments it had disappeared from the view of the gathered crowd.

Tiago Machado's legs turned bright red, and it was obvious to all the witnesses that his legs were painfully swollen.

Although many thought that Tiago's injuries resembled an electrical burn, Dr. Henrique Reis, who attended to Tiago at a local hospital, found no visible wounds or marks to account for the bright red swelling.

UFO Abductions as a Bizarre Alien Initiation Ritual

Some years ago, after we had interviewed numerous alleged abductees, we were struck by the thought that there is something almost primeval in the claims of examinations aboard UFOs. In primitive societies that emphasize pubertal initiations or rites of passage, the young child or the adult supplicant is often snatched away by masked members of a secret society or by stony-faced elders. The initiate is then taken to a place of ordeal or testing, often unconsciously womblike in design or shape. When the initiate has endured the testing process, the rites of initiation, he or she is returned to the village, a new and transformed person.

So, too, is the UFO abductee taken away by secret people whose faces, with their large, expressionless eyes and slitlike mouths, appear masklike.

The place of testing and ordeal is not only womblike in appearance, but it is often an egg-shaped enclosure. And after the abductee survives the testing process, he or she is returned to society as a transformed individual.

Abductions—In or Out of the Physical Body?

It may well be that the abductees are having genuine encounters, but of a nature whose true and total significance may be very different from what they suspect.

In his second letter to the Corinthians [12:2-5], the apostle Paul confides to his readers that he was once taken up into Heaven. But even in an age far more tolerant of supernatural occurrences and far less exacting in its scientific requirements than our own, Paul provides a number of qualifying statements that many of our contemporary abductees and contactees would do well to emulate. The apostle admits that he may have been "out of the body" during his ascent to Paradise and that it may have been a vision.

When we listen to abductees and UFO researchers telling us about being taken up through ceilings, out through walls, and levitated out windows, might we not just as likely be hearing accounts of experiences that took place in dreams, visions, or astral travel?

If it is possible that the human essence can soar free of the accepted limitations of time and space imposed on it by the physical body and truly engage in astral projection [or the more academic "out-of-body experience"], then it may well be that the paraphysical aspect of humankind may more easily interact with the multidimensional being that we commonly identify as a UFOnaut. Indeed, many accounts that tell of a subject being abducted aboard a UFO might actually be descriptions of a mental/spiritual/nonmaterial experience, rather than an actual physical/material one.

"I was lying on a couch in the living room, and I felt myself being squeezed out of my body," one abductee told us. "It felt like my head was being pulled back and two electric wires were touching the back of my neck.

"Then I became aware of myself in a dome-shaped room.

There were machines and computers on each side of me. Smallish entities in colored jackets, like smocks, were operating them. I was unable to move, as if some kind of paralysis had come over me. The beings at the machines turned toward me. Although they seemed almost expressionless, they put me at ease and I felt they were friendly. They told me something that I could not later remember, and I think they put some kind of homing device somewhere in my body."

Another abductee, a policeman from Atlanta, gave us the following report of his experience:

"I know that I was not asleep, but I was sitting comfortably in my favorite easy chair, facing the open window and the night sky. An erratically moving light caught my attention.

"Then a strange thing happened. At first I thought I was fainting. My entire being seemed to be rolling up from my feet as if my body were a toothpaste tube and my consciousness was the paste being squeezed from it. Finally my consciousness seemed to burst free and soar through space. The next thing I knew, I was standing inside some kind of craft. I was aware of a lot of smallish people with big heads standing around me, but I could not seem to focus on either their faces or their forms. I was being touched, stroked, poked, and prodded. A voice was speaking to me earnestly, but I cannot seem to recall exactly what he was saying. I know that it had to do with some special mission that I am to perform.

"Then I was aware of my wife shaking my shoulder and telling me that I should come to bed instead of sitting there dozing. I looked at my watch, and I was surprised to see that I had been in that state of consciousness—or whatever it was—for nearly three hours."

UFO Researchers Must Learn to Be Open-minded

One thing that you must quickly learn in the UFO field is to stay as open-minded as possible and to avoid focusing your attention on any one theory regarding the modus operandi of the Other, the aliens—whoever they may really be. Just when it would seem that astral projection might allow us to view abduction experiences as being more often nonmaterial experiences than physical ones, we run up against a bizarre case that bends and distorts the laws of physics and the rules of reality as we currently understand them. Although the story is told in greater length in Brad's Mysteries of Time and Space, it bears summarizing here:

William, a medical professional associated with one of the largest, most prestigious hospitals in the Midwest, related this account of a most extraordinary incident that occurred in 1968, when he was serving in the Medical Corps and assigned to the military section of a hospital in Hawaii.

One night a bedridden patient in traction and totally unable to move, with pins through his tibiae and femurs, told William that he would be gone that evening for a few hours while he joined his alien friends in a UFO. He said that William might accompany him if he truly believed in UFOs. William declined the invitation, stating that he would be on duty that night.

The patient, a man in his early sixties, was a veteran of World War II. He'd walked in front of a tractor-trailer, broken both his legs in several places, and was completely immobile.

"When I made the initial bed check that night, the patient reminded me that he would be gone for about an hour, and he repeated the invitation that I could come along in the UFO if I wanted to," William said. "I chuckled and walked on to see about the rest of the patients."

The UFO-obsessed patient was in a six-man room, but that night he was alone. William's post was across from his room. When he sat at his desk, he could survey the entire corridor. No one could get on or off the floor without his seeing them. And, of course, at the same time there were nurses, doctors, interns, and MPs walking around.

Later, during a second bed check, William was startled to see that the patient had disappeared from his bed. The traction weights were hanging there; the metal pins were on the bed. But the patient was gone!

An extensive search of the hospital and the surrounding grounds by military police failed to discover any trace of the bedridden man. Other patients said that they had seen a bright light around the time the man in traction had disappeared.

"It would have been impossible for anyone to have pulled the pins out by himself," William said. "You'd just faint from the pain. This guy had been lying in bed with both legs up, his femurs broken. He couldn't move. And if he had fallen out of bed and had tried to crawl, the pain would have been terrible."

When William, other hospital personnel, and MPs next checked the disappearing patient's room, they found that he was back in traction, pins in place. He had been gone for exactly an hour.

A doctor on the floor was completely baffled. He said that while it might be possible for a man to pull the pins out, it would be impossible for anyone to shove them back in by himself.

Four MPs grilled the patient for hours, but the man wouldn't reply to their questions. He would only say that he had been with his "friends."

When William was alone with the patient, the man sheepishly reminded him that he could have come along. But since it was apparent that his disappearance had created such a disturbance in the hospital, the next time he went flying with his "friends," he would leave his body there in traction and just go with them in his mind.

The Others' Extraordinary Interest in Human Sexuality

As the more discreet UFO investigators have phrased it, the aliens appear to express an "extraordinary interest in human sexuality." Hypnotic regressions conducted with abductees have produced the somewhat lurid details of a wide variety of means of impregnating Earth females, milking semen from Earth males, and creating a hybrid species.

UFO author-researcher John A. Keel once told us his conclusion that cases of UFO sexual liaisons are actually a variation on the age-old incubus phenomenon. "Induced hallucinations seem to play a major role in these cases," he said. "There may be considerable validity to the theory you expounded in one of Brad's books [Demon Lovers] ... that semen is extracted from human males in some succubi events and that this same semen is then introduced into human females in incubi incidents. The true nature and purpose of this operation is completely concealed behind a screen of deliberately deceptive induced hallucinations. Early fairy lore is filled with identical cases, as you know. And such sexual manipulations are an integral part of witchcraft lore."

Although vividly sensual descriptions of intercourse with demons was wrung from witches during the terrible tortures of the Inquisition by priests seeking confessions of their sins—and the graphic accounts of sexual molestation by alien intruders is wrung from the subconscious of abductees during hypnotic sessions by UFO researchers seeking confirmation of their theories-fair-minded students of either, or both, phenomena would have to concede the enormous number of similarities between being impregnated for Satan's pleasure or being fertilized to produce hybrid soldiers for an alien takeover of Earth. Indeed, according to some researchers, the two violators may be one and the same demonic entity, and the complete domination of Earth may be the identical goal.

Let us briefly consider a parallel between contemporary accounts of UFO abductions and the legends that grew up around the old religion of witchcraft in the mid-1400s. For centuries the Christian Church had officially ignored the practitioners of the ancient ways. But at the dawn of the Age of Enlightenment, when an emerging science was beginning to consider seriously the structure of the universe, certain of the Church hierarchy suddenly became obsessed with devils and their lustful designs upon Earth women.

In his AntiChrist and the Millenium, E. R. Chamberlin makes an excellent point that should be kept in mind while considering the ever-increasing reports of UFO abductions, alien impregnations, and sexual molestations by ETs:

"Paradoxically, it was the Christian Church which, seeking with all its powers to combact the practice of satanism, gave that same practice a form. It was necessary to define witchcraft in order to combat it, and by so defining, the Church gave shape to what had been little more than folklore. Most of the elements that eventually went to make up witchcraft had long been abroad in Europe, but for centuries the Church had been content to dismiss them as mere fantasy. The legend of the women who flew by night came in for particular scorn. 'Who is such a fool that he believes that to happen in the body which is done only in the spirit?' Such sturdy common sense was forced to give ground at last to a rising tide of fanaticism."

When it comes to the charges raised by some UFO investigators that the aliens in general—and the Grays in particular—are conducting genetic experiments to alter human evolution, we must speculate—based on our own extensive research—whether the extraterrestrial geneticists might not be completing a centuries-old project, rather than initiating a new one.

Rather than focusing on whether or not the UFO intelligences are conducting genetic experiments with unwilling men and women in 2012, the more powerful query is whether humankind might have been structured by the Visitors, the Watchers, the Extraterrestrials, the Multidimensional intelligences from the very beginning of our evolutionary trek. What remains to be discovered is whether their purpose is benevolent or malevolent.

CONTRIBUTORS

Timothy Green Beckley

Sean Casteel

Dr. Karla Turner

Tim R. Swartz

Brad & Sherry Steiger

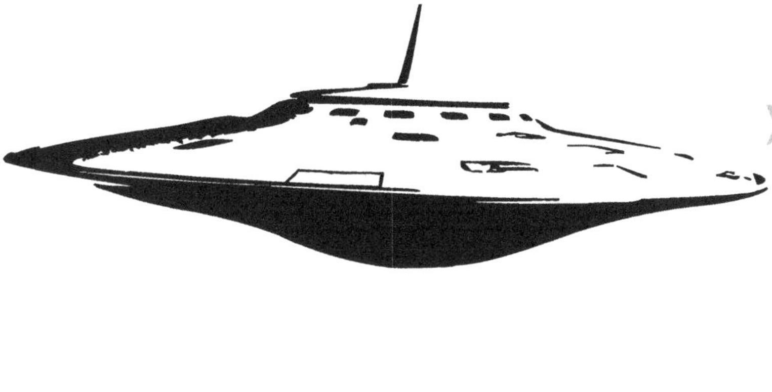

THE CONTRIBUTORS

SEAN CASTEEL is a freelance journalist who has written about UFOs, alien abduction and related phenomena since 1989. He has contributed to ***UFO Magazine***, the now-defunct ***UFO Universe, FATE Magazine*** and ***Open Minds Magazine***. Sean has also written several books for Global Communications, including ***UFOs, Prophecy and the End of Time*** and ***The Excluded Books of the Bible***. He has a website at www.seancasteel.com

TIMOTHY GREEN BECKLEY has been described as the Hunter Thompson of UFOlogy. Since an early age his life has more or less revolved around the paranormal. The house he was raised in was thought to be haunted. Tim saw his first of three UFOs when he was but ten, and has had two more sightings since – including an attempt to communicate with one of these objects. Tim grew up listening to the only all night talk show in the country that revolved around the strange and unexplained. Long John Nebel's guests included the early UFO contactees who claimed to have visited other planets and built time machines in the desert. Tim was fascinated by everything that went bump in the night – or even in the daylight for that matter.

Over the years he has written over 25 books on everything from rock music to the secret MJ12 papers. He has been a stringer for the national tabloids such as the Enquirer and editor of over 30 different magazines (most of which never lasted more than a couple of issues). His longest running effort was the newsstand publication ***UFO UNIVERSE*** which went for 11 years. Today he is the president of ***Inner Light/Global Communications*** and editor of the ***Conspiracy Journal*** and ***Bizarre Bazaar.***

He is one of the few Americans ever to be invited to speak before closed door meetings on UFOs presided over by the late Earl of Clancarty at the House of Lords in England. The Inner Light Publications and Global Communiations' catalog of books and video titles now number over 200, including the works of Tim Swartz, Sean Casteel, T. Lobsang Rampa, Commander X, Brad Steiger, John Keel, Tracy Twyman, Wendelle Stevens and a host of many other authors. He is also the host of numerous horror films under the moniker of Mr. Creepo.

KARLA TURNER —

If you wanted to find four words to describe the life of alien abduction investigator Karla Turner, Ph.D., those words might be intrepid human rights activist. A former college instructor who held a doctorate in Old English Studies from the University of North Texas, Turner had authored three books on the abduction phenomenon, ***Into the Fringe*** (1992), ***Taken*** (1994), and, with psychic Ted Rice, ***Masquerade of Angels*** (1994). She was convinced that the aliens were here not to help us out, but to steal from us the sovereignty of our souls. She wanted us to fight back – with the same courage that she herself showed when, after a period of struggle – just like Mae Brussell and Ann Livingston– she succumbed to a particularly virulent, fast-acting form of breast cancer, on Jan. 9, 1996.

The diminutive scholar, author and activist, who was born in 1947 and made her home in Roland, Arkansas, had been involved in alien abduction work since 1988. Two traits, she had come to conclude, characterized alien behavior above all: deceitfulness and cruelty. In ***Into the Fringe***, she recounted the abduction experiences of herself, her husband Casey (an assumed name), and several other members of her family. The family had first became aware of their experiences in 1988. Later, they were able to recall abduction events going back to their childhoods; the experiences were uniformly disturbing. In her second book, ***Taken*** (published, like ***Masquerade of Angels***, by her own press, Kelt Works, in Roland), Turner told the stories of eight female abductees who had contacted her after the publication of her first book. ***Masquerade of Angels*** was the biography of Louisiana psychic Ted Rice, who, used to channeling benevolent entities, then becoming aware of his alien abduction experiences, first believed the aliens were benign, then came to the conclusion that they were no more than remorseless predators.

TIM R. SWARTZ is an Indiana native and Emmy-Award winning television producer/videographer. Tim is the author of a number of popular books including ***The Lost Journals of Nikola Tesla, Time Travel: A How-To-Guide, Richard Shaver-Reality of the Inner Earth, Admiral Byrd's Secret Journey Beyond the Poles***. He is a contributing writer for: ***Sir Arthur Conan Doyle: The First Ghostbuster***, and Brad Steiger's ***Real Monsters, Gruesome Critters, and Beasts from the Darkside***. As a photojournalist, Tim has traveled extensively and investigated paranormal phenomena and other unusual mysteries from such diverse locations as the Great Pyramid in Egypt to the Great Wall in China. He has worked with television networks such as PBS, ABC, NBC, CBS, CNN, ESPN, Thames-TV and the BBC. His articles have been published in magazines such as ***Mysteries, FATE, Strange, Atlantis Rising, UFO Universe, Flying Saucer Review, Renaissance***, and ***Unsolved UFO Reports***. View his website at: www.conspiracyjournal.com

BRAD AND SHERRY STEIGER –

BRAD STEIGER is the author/coauthor of 170 books with over 17 million copies in print.

Steiger's first published articles on the unexplained appeared in 1956, and he has now written more than 2,000 articles with UFO or paranormal themes. From 1970-'73, his weekly newspaper column, ***The Strange World of Brad Steiger***, was carried domestically in over 80 newspapers and overseas from Bombay to Tokyo. Among his books are ***Revelation: The Divine Fire, The Werewolf Book: An Encyclopedia of Shapeshifting Beings; Real Ghosts, Restless Spirits***, and ***Haunted Places; Shadow World***, and, with his wife Sherry, ***UFOs Are Here, UFO Odyssey, The Gale Encyclopedia*** [three volumes] ***of the Unusual and Unexplained; Conspiracies and Secret Societies: The Complete Dossier***. Sherry is herself the author or coauthor of over 40 books. From the mid-1980s through 2002, they lectured and conducted seminars throughout the United States and overseas. They have two sons, three daughters, and nine grandchildren, eight girls, and one boy. www.BradandSherry.com

Sherry Steiger has for over 30 years actively studied the dynamic interaction between the body, mind and spirit in health-related matters as well as the effects of environment and technology on health and wellness. Sherry has addressed audiences and corporate groups from coast to coast. In the early 1970's, through SmithHaven Ministries of Long Island, New York, an ecumenical outreach, specializing in crisis and family counseling. Sherry worked with runaway teens, drug and alcohol abuse, suicide attempts and abused teens, children and women. She also taught special classes, such as the highly successful ***On Being a Woman***. Open to only teenage girls at first, her class was in such great demand that she eventually adapted the class and taught it to women of all ages, then developed and taught ***On Being a Person*** for both genders of all ages. In 1972 Sherry founded one of the earliest nonprofit schools dealing with new approaches to healing and learning.

The Butterfly Center for Transformation. In the late 1970s, Sherry was invited to serve as a member of the original Board of Directors for a Wellness Center, consisting of health professionals and M.D.s from the Institutes of Health, Education and Welfare in Bethesda, Maryland. The group met monthly in the Washington D.C. area for meetings and retreats for the sole purpose of exploring stress and disease, their causes and roots, and to evaluate varieties of healing techniques and their efficacy in order to create a new concept in medicine and healing: a Wellness Center. The many alternative therapies researched and studied led to the 1992 official creation of The Office of Alternative Medicine under the Institutes of Health, Education and Welfare in Bethesda, Maryland.

Send an email for a free subscription to our weekly Conspiracy Journal to –MRUFO8@hotmail.com

Web Sites: www.ConspiracyJournal.com www.TeslasSecretLab.Com

We publish many books, catalogs, audio CDs and DVDs on a wide variety of topics. Please contact us at above or thru the mail at

Global Communications
Box 753
New Brunswick, NJ 08903